The Politics of Murder

THE POLITICS OF MURDER

Organized Crime in Barry Goldwater's Arizona

DAVE WAGNER

Gracenote

Gracenote Books
PO Box 27707
Tempe, AZ 85285

480.454.6266

Also by Dave Wagner

A Very Dangerous Citizen: Abraham Lincoln Polonksy and the Hollywood Left (with Paul Buhle)

Radical Hollywood (with Paul Buhle)

Hide in Plain Sight: The Hollywood Blacklistees in Film and Television, 1950–2002 (with Paul Buhle)

Jews in American Popular Culture (associate editor)

For the newspaper reporters and editors I have worked with And for my grandchildren,
Arizonans all

Kennst du das Land wo die Zitronen blühen?
(Do you know the land where the citrus blooms?)
—Goethe

TABLE OF CONTENTS

Land Fraud Embarrasses Goldwater. An Accountant's Murder Raises the Stakes. A Security Leak to Warren. The Prosecutor's Confession.

INTRODUCTION:
JOURNALISM AND HISTORY

After eleven days, the deathwatch broke. On June 13, 1976, *The New York Times* announced the death on an inside page next to a long sidebar by Robert Lindsey, who had used the week and a half since the car bomb exploded to find out who wanted Arizona reporter Don Bolles dead. Lindsey introduced the sidebar with what newspaper editors in those days called "swoop":

> Under the gaze of a sweltering desert sun, a hybrid breed of organized crime—including Mafia-style émigrés from elsewhere and a homegrown species of seemingly respectable business and professional men—is blossoming in Arizona, the nation's fastest-growing state.
>
> Largely through vast fraudulent land deals, securities frauds and other, often-related "white collar crimes," criminal groups are turning over many millions of dollars a year in illicit profits, bringing gangland-style violence to this fast-urbanizing frontier state and provoking [here, Lindsey tapped the brakes] unresolved charges of official corruption.

Unresolved. It was a nervous word, perhaps inserted by an editor who doubted whether Lindsey could fairly describe Arizona as a landscape of fraud, violence, and official corruption.

It was true that Phoenix had a history of high-profile assassinations, some of them operatically staged message murders. The killers used a truck bomb to scatter the remains of the socially prominent gangster Willie Bioff across his neat suburban lawn. They decapitated Gus Greenbaum, the state's most powerful crime boss, and then turned the knife on his wife. A year before Bolles's murder, a pair of gunmen from Chicago Heights used a .22-caliber pistol to kill an accountant only hours before he was to tell a grand jury what he knew about land fraud in Arizona. As they stepped over his body, the gunmen dropped a few coins.

The mobsters' confidence that they had little to fear from the law in Phoenix appeared justified. Although the US Senate had held three major committee hearings on organized crime in the United States since World War II, with an Arizona senator sitting on each of them, the state was barely mentioned. A House hearing in the 1970s at which Bolles testified came to ruin, perhaps because of sabotage by an Arizona congressman who was a member of the committee.

Within hours after Bolles died, Phoenix police arrested the chief assassin, John Harvey Adamson, and detectives told *The Times'* Lindsey that they were closing in on other conspirators. "Their investigation was centering on prominent, influential people," Lindsey wrote, "including some with important political ties."

Quoting police sources, Lindsey named Kemper Marley, a rich and powerful rancher, as the leading suspect in the Bolles assassination. He identified Marley's protégé as the man who carried the payoff money from Marley to Adamson. Soon after the *Times* story appeared, Marley fled to Mexico.

In February 1977, *The New York Times Magazine* published a long news feature from Lindsey that opened with a contrast between the dive bar where assassin Adamson drank and the tony country club where Marley was a member.

PHOENIX—The Ivanhoe is a cocktail lounge at 3033 North Central Avenue. It is a dark place with red carpets and late medieval décor. The wood paneling is plastic, the antique brick on the walls is imitation, and the fire that seems to flicker in the fireplace is a rotating lightbulb. The Ivanhoe opens each morning about six-thirty, and before long it begins to fill up with the regulars, who while away their mornings, and then their afternoons, drinking, talking, playing cards, and trying to make deals, using the two telephones placed on the bar for the customers' use.

For the most part, they are people who are losers in life, waiting for a big score. It is a place where there has been talk of burning down buildings for a price, of smuggling drugs and caches of silver from Mexico, of hijacking trucks and disposing of stolen goods—and, on occasion, of committing murder for a price.

Several miles from the Ivanhoe, outside Phoenix, amid a scattering of expensive ranch-style homes, the Paradise Valley Country Club nestles at the bottom of Marshmallow Hill. Richly decorated in earthy colors and native stone selected to match the stark but peculiarly beguiling desert, the country club is the centerpiece of the good life in this, the largest city in America's fastest-growing state. It is the playground of upper-crust Phoenicians, as they call themselves—the top bankers, lawyers, merchants, ranchers, and mining men.

Some are well known, like Senator Barry Goldwater and his brother, Robert, or the former [US] Attorney General, Richard Kleindienst. But there are many lesser-known people who have made it in Arizona—men like Kemper Marley Sr., a millionaire rancher, landowner, and businessman, the son of an Arizona pioneer.

The Ivanhoe and the Paradise Valley Country Club belong to two different worlds. But last June 2, the two worlds intersected when a bomb went off in a Phoenix parking lot.

Lindsey's profile of Marley reviewed the evidence for his role in the murder, including the trail of $5,000 from the old rancher through his protégé and business partner, Max Dunlap, to Adamson. (It was intended for "machinery repairs," Marley told police.) Lindsey suggested that events were moving quickly toward a moment of accountability for the assassination.

Eleven months after writing his first article, however (the one with the sweeping lead), Lindsey changed his mind. Detectives had lost their optimism about solving the case. Their investigation had not resulted in any "immediate indictments, arrests, or other major short-term effects," Lindsey wrote, "and none appear likely." After the early arrests of three men, two of whom were contract killers, none would follow. It was "a story without a dénouement, a thriller without a final chapter."

Lindsey went on to write a number of bestselling books, including 1979's *The Falcon and the Snowman: A True Story of Friendship and Espionage* about two young men who sold US security secrets to the Soviets. Ten years after his first piece on the Bolles murder, Lindsey made a declaration that is as true now as it was in 1986: "Mr. Bolles's murder is still unsolved."

There were two insults to justice in the Bolles case. The first was a failure to investigate the actions or the motive of Marley, the chief suspect in the case, even though the motive was unambiguous. He had been taking sizeable payoffs from high-level members of organized crime in Las Vegas in exchange for laundering casino profits at a local racetrack. It was the story Bolles was working on when his car exploded.

The second insult to justice was leaving the Bolles murder unsolved to keep from the public a politically explosive story involving the bomb-maker, John Adamson. Six months before Bolles was killed, the assassin had been part of a plan devised by Senator Barry Goldwater's political operation to overthrow the elected Navajo tribal government.

The connecting link between the Bolles case and the Navajo plot was a shabby lawyer named Neal Roberts, who worked covertly for Goldwater. It was Roberts who hired the getaway plane for Adamson in the Bolles murder, and it was Roberts who recruited Adamson for his part in Goldwater's Navajo operation. The story about Roberts had to be suppressed to prevent a serious, perhaps career-ending scandal for Goldwater.

All of this required the cooperation and silence not only of influential insiders but the assent of members of the political and the juridical class whose loyalty to Goldwater outweighed whatever obligations they felt to the Arizona public.

ORGANIZED CRIME AS A POLITICAL SYSTEM

"For much of history-writing," historian Renate Bridenthal observed, "the relationship of crime and corruption to state and society has been resolutely ignored as little more than marginal or anecdotal phenomena." Bridenthal blamed this professional detachment of the history profession on the scarcity of sources. "Illicit practices leave few trails." Criminologists, notably Alan A. Block and William J. Chambliss, pointed to the inadequacy of the reigning "law-enforcement model" of organized crime adopted by police, prosecutors, and journalists as well as most criminologists of the later twentieth century. But the law-enforcement model limited their understanding of organized crime to the behavior of social outsiders, principally members of ethnic minorities who engaged in violence. Block and Chambliss, by contrast, showed that in practice, organized crime is a social system that thrives on the cooperation of powerful and socially prominent insiders, with no restrictions in regard to class, race, or ethnicity.

Block and Chambliss presented an alternative, "the patron-client model" of organized crime. A study of how it worked in the large cities in the United States in the second half of the twentieth century, including Phoenix, was Chambliss's *On the Take: From Petty Crooks to Presidents* (1978), an investigation of the inner workings of organized crime in Seattle, which at the time was a city about the same size as Phoenix. *On the Take* was a cornerstone of modern criminology and a rare piece of investigative journalism. It explained how an invisible network of insiders, using secrecy, rewards, and intimidation, turned the governing power of public institutions in the State of Washington to their own benefit.

Chambliss defined organized crime as "a political phenomenon that takes its character from the economic institutions" of a particular place and time. "I do not believe that organized crime is run and controlled by a national syndicate with a 'commission' or 'board of directors' who have feudal-like control over underlings spread across the nation," he wrote. Rather, "organized crime really consists of a coalition of politicians, law-enforcement people, businessmen, union leaders, (and in some ways least of all) racketeers..." In Seattle, "representatives from each of the groups engaged in organized crime made up the political and economic power centers of the community, met regularly to distribute profits, discussed problems, and made the necessary organization and policy decisions essential to the maintenance of a profitable, trouble-free business." But the organization was not monolithic. It included a number of power centers whose bosses could act independently, particularly in an emergency, to silence someone who represented an immediate threat.

The profits were the payoff, or the *take* of Chambliss's title. The payoff was simultaneously a system, its means, and its end. Protecting the payoff required the help and involvement of people in power. "Politicians, law-enforcement officials, professionals (especially lawyers, accountants, bankers, and Realtors), and 'legitimate' businessmen become partners in the illegal industry."

As Chambliss was finishing his book, the events described in these pages were unfolding in Phoenix, and he was aware of them. "As this book is going to the printer," he wrote in the preface to *On the Take*, "a group of journalists [Investigative Reporters and Editors, Inc.] has recently published materials detailing illegal businesses and crimes in Arizona that implicate some of the most prominent politicians and businessmen in the United States. With a few changes of names and political affiliation, the Arizona materials could be piped into the findings from Seattle, Chicago, Newark, or anywhere else."

Like most journalists, then as now, Bolles followed the law-enforcement model in his reporting. In 1976, most police officers and prosecutors still assumed that organized crime was the exclusive province of ethnic groups, and it was from the most conscientious investigators among police detectives that Bolles developed most of his information. It would be no surprise that he organized his research into lists of mostly Italian- and (less often) Jewish-surnamed associates of organized crime, including members or allies of the then-little-understood Chicago Heights crew of that city's Mafia that established a powerful street presence in Phoenix. Drawing on these sources, Bolles wrote groundbreaking pieces on ethnic crime groups in Arizona. He was the first writer in Arizona, for example, to report on land-fraud king Nathan Waxman (known in Phoenix as Ned Warren) and the Italian-American restaurateur Joe Tocco, brother of the Chicago Heights crime boss.

It would be inaccurate to say that an ethnic definition of organized crime had no relevance to events in Phoenix. On the contrary, Italian-American gangsters played a leading role in each of the message murders and in at least some of the homicides of people who threatened to expose Ned Warren. There were strong ties among some members of the Chicago Heights crew and the Warren gang, relationships that are helpful in understanding the Bolles murder and the history of the period. But ethnicity has little value in understanding who wanted to acquire control over the investigation into Bolles's killing and why.

Phoenix is one of the few large cities in the country that lacks a written history of its organized crime. The reason might be related to an observation made by W. H. Moore, historian of Senator Estes Kefauver's famous hearings on the rackets in the 1950s, who wrote that crime could not have flourished in major US cities without political protection from "the individual who controlled the local law-enforcement officials."

In Phoenix, the term of art for this kind of protection was "keeping the lid on." To keep the lid on the Bolles murder, the Phoenix network had a power perhaps unique at the time, namely, a deep and continuing influence over history as well as journalism. When the journalists of Investigative Reporters and Editors (IRE) decided they would pursue the stories Bolles was working on when he died and leave the investigation of his murder to law enforcement, they seriously overestimated the independence of Arizona's judicature, its political class and, at times, its press.

Chapter 1

THE SOCIETY GANGSTER—WILLIE BIOFF

The discreet public silence about organized crime in Phoenix was shattered in 1955 with the murder of a loquacious, pudgy, and myopic citizen when he stepped on the gas pedal of his pickup truck. A bomb attached to his starter motor scattered parts of him across his driveway, and the lower branches of the trees in front of his house.

Nelson, as he called himself, was in fact Willie Bioff, the star witness in a Hollywood scandal that was widely covered by newspapers around the country on the eve of World War II. Bioff eluded a long prison sentence by turning informer on his fellow mobsters, and he found a refuge in Arizona. For almost a decade, he attracted little if any public notice, but news stories about his murder alluded for the first time to his friendships with some of the most prominent people in Arizona, including Barry Goldwater.

Bioff changed his name and abandoned the role of the swaggering gangster he'd cultivated in Chicago and Los Angeles. In public, he played the role of the regular Joe, but in elevated circles, his identity was known and even celebrated. One of the state's wealthiest men, an early funder of Arizona's conservative movement, arranged for the governor of Sonora, a Mexican border state, to welcome Bioff with honors when he visited there. He was on a first-name basis with lawyers and judges at one of the best country clubs in Phoenix. He gambled in Las Vegas casinos run by the Chicago mob and at least once flew home to Phoenix in Goldwater's Beechcraft, with the senator at the stick.

Willie Bioff's access to the rich and powerful in Phoenix could be attributed in part to the celebrity status of gangsters in the postwar period. Thanks to the publicity surrounding his shakedown of Hollywood studios, Bioff had a national reputation. But in Phoenix, he was *meshpucha*, a member of the family.

Bioff got his start in Chicago in the 1920s as a pimp and brothel owner on the bottom rung of the Al Capone organization. During the Depression, he began to specialize in extortion. Through bribes and beatings, he acquired control of the screen-projectionists union in the upper Midwest, and in 1936, he demonstrated his muscle by ordering a strike that shut down every movie theater between Saint Louis and Chicago. Later that year, Bioff called on Nicholas Schenk, president of Loews Theaters and chief negotiator with the Hollywood craft unions for the studio owners. "You have a prosperous business here," Bioff told Schenk as he swept an appreciative eye across the mogul's Los Angeles office. Unless industry payoffs started rolling in to the Capone gang through him, Bioff threatened, he would close every theater in the country. "I am the boss, and I want two million dollars out of the movie industry," Bioff told Schenk. *I* meant *Chicago*.

To Bioff's surprise, Schenk was happy to take the deal. The heads of Twentieth Century Fox and RKO preferred to negotiate with the mob rather than the unions. Each of the major studios agreed to pay Bioff $50,000 a year, and the minor studios half that amount. To seal the agreement, the producers presented Bioff with a down payment of $75,000 in a New York hotel room. Bioff accepted a suitcase full of cash, opened it, and dumped it on the bed as the studio chiefs looked on.

Bioff's growing notoriety in Hollywood attracted the attention of an influential newspaper columnist, which led to scrutiny from the US Department of Justice. A few years later, Bioff and his fellow gangsters went to trial. Bioff cut a deal and appeared as a witness against his old pals. On the witness stand, he boasted, smoked, and leered at the mobsters as he pointed them out and named them, one by one.

In 1943, Bioff and ten other Chicagoans were convicted and sentenced to the federal pen, most of them with reputations much larger than Bioff's. The most notorious was Frank Nitti, Capone's designated successor, who killed himself rather than serve prison time. Bioff's testimony also sent up Paul Ricca, Louis Campagna, and a more obscure figure, Philip D'Andrea, whose family would play an important role in Arizona in decades to come. While his old associates cooled their heels in Atlanta and Leavenworth, Bioff was released after a brief stay behind bars.

On his release, Bioff moved directly to Arizona, where he already knew an old associate from his earliest days in Chicago, Gus Greenbaum, who by this time was a member of the Goldwater-Rosenzweig circle. Bioff adopted Nelson, the maiden name of his wife, Laurie. Most of those who knew "Bill Nelson" well enough to shake his hand also knew his real name.

Laurie Bioff later devised a list of her husband's closest friends in Phoenix. They included L. C. "Jake" Jacobson, a partner of Del Webb, developer of Sun City and the Flamingo Las Vegas Hotel and Casino. Another was William Luzzo of First Security Transfer, who like Bioff did business under a pseudonym. Rounding out the list were Greenbaum, Rosenzweig, and Mike Newman, like Rosenzweig a close friend of Goldwater since childhood.

The end for Bioff came on November 4, 1955, a Thursday. Shortly after 8:00 p.m., Bioff dropped by Mike Newman's house in the Bethany Home neighborhood, a comfortable area just north of Camelback Road. Gathered at Newman's home that night were Herman Matz, owner of a used-car lot downtown; Bennie Rosner, a buyer for Rosenzweig's jewelry store; and two out-of-town watch salesmen.

Rosner later described Newman's Thursday-night gathering as a casual affair, a dinner of cold cuts and conversation, nothing more. There was no liquor, no drinking of any kind. Before long, the two watch salesmen grew restless and proposed a trip to a nightclub called the Steak House, noted for gambling and other attractions. Rosner told the salesmen he didn't feel like going and said to the others, "One of you will have to take me home. I don't have a car."

Bioff told Rosner, "Take my pickup truck to your house. One of the other men can take me by to get it when I'm ready to go home."

Rosner drove Bioff's truck to his home around 9:30 p.m. Sometime after ten thirty, as Rosner and his wife sat up reading a newspaper, Matz's car pulled into their driveway. Bioff's truck started up soon after and drove off. Laurie Bioff said later that her husband arrived safely at home, where he pulled his pickup into the driveway of their tidy home, nestled in the embrace of plumbago and lantana bushes that Bioff had planted with his own hands.

Late the next morning, a Friday, Bioff climbed into the front seat of his pickup and waved to Laurie through the windshield. She watched him through the kitchen window. As she waved back, Bioff stepped on the starter button.

The blast "rocked northeast Phoenix," *The Phoenix Gazette* reported that evening. The paper fixed the time of the explosion at 11:59 a.m. In the front yard, police found two legs and a right hand. It was on one of the fingers on this hand that Bioff wore a six-carat diamond ring that became the subject of conflicting stories. In their incident report, police said it was Ben Rosner who found the ring after a careful search on hands and knees through the Bermuda grass on Bioff's lawn. In an interview five months later, Rosenzweig gave a different version. "A colored window washer" discovered it after he was hired to replace the windowpanes blown out by the blast.

THE ONE LABOR BOSS GOLDWATER ADMIRED

Some of Bioff's national celebrity derived from a book published in 1950, journalist Malcolm Johnson's bestseller, *Crime on the Labor Front*, which contained a chapter on Bioff, his years in Hollywood, and the trial that made him famous. His reputation was spread further by an influential newspaper columnist.

Soon after Bioff arrived in Hollywood to shake down the studios, the news reached Westbrook Pegler, a former Chicago reporter who was then riding high as a columnist for *The New York World-Telegram* and the Scripps Howard syndicate. A foe of both the mob and the unions, the conservative Pegler made inquiries about Bioff through sources he had collected during his early days as a reporter for *The Chicago Tribune*. Pegler discovered that the Chicago police still had an outstanding warrant for Bioff on a charge of pandering. Pegler's readership went up as he used this information to campaign against Bioff and the growing influence of the Chicago mob in Hollywood. In 1941, Pegler won the Pulitzer Prize for a newspaper series on that theme. In response, the Justice Department brought new charges against Bioff and the Chicago gang, including in their brief not only crimes in Hollywood but racketeering, tax evasion, and mail fraud. As though to celebrate his Pulitzer, Pegler moved his column from New York to a new home he bought in Tucson.

Naturally, Pegler took an interest in the Bioff murder. By 1955, his column was syndicated by Hearst and was a prominent feature in *The Arizona Republic*, among many other papers. He was also an occasional contributor to *American Opinion* magazine, published by the John Birch Society, then a rising force in Arizona's conservative circles. Organized labor was Pegler's declared enemy. He was particularly incensed by any form of politically engaged unionism. So, when the bomb that killed Bioff led to the awkward revelation in news reports that gangster and labor leader Bioff was close to Goldwater, readers in Phoenix eagerly turned to Pegler's column to see how he would handle it.

Pegler had a surprise for them. "It may now be related without reflection on Barry Goldwater," Pegler observed, that Goldwater's friendship with Bioff was an artifice. The gangster had been working with the senator in an investigative role. "Barry has been defending the right-to-work laws in all the states which have adopted them, including Arizona," Pegler wrote, and Bioff had served as an undercover expert for Goldwater, providing expert advice on labor corruption. In Pegler's view, Goldwater was a rare example of an elected official who was willing to risk his political reputation by associating with a criminal in the cause of uncovering "the parasites of political unionism."

Pegler returned to the Bioff murder a few months later to address the question of the mobster's friendship with Harry Rosenzweig. According to Pegler, Rosenzweig was the civic leader who had welcomed Bioff to Phoenix. "Bioff said he was lonesome. Rosenzweig made him welcome and took him to lunch." Pegler described Rosenzweig as "an occasional politician engaged in reform projects." Among these projects, wrote Pegler, was "the banishment of prostitution and open gambling," a claim that could be regarded as droll even before the reader reached the end of the column to learn that its source was Rosenzweig himself.

RUSSIAN URNS AND CLOISONNÉ VASES

The Goldwater circle's relations with Bioff were a good deal more extensive than Pegler had represented. After the gangster's murder, an item in the *Republic* announced that the county probate court appointed Harry Rosenzweig and Valley National Bank Vice President Thomas Goodnight to serve as examiners and appraisers of Bioff's estate. It was their task to go through Bioff's possessions, papers, and holdings; catalogue them; establish an approximate value for each item; and report their findings to the court. Three years later, after Gus and Bess Greenbaum were killed in their home in another gruesome assassination, the probate court once again appointed Rosenzweig and Goodnight (who was also Kemper Marley's brother-in-law), to perform the same tasks for the Greenbaum estate as well.

Rosenzweig and Goodnight reported to the court that they found little of interest among Bioff's effects. There was not much money, either. For a successful extortionist who collected payoffs of tens of thousands of dollars in his high-earning years, it appeared that Bioff lived modestly. His estate amounted to $60,000, about a third of it tied up in the family home.

In their inventory of the Bioff estate, Rosenzweig and Goodnight itemized $956.30 in cash, a silver belt buckle set with precious stones, and a .38-caliber Colt pistol. The couple's furnishings ran to French tapestry chairs, Russian urns, and sentimental nineteenth-century oil paintings (among them Hugo Engl's *Family Scene*), including one that buyers rejected as a fake when it was put up at auction in Scottsdale in 1957. The Bioffs lived in a style that might be expected from a moderately successful businessman who appreciated jade knickknacks, Chinese cloisonné vases, and Czechoslovakian crystal ware. There were no papers to compromise any of Bioff's Phoenix friends, including Rosenzweig. For that matter, the two estate examiners listed no papers of any kind in their report. When Laurie Bioff petitioned the court to name her administrator of her husband's estate, the only records she provided were insurance claims for the truck and the diamond ring and a note for $5,500 from an unidentified creditor. No checking or savings accounts or securities were reported.

There was one mystery, however. In a brief account of the 1957 auction of Bioff's paintings, the *Republic* noted that the auction included some unidentified possessions of a prominent Californian, Mickey Cohen. How their effects came to be auctioned together remains unknown.

'A RATHER SUBSTANTIAL BANK ACCOUNT'

The search for Bioff's money did not end with the Rosenzweig and Goodnight report, which turned out to have overlooked some items. A few days before Thanksgiving, the *Republic* reported that two captains from the Maricopa County Sheriff's Office, while combing through Bioff's records at the Phoenix branch of the Bank of Douglas, found what they called "a rather active and substantial bank account." The savings account was opened in 1947 with $500 and soon received a series of handsome deposits. On one day, $28,000 was recorded; on another, $16,000. Later entries showed several individual deposits of $10,000. Bioff opened a checking account in 1950 with $5,000, which built up to $60,000 in less than two years. The single largest deposit was $35,000. By the time the sheriff's men got to the bank, both accounts had been drained of all but $108. The person who made off with the money was never identified.

The sheriff's men were elusive about sharing anything else they might have found, but they did pass on to Phoenix police one intriguing detail. In running through the microfilm record of canceled checks, the deputies discovered one for $5,500. A partial underexposure made it impossible to determine to whom the check was payable. But the next frame of the microfilm clearly showed that Rosenzweig endorsed it on October 25, 1955. Records showed two other checks made out to Rosenzweig: one for $1,000 in 1952, and another for $3,000 in early 1955.

The Bank of Douglas was unique in Arizona; its owners were a pioneer family, the Brophys, whose ancestors, like the Goldwaters', were San Francisco grandees. In the 1950s and '60s, Frank Cullen Brophy emerged as one of the most influential men in Arizona and one of its wealthiest landowners. It was Brophy, for instance, who sold Goldwater the hilltop lot in Scottsdale, near Camelback Mountain, where Goldwater built *Be-Nun-I-Kin*, the home on which be bestowed a Navajo name. Brophy owned a swath of land in southern Arizona three miles wide and twenty-four miles long, rivaling Marley's largest parcels. Like Goldwater, Brophy was a man of immense, roguish charm. Both men shared a passion for Arizona history and an interest in politics that extended to the most prominent conservative organizations of the day. Brophy, too, was a friend of Willie Bioff.

The relationship between Brophy and Bioff remains elusive. Evidence that it existed at all is contained in a letter to Goldwater from a Phoenix property broker who said he had sold a house to Bioff and his wife in 1945 and got to know the couple over dozens of lunches at the San Carlos Hotel. At one point, Goldwater's correspondent reported, Bioff visited the broker at his office in the Bank of Douglas on Camelback Road and pulled out a sack of diamonds worth $125,000. In the conversation that followed, the broker said, Bioff told him that Brophy had been kind to him socially. Sometime between 1945 and 1948, at Bioff's request, Brophy arranged for an official state document to be drawn up, "a very formal introduction, with ribbons and the Great Seal of Arizona, from Governor [Sidney] Osborn to the Governor of Sonora for Mr. Nelson." Bioff asked Brophy to ask Osborn to sign the introduction, the real estate man wrote, because "it was his first visit to Mexico and he wanted to go in style." Goldwater responded affably. He thanked the broker for the "interesting letter about Willie Bioff. I knew that Frank Brophy knew him. In fact, most of the judges and half of the country club knew him."

BEHIND THE BIOFF MURDER

Some writers assume that someone in the Chicago Mafia organized Bioff's murder as a revenge killing for his role as informer in the Hollywood-extortion trial. But according to *The Chicago Tribune*'s Herb Lyon, an influential columnist who frequently wrote about the mob in his city, the perpetrators were probably members of the Detroit-Cleveland mob who had moved to Tucson in the early 1940s. Lyon quoted a Phoenix police source who said Tucson boss Peter Licavoli gave Bioff $300,000 to buy points in a horse track in Las Vegas and was incensed when he discovered that Bioff had diverted the money to another project. "They tell me the late Willie Bioff sealed his doom when he bought a chunk of a Las Vegas gambling casino shortly before his demise," Lyon wrote. "He is reported to have done it with loot the syndicate was anxious to get back. (The Chicago boys, it is said, took over his interest the day after Willie departed.)" The casino was not identified.

Meanwhile, a "confidential caller" told the Maricopa County Sheriff's Office that Licavoli was behind the killing but gave a different motive. The Tucson boss had ordered Bioff's death because he refused to repay the money. The $300,000 had been intended not for Las Vegas but for the expansion of a short-lived racing organization called Arizona Downs.

In the spring of 1968, the *Republic* acknowledged that Willie Bioff had been an unsavory character but suggested that Goldwater had managed to rehabilitate him. The *Republic* described Bioff as "a law-abiding, tax-paying citizen [who] had lived in Phoenix for seven years and behaved wisely. A staunch Republican, he could nod to men like GOP leaders Harry Rosenzweig and even contributed $500 to Barry Goldwater's 1952 campaign for the US Senate." But Bioff's life in Phoenix and his violent death suggested something darker.

The portrayal of Bioff as a lost criminal reformed by sympathetic attention from municipal reformers was an official fiction. In this, it had much in common with the spirit of the document with the Arizona state seal he presented to the Sonoran governor. The same fiction could be found in the examiners' report on his estate's assets written by Rosenzweig and Goodnight, and in Pegler's unnervingly cynical explanation for Bioff's friendship with Goldwater.

If glimpses of deeper ties between Bioff and the Phoenix network rarely reached the public, there was evidence that law enforcement was aware of them. One of the more pertinent surfaced after Goldwater's death in 1998. When the FBI released its files on the senator, bureau correspondence revealed that the bureau was aware that the relationship between Goldwater and Bioff was closer than the official accounts allowed. "It cannot be said that the senator knew nothing about Willie's background because from what I can gather, Goldwater at one time was trying to help Bioff get a presidential pardon," an anonymous FBI agent wrote. Goldwater's request was dated November 4, 1954, the year before Bioff's death.

Chapter 2

THE EXECUTIVE GANGSTER—
GUS GREENBAUM

In the two decades after World War II, a casual connection to gangsters added a dash of glamour to the normal middle-class life of some Phoenicians. Arizona historian Thomas E. Sheridan described his family's brush with it. "[A] friend with unexplained entrees into unusual places would call up the day after Christmas and say, 'Let's fly to Las Vegas for New Year's Eve.' They'd get front-row seats" at a casino floor show. "Anyone who didn't live in Phoenix during the boom has a hard time understanding how honest businessmen and business-women could rub shoulders with people like Bugsy Siegel and Ned Warren. But they did. It was a wide-open town."

Southwestern swank in the Sinatra era reflected the new respectability of organized crime. But Phoenix had been an open city for decades, if more in the style of the stogie in the back room than a cigarette in the cocktail lounge. When an interviewer for the Arizona Jewish Historical Society asked Harry Rosenzweig about the experience of living in Phoenix in the 1920s and '30s, he used Sheridan's phrase. "Gambling was wide-open here. When I grew up, they had so many bookie joints and places to bet on anything. Gambling just like you'd see in the movies. Just exactly. I can remember some of the joints we used to have around here. Nobody ever bothered them. As I said, we used to have a bookie joint right across the street from our [jewelry] store; we could go place a bet on any horse running in the country." Had Rosenzweig ever run for public office? "Yes," Rosenzweig replied, "on the city council. Barry and I ran. We were against gambling, prostitution and vice...And Barry said, 'The three things we like best.'"

For the generation of Phoenicians who could properly be called pioneers— Arizonans born before statehood in 1912—the saloon culture of the frontier was a fondly recalled way of life. The Goldwaters, Rosenzweigs, and Marleys, pioneer families all, were bound by memories that grew more revered as urban growth overwhelmed the romanticized liberties of the Old Territory. What remained among the pioneer descendants was a mutual respect that transcended faction and an attachment to an older culture that in its manly habits would not have been unfamiliar to organized crime figures like Willie Bioff and Gus Greenbaum. Even the political culture would have been recognizable. During the 1930s and '40s, the Democratic Party looked on benignly as its municipal government shared discreetly in the profits of dozens of flourishing brothels, whose female employees reported to the police station once a week to pay a fine of fifty dollars. Some taverns specialized in gambling; others combined gambling with prostitution. It was indeed a wide-open town, the crucible of the original Phoenix network.

In a transforming moment during World War II, officers in command of a US Army infantry regiment stationed at Papago Park forbade their soldiers from drinking or socializing in Phoenix after a racial incident triggered a riot and led to an army boycott of the city. The threat to the local economy was so alarming to the respectable citizens of Phoenix that they organized a citizens-reform movement called Charter Government and put Barry Goldwater at its head. In 1948, the Charter movement swept the Democrats from office.

Charter Government embraced an awkward paradox. Its membership included some of the very people its founders wanted to expel from public life. While one wing of the coalition was made up of real reformers, another belonged to surviving members of the old Democratic machine.

In 1948, a central figure in the older network, Gus Greenbaum, offered to shut down his gambling operations in Phoenix if the Charter Government ticket prevailed in that year's elections. Goldwater biographer Robert Alan Goldberg noted, "[T]o avoid embarrassing Harry and Barry, Greenbaum let Rosenzweig know that when the Charter Government ticket won in November, he would 'wrap up' his gambling operation and 'take it all back to Vegas.'" The same Greenbaum who had been a donor of large sums to Democrats running for state and federal office became a key contributor to Republican causes. Greenbaum gave "a significant portion of the nearly $18,000 the [Charter] slate spent during the [1948] campaign," Goldberg wrote. "Goldwater was aware of Greenbaum's contributions but denied knowledge of his criminal activities. 'He was a generous person,' Barry remarked. 'I'm not a gambler. I didn't know about that.'"

Charter Government represented an authentic form of Western reform politics. "We cleaned the city up," Rosenzweig told an interviewer. "We had twenty-seven different [city] departments when we went in, and by the time we went out, we had it down to eleven. [We] got a real special city manager who stayed fourteen years. Prior to that there were thirty-five city managers in thirty years. None of them lasted, because everything was a 'fix.' In other words, you could get anything you wanted if you paid for it under the table." Nonetheless, the survival of the older network within the Charter Government was only rarely mentioned in the press until the murders of Bioff and Greenbaum.

In his study of the social changes inside organized crime after World War II, sociologist Alan A. Block described how criminals trained in the older, established underworlds of the East spread across the West to conquer its largest cities. The Easterners had made their fortunes as managers of large, complex bootlegging operations during the 1920s, and after Prohibition ended, they increased their wealth and power by running equally large and complicated gambling operations. The most enterprising of these men moved west to Los Angeles, New Orleans, Las Vegas, and Reno, where they forged partnerships with local figures. The skills they mastered over fifteen years in Eastern cities would help the new, hybrid capitalism emerging in the Southwest. "This wider world of action," Block wrote, "brought with it scores of new customers, more and more politicians, land developers, corporate and tax attorneys, banks, brokerage houses, and bond salesmen, all anxious to participate in a variety of projects with the new criminal confraternities."

Many of the areas Block named as expansion cities for organized crime had their own bookmaking operations in place before the criminal migration.

In Phoenix, Meyer Lansky had his representative, Gus Greenbaum, in place by 1928. Greenbaum had already worked his way up from his bookie joints in downtown Phoenix cigar stores and pool halls to more elevated circles. By the mid-1940s, he was a leader of the urban Democrats and a rival to Kemper Marley, who led the "Pinto" Democrats, the party's conservative, rural faction. But by the end of the war, things began to change for Greenbaum.

Marley saw an opportunity to challenge Greenbaum by taking control of his racing wire just as the Chicago bosses were losing interest in horse racing and turning their attention to Las Vegas, where they wanted Greenbaum to assume large responsibilities. This prospect, along with the rise of the political fortunes of his friend Goldwater in 1948, persuaded Greenbaum that it would be a smart bet to change parties. Soon, the gangster would be a respectable citizen and a "reformer." Soon, Phoenix bankers would insist that he cosign loans underwriting the construction of casinos in Las Vegas before they approved deals worth hundreds of thousands of dollars. Few men in Arizona were so strategically placed in the postwar Phoenix economy.

THE GREENBAUM CLAN FINDS A HOME

In his prime, Greenbaum was a big man with a growly voice and a wide, over-large mouth. His ears hung like pendulums on either side of a balding head. He brushed the few strands of his forelock up, over, and back. There was little else that distinguished his appearance. He was simultaneously gangly and paunchy, but he knew how to dress.

In a photo taken on the lawn of the Flamingo Las Vegas in the 1950s, Greenbaum is visibly at ease—no tie, shirt buttoned at the neck, a light sports coat with a white hankie peeking out of the breast pocket, and ample but well-fitted, creased trousers breaking over expensive shoes. Next to him in the photo, his mobster pals from Minneapolis and New York favor dark suits with silk ties. They grimace involuntarily in the sharp desert light, but Greenbaum beams for the camera. He's dressed for the heat, looking every inch the experienced Southwesterner, which is what he had become.

"Gus," as Gustave Greenbaum was universally known, determined early on that Phoenix was home. In the leanest Depression years, he sent for his extended family to join him and his wife, Bess. His three brothers and their wives followed in short order: Sam and Bertha, William and Gertrude, and, a little later, the youngest couple, Charley and Leone. They all found homes in the fashionable Encanto neighborhood of central Phoenix.

Gus excelled at his profession of providing whiskey, women, and odds. Charlie opened a cigar store that took horse-racing bets that he ran through Gus's wire room. (In 1948, a writer for *The Phoenix Gazette* noted coyly that Charley was "a smoke-shop proprietor widely known in sporting circles.") Sam set up a bail-bond company and, when called upon, helped Gus run the wire.

After the three brothers arrived in Phoenix, the Greenbaums set about organizing quasi-legitimate businesses, including an ambitious grocery chain with about twenty outlets. It was to this operation that Goldwater was referring years later, perhaps tongue in cheek, when he said he had known Gus Greenbaum but only as a "grocer." The business managed to stay afloat for a little more than two years, but in November 1934, after the government turned Greenbaum's business manager into a cooperative witness, a federal grand jury indicted Gus, Sam, and William on seventeen counts of securities fraud. The case earned the Greenbaums local notoriety when they were convicted after a six week trial. They appealed to the Ninth Circuit in San Francisco, which overturned the conviction and ordered a new trial. Their notoriety turned into something closer to respect when the brothers, after a retrial in 1937 that resulted in a second conviction, appealed to the Ninth Circuit once again. This time, the case was dismissed outright. It was the one time that Gus, or for that matter, any of his brothers, would be troubled by Arizona law enforcement. In the late 1940s, there were sporadic mentions of the Greenbaums and the racing wire in *The Arizona News*, a fearless, conservative muckraking weekly, and increasing attention from *The Arizona Times*, a short-lived Democratic daily newspaper owned by Anna Roosevelt, daughter of President Franklin Delano Roosevelt. But after those few skirmishes, the Greenbaum brothers subsided into obscurity. The death of William from a heart attack in 1940 passed without notice in the daily press.

GUS CLIMBS TO THE TOP

Once he was established, Greenbaum presided over most of the city's illegal-gambling operations from his offices high in the Luhrs Tower, a Florentine layer cake cut out of stone that was regarded as the architectural jewel of downtown Phoenix. The dark interiors resembled a film-noir set, especially the ninth floor, which Greenbaum rented for his horse-racing wire and book. When it was busy, the place could be noisy, with a dozen or more people barking on telephones, a kitchen staff clanking silverware and plates as they served meals to players. A teletype rattled off the odds, race by race, from Chicago. On the other end of the phone lines were bookies from around the city and occasionally from Tucson and Yuma, the state's smaller gambling centers, when they needed to lay off bets. Greenbaum was a bookie's bookie, a gambler with enough capital, or access to it (through Meyer Lansky, CFO of the national mob), to handle as much action as Arizona cared to provide. Among his closest lieutenants were two gamblers who shared the same first name and middle initial, "Clarence E." This curious fact forced a moniker on each of them. Clarence E. Baldwin was "Teak," and Clarence E. Newman was "Mike." The two Clarences were twin moons orbiting Greenbaum.

When he wanted to get away from the noise of the betting room, Greenbaum retreated to his private sanctum on the fifteenth floor, the tiny, top layer of the stone cake. From there, he could survey the entire metropolis, such as it was, including city hall, the county courthouse, and the dome of the state capitol a mile or so due west. There was great curiosity around town about what went on in Greenbaum's penthouse. It had no elevator access and could be reached only by a narrow stairway from the fourteenth floor. Newspaper reporters sometimes imagined that this was the mysterious chamber in which bundles of cash were pressed into the hands of politicians. At least once, a reporter tried to bribe a Luhrs employee into letting him have a peek into the aerie, but even if he had succeeded, he would have been disappointed. Although the room was dressed with expensive drapes and carpeting, the main feature was a modest round card table with four chairs and a small refrigerator stocked with snacks and drinks. It was here that Greenbaum, a passionate bridge player, escaped the din of the wire room. When there weren't enough bridge players around, he settled for pinochle, playing for hours on end with friendly pols or businessmen or visiting underworld dignitaries from Las Vegas, Los Angeles, and sometimes New York.

In the days shortly after the war, Greenbaum knew everyone worth knowing in Phoenix, not just politicians and not only Democrats. The prestigious Arizona Club, founded in the early 1890s, well before statehood, occupied several floors of the adjoining and much-larger architectural companion of the Tower, the Luhrs Building proper. Club presidents who gaveled meetings to order in the earliest days of the Arizona Club included three members of the Territorial Supreme Court and Baron Goldwater, father of the future US senator. From its dining room, members could see cattle ranches stretching south to the Salt River and, in the distance, the jagged, blue horizon line of South Mountain.

THE HORSE WIRE IN PHOENIX

The end of Prohibition was still five years in the future when Meyer Lansky began to plan for the impending loss of the mob's vast profits from bootleg liquor. Criminal gangs had always made money from whiskey, prostitution, and gambling, but Lansky was convinced that with the end of speakeasies, the most promising source for new windfalls lay elsewhere and required a move from the nighttime into daylight, from the furtive to the legal. That meant betting on horses. That, in turn, required a single, bold strategy—gaining control of most of the fifteen thousand bookies in the country and a percentage of their profits. To accomplish that, Lansky had to take over the horse-racing news wire that made the betting possible and tied the bookies together into a single industry.

In 1928, Chicago was the home of the only nationwide racing wire, the General News Bureau, owned by the politically influential Moses Annenberg. Lansky could do little more than watch as Annenberg absorbed small regional wires around the country and shaped General News into a monopoly. For most of the 1930s, Lansky had to be satisfied with hanging on to his regional wire, the Greater New York News Service.

Lansky thought his chance had come in 1934, when Annenberg had a falling out with his partner, James Ragan, who managed General News for him out of Chicago. Chicago boss Frank Nitti tried to force Ragan to join in the creation of a mob-owned national wire service to compete with Annenberg, but Ragan refused. He had little time for gangsters because, he said, they used racing money to launder profits and capitalize prostitution and drugs. Instead, Ragan opened a new national racing wire under the name Continental Press Service and remained independent of both Annenberg and the mob. Annenberg went on to become one of the country's most successful publishers, built on the success of the "bible" of the horse-racing industry, *The Daily Racing Form.*

Lansky challenged Ragan's Continental almost immediately. In 1940, he set up the rival Trans-American Wire, an undisguised effort to force Continental out of business. But Lansky didn't rush. For the first few years, he required bookies under his control to take on the new wire merely as a supplemental subscription. He placed the Trans-American in the willing hands of Ben Siegel, whom Lansky had ordered to California in 1937 with the goal, among others, of selling Trans-American to bookies in cities around the Southwest, including Phoenix.

Through a combination of ruthlessness and guile and with the profits from an occasional large heroin deal in Mexico, Siegel developed the once mutually remote fiefdoms of southern California, Arizona, and New Mexico into a single coherent gambling operation under his control. The moment Lansky chose to deliver the coup de grace to Ragan can be established almost to the day.

In 1950, Arizona's own US senator Ernest MacFarland led the first national probe of interstate gambling in the horse-racing business. MacFarland's investigation ignored Phoenix and Greenbaum with the exception of a single reference that establishes the day when Lansky started his attack on Ragan. A list of companies subscribing to Ragan's Continental Press Service in 1943 included the Washoe Publishing Co. of Phoenix, domiciled in room 909 of the Luhrs Tower. There was a footnote: Washoe was "discontinued November 24, 1943," the Wednesday before the start of the Thanksgiving holiday. After dropping

Ragan's wire, Greenbaum subscribed exclusively to Lansky's Trans-American, and Lansky expected all the bookies to follow suit. He had a warning for hold-outs who refused to drop Ragan's wire. Bookies in southern California would have to pay an immediate $25,000 fine. Others would get a beating in addition to the fine.

Within a few years, Ragan would be dead, the victim of a mob hit in which Greenbaum had a direct hand.

BUGSY SIEGEL IN THE LUHRS TOWER

Through the war years, Ben Siegel used Gus Greenbaum's offices in the Luhrs Tower as his Phoenix headquarters. When he was not able to visit, he kept an eye on the operation through Virginia Hill, his notorious girlfriend. Hill sometimes worked directly for Lansky as a courier, traveling around the country to deliver money and heroin and to pass on his instructions to mob associates face-to-face. During visits to Greenbaum in Phoenix, Hill liked to stay in the adobe resort in Scottsdale called the Paradise Inn. In November and December of 1947, seventeen months after Siegel was mur-dered in her living room in Los Angeles, Hill returned to the Paradise Inn to escape press attention, only to make national headlines when she was found unconscious in her room after taking an overdose of what was described as sleeping pills.

From time to time, when Siegel visited the Luhrs Tower, he brought a part-ner, Mickey Cohen, a Hollywood celebrity gangster like Siegel. At other times, Siegel showed up in the company of Hollywood pal George Raft, a movie star who played Siegel-like characters in B films. Raft spread a ripple of glamour during his visits to the tower by buying flowers in the gift shop and presenting them, with a flourish, to the young women who operated the elevators. Raft had friends of his own in town, among them Jack Chiate, a member of a family of Angeleans, cash-poor but land-rich, who left California to join Greenbaum's growing circle in Phoenix.

In 1951, Mickey Cohen provided a glimpse into life on the ninth and fifteenth floors of the Luhrs Tower when the Kefauver Committee heard testimony that included a rare bit of news about Arizona. "I was down there about eight months, on the lam," Cohen told the committee during a hearing in Los Angeles, where he saw things in Greenbaum's operation that astonished him.

"Listen, Ben Siegel and I sat in an office in Phoenix, and I heard a man deal with a congressman in Washington and some senators. He had maybe ten guys working for him in his office in downtown Phoenix, and it had kitchens and everything else. It was air-conditioned, and here was the tops in our govern- ment doing business with the underworld. Placing bets and talking, and actu- ally, they were dealing, and Siegel had a piece of this. Like the guy would say, 'Senator, take this advice and make this move.' He was a part of the underworld and advising a senator."

Who were the congressman and senators Cohen saw at the Luhrs Tower? For his 1967 biography of Siegel, Dean Jennings interviewed Cohen and pressed him on the identity of the politicians he mentioned in the congressional hear- ings. Jennings asked him whether the man he had referred to was "an Arizona or a California senator."

"There were so many of them," Cohen said. "I sat there amazed. I was still a punk, you know. There was some high muckety-mucks that came into the office at different times and had lunch—it was air-conditioned, the most beautiful thing you ever seen."

One thing was clear: the senator in question could not have been Barry Goldwater, who first took national office in 1953, nearly two years after Cohen testified to Congress. The more probable interpretation of the scene is that the "senators" Cohen saw were members not of the US Congress but of the upper house of the Arizona legislature. In 1976, an IRE journalist interviewed Adam Diaz, once a Luhrs elevator operator and later a member of the Phoenix City Council who was recruited to run as a Charter candidate by Goldwater himself. Diaz reported that Greenbaum spent long hours on the fifteenth floor playing pinochle with "his good friend" Joe Haldiman.

In the 1930s and '40s, Haldiman served three terms in the Arizona sen- ate, the second term as senate president. During the years he wielded the gavel, Haldiman ran an insurance company from offices on the ground floor of the Luhrs Tower and was often available to Greenbaum for a quick card game and political advice. Haldiman was a man of more than marginal influence. The year Greenbaum arrived in Phoenix, Haldiman was the owner and publisher of the *Arizona Farmer* and a majority stockholder in *The Phoenix Evening Gazette.* As for the US Congressman, *The Arizona News* reported in September 1948 that Greenbaum and a brother of Arizona Governor Sidney Osborn were negotiating over the rewards that might follow if each of them contributed $25,000 to the campaign of Democratic Congressman Richard F. Harless for governor. Greenbaum and Neri Osborn, Sidney Osborn's brother and also a Democrat, deadlocked for eight months on the terms of their proposed $50,000 contribution to Harless. Greenbaum was said to be troubled by Harless's ambition; he wanted assurances that he would remain in the governor's chair even if a US Senate seat opened up to make sure Greenbaum got his money's worth.

GREENBAUM IS ORDERED TO LAS VEGAS

In 1945, Meyer Lansky made a fateful business decision that changed the direction of Gus Greenbaum's career and with it the future of organized crime in Phoenix. Just as Lansky and Lucky Luciano decided in 1928 that the best prospects for post-Prohibition profits lay in racetrack gambling rather than in liquor, they foresaw that after World War II horse racing would decline in popularity and that the future of gambling lay in casinos. They also perceived that the biggest profits would come from legalized upscale gambling of the European sort. For Greenbaum, that meant reassignment to an executive-management position in the mob-owned casinos of Las Vegas. Greenbaum resisted. In Phoenix, he had built a life for himself and his brothers and their families, and he did not want to leave. It would not be the last time Greenbaum found that what he wanted conflicted with his bosses' desires. But for the moment, he complied, and in January 1945, Greenbaum packed up his handbook equipment, moved it out of the Luhrs Tower, and stored it in a warehouse.

Greenbaum was already familiar with southern Nevada. He and Ben Siegel had cased Las Vegas as early as November 1941, when resort hotels and downscale gambling houses promoted their games with cowboy themes. Among them were El Rancho and the Last Frontier, which catered to officers training at the nearby US Army Gunnery School.

A less fashionable spot was El Cortez in downtown Vegas on Fremont and Sixth streets. Siegel waited for the closing months of the war to acquire it. Lansky installed Greenbaum as the manager and for support added a few associates from the Minneapolis mob, led by the capable Moe Sedway. Before long, Siegel used the profits from El Cortez to acquire three more nightclubs: the Frontier Turf, El Dorado, and the Las Vegas. Siegel had at least one-quarter interest in each of them, and he shared an undisclosed percentage of the ownership with Greenbaum, who assumed management of all four clubs. The commitment of time and energy was so large that Greenbaum was able to return to Phoenix only infrequently. His wife and brothers, with the exception of the deceased William, continued to live there.

Meanwhile, Greenbaum nursed the hope that he could go home and reopen the old handbook. Soon after the purchase of El Cortez, Greenbaum ordered Teak Baldwin, Mike Newman, and a new partner, Jimmy Aaron, to haul the handbook equipment out of the warehouse and reopen in the Saint James Hotel. The corporate name was changed from Washoe News to the Western News Exchange.

GREENBAUM AND MARLEY BATTLE FOR INFLUENCE

Reopening his Phoenix racing book while he was responsible for managing four clubs in Las Vegas was likely the first of a series of Gus Greenbaum's errors in judgment. For one thing, Kemper Marley, his rival for control of the Democratic Party, coveted the mob-approved racing wire in Phoenix, and he usually got what he wanted.

Marley was, first and foremost, a man of the soil. He owned cattle and sheep ranches, urban feedlots, meatpacking houses, cotton fields and cotton gins, and hundreds of sections of farmland in central Arizona and the Imperial Valley of southern California. He was co-owner of large and valuable tracts of land in north Scottsdale. He controlled the lion's share of alcohol production in the state, including the importing and bottling of the leading international brands of spirits, an advantage he acquired as the first Arizonan after the demise of Prohibition to buy up licenses for liquor wholesaling. He sat on the boards of banks, water and utility cooperatives, and various state commissions. Shortly before World War II, he was the employer of a group of quasi-legal vigilantes who used ax handles to break up strikes by migrant strawberry pickers, and when the notoriety that followed seemed to exclude his chances for a political career, he financed his preferred candidates for the highest public offices, often in direct conflict with Greenbaum's union-supported choices.

In the 1950s, at the peak of Marley's influence, one of the West's most exclusive social clubs invited him to join. Membership in the Rancheros Visitadores allowed him to rub shoulders with Ronald Reagan, George Hearst Jr., and Western owners of land, capital, and industry. His personal attorney in this period was a young lawyer who graduated at the top of his class at Stanford, a future chief justice of the US Supreme Court, William Rehnquist. In the late 1950s, Rehnquist defended Marley against a charge that he owned a pair of cinderblock brothels next to the railroad tracks in the south Phoenix barrio.

It is far from clear why a man of Marley's wealth and political influence would want to own a depreciating asset like the postwar horse wire in Phoenix. Still, law enforcement watched carefully as Marley, around the time Siegel was buying El Cortez, reinstalled Meyer Lansky's Trans-American wire service in downtown Phoenix.

In November 1945, nine months after Greenbaum moved his wire operation out of the Luhrs Tower, agent Jack Wallace wrote in the FBI Phoenix Bureau's annual crime survey that Marley had "announced" to an unidentified FBI informant that his "intention was to replace that [wire] abandoned by Greenbaum...Marley indicated he intended to install a wire service at 719 East Jackson Street." This was the Marley-owned American Bottling Exchange, a warehouse known informally as the bottling works. Marley once described the place as a "junkyard and glass-collection facility," which abutted the tracks of the Southern Pacific Railroad. The "works" lay just three blocks from Marley's brothels at 119 and 121 South Sixth Street in the immediate neighborhood of what would become decades later the Diamondbacks baseball stadium. It was a rough area, but Marley was prepared for trouble. Agent Wallace wrote that Marley was "often in the company of A. F. Cowan [actually Alex Cohen], alias 'Fats,' his strong-arm man." Cohen, the FBI report said, "has long been a local hoodlum and gambler at Phoenix, with a record of manslaughter," about whom very little information has survived.

The FBI informant also provided the opinion that Marley's "source of news, presumably, was to be the same as that employed by Greenbaum," that is, the Trans-American wire. In 1977, police sources who had studied public records, now apparently lost, said that in 1946, Marley "and several others, including Cosa Nostra mobster Peter Licavoli, took over the racing wire service for bookies in Arizona…Marley and his associates were instructed by the Chicago Syndicate to move Greenbaum out of the wire, and they did so." Peter Licavoli was the head of the mob in Tucson. His relationship with the Detroit-Cleveland Mafia was comparable to Greenbaum's with Chicago.

If Licavoli and Marley were cooperating to revive the Trans-American wire in Phoenix, they had to have the blessing not only of Chicago but of Lansky and probably even Luciano as well. That meant the entire national-gambling organization wanted Greenbaum out of Phoenix and back at work in Las Vegas. Greenbaum did not take the hint.

Sometime in the spring of 1946, according to an FBI report dated August 28, 1946, Greenbaum defied the mob leadership and again subscribed to the hated James Ragan's Continental Press Service with the intention of going into direct competition with Marley. Greenbaum would have been too valuable a casino manager to be roughed up, but he was given a lesson. Phoenix FBI Special Agent in Charge William E. Miller reported the incident to Washington on Aug. 21. "Some of the gamblers had been 'taking Gus' recently by obtaining the results of races and then placing bets on the winning horses before Gus received the report on the race." Miller wrote that the cheating might have been "part of a campaign to force Gus to sell out," noting that Marley and Alex Cohen "have wire service into Phoenix, and it is possible there is some connection between this wire service and Gus Greenbaum's recent losses." In other words, the national mob had made its ruling: Marley would replace Greenbaum as the head of its gambling operation in Phoenix. Marley would teach Greenbaum the necessary lesson by cheating him out of money.

GREENBAUM DIRECTS A MURDER

By summer, the pace of events picked up. James Ragan was gunned down in an ambush. It immediately brought Greenbaum under closer scrutiny from federal authorities.

On June 24, 1946, Ragan pulled up at the stoplight at State Street and Pershing Avenue in Chicago. Directly in front of him, waiting for the light to change, sat a gray sedan, stalled. An old delivery truck covered with a tarpaulin pulled up in the right lane next to Ragan's car. Suddenly, the tarpaulin flew up on the left side of the truck. Someone fired two shotgun blasts. One of them cut open Ragan's right shoulder, shattering his collarbone and breaking his humerus. The truck sped off and was later found abandoned.

Ragan was rushed to the hospital and put in an oxygen tent, where he clung to life with the help of blood transfusions.

In Las Vegas, Greenbaum got the news that Ragan had survived the attack. According to the daughter of Dave Berman, who had helped manage some of Siegel's Las Vegas properties, Greenbaum was standing in the pit of the Las Vegas Club when he learned that Ragan had survived the effects of his wounds. Greenbaum picked up the pit phone and called Chicago. In a fury, apparently not caring who heard him, Greenbaum associated himself directly with the murder. "You didn't finish the job," Greenbaum barked to someone. "Either Ragan dies, or you do."

Within the span of a little more than five weeks, on August 8, Ragan was dead, finished off by a favorite mob poison of the time, tablets of bichloride of mercury. A Greenbaum confederate had managed to evade a police guard and get into Ragan's hospital room to force the mercury pills down his throat. "They slipped him the salt," one of the pit men boasted when Greenbaum and the others got the news that Ragan was dead. That evening the gangsters celebrated. Waiters in tall chef hats served canapés on silver platters.

The mob's defiance in killing Ragan rattled federal law enforcement. The FBI responded with a series of urgent inquiries to the local bureaus. Long summaries of files on the local racing wires soon arrived at FBI headquarters in Washington. The murder confirmed that Lansky had acquired significant control over the illegal off-track-betting industry. National publicity about Ragan put pressure on Congress, whose members began to think of the racing wire as a subject for investigation.

WHY GREENBAUM JOINED THE GOP

Thirteen days after James Ragan was "slipped the salt" in his Chicago hospital bed, William Miller filed his report on the rivalry between Greenbaum and Marley for control of the wire. Through July and August 1946, reports flew between Washington and national gambling centers, including Phoenix, Chicago, Salt Lake, and Detroit. The FBI replaced its file acronym from the routine-sounding "Crime Survey" to the acronym CAPGA, short for "Reactivation of the Capone Gang," a sign of the urgent mood in the bureau after the Ragan murder.

Eight days after reporting that Marley had used the Trans-American wire to cheat Greenbaum, Miller prepared a comprehensive review of the local files for the CAPGA report and summarized everything that was known about the Phoenix gambling scene. Even in the heavily redacted form in which it surfaced thirty-five years later, the FBI review contained some startling information. Somehow, Greenbaum had prevailed. Marley removed the wire from the bottling works on East Jackson Street. "Since Gus Greenbaum restored his wire service at Phoenix," an FBI agent wrote for Miller, "the wire service of Cowan and Marley has been discontinued, and [informant] has not heard of anyone trying to establish any additional wire service since."

No record has survived to explain how Greenbaum turned the tables on Marley, but this much is known: sometime late in 1946, Greenbaum signed over his stake in the wire to Teak Baldwin and Mike Newman. They reinstalled it at the new restaurant and bar on north Central Avenue called the Steak Club. It didn't last long, however. Placing illegal bets on the ponies was losing its allure and would all but expire by the late 1940s. The FBI speculated that Marley had either been bought out or had simply lost interest and let the wire die. In any case, it was around this time that Mike Newman moved to Las Vegas; an arrest on a tax charge made Phoenix too hot for him. He joined Greenbaum at the Riviera, where he ran junkets for tourists. Teak Baldwin remained in Phoenix and became a member of Marley's operation.

Publicity over the gangland killing of Ragan, combined with national headlines kicked up by MacFarland's and then Kefauver's senate investigating committees, put the racing wire in a bad odor with the public. Even in Nevada, bloodshed over control of the horse wire led to hearings before the State Tax Commission and in 1949 to the enactment of a law giving the commission the authority to require all wire services to be sold to any willing customer. The romance of the horses in the gangster era was gone for good, to be replaced by legalized gambling and casino profits so vast that they would become the cornerstone of a new underworld banking system.

All through its careful narrative of the struggle among leading gangsters for control of the racing wire in Phoenix, the FBI seemed to avoid the deeper question, which was not who had possession of the teletype tickers but who was providing police protection. That issue was resolved in Greenbaum's favor. Before leaving for Las Vegas and the Flamingo, Greenbaum formally joined the rising reform movement in Arizona by giving Harry Rosenzweig $10,000 for the Republican Party, earmarked specifically for the campaign for city council led by the rising star of Arizona politics, Barry Goldwater. It was a move with local consequences that could hardly have been foreseen.

"Gus said he'd put up some money for us," Harry Rosenzweig told *New Yorker* reporter Burton Bernstein, "and at his brother's anniversary party, he handed me a package, which I didn't look at until I got home. He said, 'You can get this amount of money every month for the next six months.' I said that we'd take this amount, but we don't want the rest of it, since it wouldn't look right." Rosenzweig wasn't asked why it was acceptable to take $10,000 in cash from an emissary of Meyer Lansky but not $70,000. Still, he understood that some proprieties were needed. "To hide who gave it," Rosenzweig told *The New Yorker*, "I called up ten Democrats and put it under their names," in amounts of

$1,000 each. The scrupulous touch was Rosenzweig's insistence that all ten of the phony campaign donors be real Democrats.

A PHOENIX BANK SAVES THE FLAMINGO

The origin of the Flamingo is established lore. Perhaps the best retelling was Hollywood's adaptation (*Bugsy*, 1991) of Dean Jennings's biography of Ben Siegel. The last scene occurs on the Flamingo's opening night on the day after Christmas in 1946. Moe Sedway and a portly figure climb out of a coupe carrying California plates in rare rainy and windy weather for southern Nevada. The two men stride through the Flamingo entrance and stop at a blackjack table to ask directions. The dealer points to the back, where Siegel's girlfriend, Virginia Hill, draped in a violet gown with a brooch pinned at the neckline, sits at a table reckoning casino accounts. "Hello, Virginia," says Sedway. Then, pointing to his silent companion, adds, "This is Gus Greenbaum. Meyer Lansky sent us. We're taking control of the Flamingo Hotel." When Hill protests, Greenbaum explains that Ben Siegel is dead. Hill's stunned take, delivered in forty wordless seconds scored with a memorable lament for flute and trumpet, closes out the movie. It is memorable filmmaking, even with the misleading invention that Virginia, in reality an occasional visitor to Gus Greenbaum's office in the Luhrs Tower, would need an introduction to the Phoenix gangster. Still, *Bugsy* might have contained the first reference in popular culture to the role Phoenicians played in building the Flamingo. Several times the camera is positioned to capture Phoenix developer Del Webb's name hand-lettered on the doors of construction vehicles. Greenbaum's presence in the final scene makes the point that it was two Phoenicians, Greenbaum and Webb, who saved Siegel's dream.

The financial history of the Flamingo reveals that, by the time Lansky ordered Greenbaum to move to Las Vegas, he was a much more influential citizen than his career as a handbook operator would have suggested. In the summer of 1946, as Baldwin and Newman were removing Greenbaum's gambling equipment from storage, Siegel and Lansky were arranging loans to finance the Flamingo. Both men had already invested their corporate profits from the sale of El Cortez in July, a comely $166,000 return on a six-month investment of $600,000. Lansky added another $62,500 from his personal funds. The entire sum capitalized a new company called the Nevada Project Corporation, formed to take advantage of an opportunity created by the owner of *The Hollywood Reporter*, Billy Wilkerson, who wanted to build the first gambling spot in Las Vegas that would borrow its glamour not from images of the Old West but from the nightclubs on the Sunset Strip.

After buying the land in a rapidly inflating market, paying for plans, and breaking ground, Wilkerson was running out of money. He took all of the Nevada Project's money, but by November needed more. On the next to last day of that month, Wilkerson signed a loan for $600,000 from the Valley National Bank in Phoenix. Greenbaum arranged the loan. Both Greenbaum and Wilkerson signed the papers for the construction contractors, former carpenters turned business partners, Del Webb and Laverne C. (Jake) Jacobson.

It is useful to consider how Greenbaum arrived at the moment in his career when he could vouch for a large loan from a leading bank, considering that for years he had been the object of FBI scrutiny for his ties to some of the most notorious organized-crime figures in the country. In 2016 dollars, the loan would have amounted to $7.2 million for what was at the time an unusually risky proposition. It was the first time a legitimate bank had funded a construction loan for a casino in Las Vegas. Yet Greenbaum's role did not appear to be a concern to Valley National bankers. On the contrary, his signature guaranteeing payment to the building contractor appeared to be a condition for the loan.

It is not too much to say that the Valley National–Flamingo deal was a turning point in Phoenix history, the moment when at least one sector of organized crime was formally accepted as part of the city's power structure. When an IRE reporter asked Thomas Goodnight in 1976 if he knew Greenbaum well, the banker responded, "Mr. Greenbaum was a very fine and respected man in this community. We had many dealings with him at the bank."

The Christmas 1946 opening at the Flamingo did not go well, at least for the owners. The guests had a fine time, showing up in droves and winning big at the casino tables, but because the Flamingo's hotel rooms were not finished, the guests took their winnings back to their rooms in downtown Las Vegas, where they enriched Siegel's competitors by losing most of their Flamingo winnings there before turning in. By February, Siegel was stalling on paying Webb about $300,000 he still owed. Siegel then obtained an additional loan for that sum from the Valley National Bank. By mid-March, when Siegel had still failed to use the Valley National money to pay him off, Webb filed a lien against the Flamingo.

Siegel's failure to pay must have made for some uneasiness on the evening of March 1, when Webb led a delegation of notable Phoenicians to a party at what was billed as the "formal" opening of the Flamingo. The guests flew in on Webb's newly organized Arizona Airways, created to carry sportsmen on weekend round-trip flights between Phoenix and Las Vegas during Arizona's winter-tourist season. Guests included the Harry Rosenzweigs, Webb lawyer Charles Strouss, and Mr. and Mrs. Bob Goldwater. The senator's younger brother had reason to celebrate: a few weeks earlier, around the signing of the bank's $300,000 loan to Siegel, Valley National Bank appointed him to its board of directors. Other notable Phoenicians on the flight included Fred Meyer, advertising director of the two Phoenix daily newspapers. Two months after the party, on May 1, Webb Co. broke ground on a $1 million new office and printing home for the *Republic* and the *Gazette* at Second and Van Buren streets in downtown Phoenix.

On the flight to Las Vegas, the pilot dipped a wing over points of interest, including the Kingman Army Air Base, where some five thousand decommissioned World War II aircraft were parked in ranks on the desert floor. There is no record of how well the Flamingo guests enjoyed the celebration apart from a clue in the Webb Co. newsletter. A planned flight over the Grand Canyon on the return leg had to be cancelled because badly hungover guests were afraid of what a glimpse of the great chasm might do to their stomachs.

TONY ACCARDO PAYS A CALL

In early 1955, claiming ill health, Greenbaum announced his retirement from the Flamingo and returned to Phoenix. It had been ten years since he took over management of the casino, which he had turned into a profitable operation in a matter of months. By the end of 1947, Greenbaum reported a casino profit of $4 million to the IRS. His success was attributed to his rapid expansion of the number of hotel rooms, his Gold Club program for high rollers, an innovation at the time, and his skill at collecting gambling debts. Before he left for Phoenix to take up the life of a retiree with wife Bess and his remaining brothers, Greenbaum buried in the desert, perhaps as life insurance, casino records containing the names and financial information of Flamingo Gold Card members.

Before long, Las Vegas intervened in Greenbaum's life once again. A syndicate of investors assembled by Los Angeles lawyer Sidney Korshak, which included key members of the Chicago Outfit and a few Hollywood stars (the Marx Brothers, Dean Martin), had decided to open a new hotel and casino, the Riviera, a $10 million high-rise designed in the style of a Miami oceanfront hotel. It was an unusual arrangement because the investment syndicate was leasing the building from a third party. Like the Flamingo, the Riviera Hotel & Casino started losing money from the moment it opened its doors on April 19, 1955. Part of the problem was that the skim was out of control. The cause was not hard to identify. The point of Chicago's participation was to skim as much money as possible from the gambling tables. By July, the Riviera was filing for bankruptcy, and the landlord was looking for a new operator.

Tony Accardo, newly in charge of the Chicago mob, showed up in Phoenix in the company of Jake Guzik. They wanted Greenbaum to return to Nevada and take charge of the Riviera. This put Greenbaum in a tight spot. Accardo had earned the nickname "Joe Batters" because his preferred instrument of persuasion was the baseball bat. A visit from him might have been considered an honor or a death threat, depending on his mood.

The Chicagoans took Greenbaum to a Phoenix restaurant, The Flame, a place close to his home that was considered a classy joint. Its main feature was a large horseshoe-shaped bar facing a wall of tropical plants behind plate glass. The mob chiefs explained to Greenbaum that to get the Riviera landlord off their backs, the Riviera needed a fresh start under his leadership. Most of all, they said, they needed him to lead them to the spot in the Mojave Desert where he buried the records of Flamingo Gold Card members.

Greenbaum declined. He was a sick man, he explained. Vegas, with its easy access to hookers and hard drugs and craps tables, had not been good for him. And he had promised Bess that he was done with all of that. After dinner, he went home and tried to sleep. "Then one night a few days later," mob writer Ed Reid reported years later, Charley Greenbaum and his wife, Leone, paid a visit to Gus. "Leone was nearly hysterical with fear." Someone had threatened her on the telephone. Whoever it was hinted that they were going to "teach Gus a lesson." Gus still wouldn't listen. "A few nights" after the meeting at The Flame, Leone was smothered to death in her Phoenix home. Gus changed his mind and took the job at the Riviera.

That is the accepted version. A closer look at the record reveals a different story. While it's true that Leone Greenbaum was asphyxiated in her Phoenix home and that Gus took over the Riviera not long after, there is reason to doubt that Leone's murder was the cause for his change of mind. For one thing, Leone was killed a week after the Riviera opened (April 27, 1955), nearly three months before it filed for bankruptcy. For another, contemporaneous news accounts of Leone's murder reported that the incident in which she had been threatened on the telephone occurred much earlier, on October 30, 1954, rather than a few nights before her murder. She had been beaten and badly bruised in a break-in at her home. She told police she believed the intruder was after her jewels. She also expressed fear that her brother-in-law's association with Ben Siegel might have had something to do with the assault; it might have been one of Siegel's "henchmen," she said. It's not difficult to imagine that this report, without the time elements, could have been mistaken later as cause and effect.

GOLDWATER ATTENDS GREENBAUM'S FUNERAL

No one but his killers knew what Gus Greenbaum was watching on television on Tuesday, December 3, 1958. At seven thirty, Gus was alone in the Greenbaum home. The maid had just finished cleaning up after dinner. She climbed into the passenger seat of Bess Greenbaum's 1957 Fleetwood Cadillac as Bess slid behind the wheel and, as was her custom, drove the maid the scant half mile to her home. Neither woman was aware that she was being watched.

After they left, Gus retired to the master bedroom, slipped into his silk pajamas, and turned on a heating pad. Before settling in, he switched on the TV, which was still on when Phoenix police arrived. It might have been tuned in to *Dragnet*, NBC's police procedural starring Jack Webb, which was just coming on as Gus got ready for bed. Or perhaps he rotated the clunky VHF dial to ABC's *Cheyenne* starring Clint Walker, who had been a familiar face in Las Vegas when he worked as a security guard at the Sands in the early 1950s.

As Greenbaum settled back to watch TV, two men slipped into the kitchen through the back door. Their hands were covered with plastic bags tied off at the wrists. One of them selected a large butcher knife. The other picked up a heavy, ornamental glass bottle. They followed the sound of the TV to the bedroom. Before Gus could get up from the bed, the bottle came down on the top of his head. Moments later, the killers applied the butcher knife to his throat.

Before they could leave the house, the hit men were surprised by the return of Bess Greenbaum. When she entered the house, they grabbed her, tied her hands behind her back with a blue necktie, and shoved her onto a couch in a den near the kitchen. One of them hit her on the head with the bottle. In a strangely tidy final gesture, before turning the butcher knife on Bess, the second killer spread out newspapers and towels on the couch under her neck.

The killers were never caught, and no one has established exactly why Greenbaum was killed. Years later, the Chicago mob's "ambassador" to Hollywood and the CIA, Johnny Roselli, told a friend, "That was Meyer's contract." Organized-crime writer John William Tuohy believes that Accardo had gone sour on Greenbaum and by 1958 wanted him out of the Riviera. In a turnabout, Greenbaum, by now hopelessly addicted to hookers and heroin, refused to leave, and Accardo ordered Las Vegas enforcer Marshall Caifano to kill him. Another account had it that Greenbaum owed Chicago as much as $1 million dollars in stolen skim, bad loans, and gambling debts. Reporters Ed Reid and Ovid Demaris, in *The Green Felt Jungle* (1963), wrote that by 1958, "his personal fortune was completely dissipated," but that turned out to be inaccurate.

As they had in the Bioff case in 1955, Harry Rosenzweig and Thomas Goodnight played the role of court-appointed examiners for the Greenbaum estate. They set the estate value at $632,000, and nothing was reported as missing. A joint checking account held $25,500. There were twenty-two thousand shares of stock in the Riviera worth $120,000 and another $150,000 in debentures from the same casino. Gus held a promissory note from the Flamingo for $92,000. Life-insurance policies paid off at about $90,000 to the Greenbaum's daughter. Apart from the gambling stock, there was little to distinguish the estate from that of any other successful corporate executive.

At the Greenbaums's funeral, three hundred people turned out to say goodbye, among them a number of prominent Phoenicians. An unknown photographer captured the scene. Brother Charles was at the head of the pallbearers as they carried Gus Greenbaum's coffin out of Temple Beth Israel. Among those standing in the background looking on, clearly visible in his black, horn-rimmed glasses, was Barry Goldwater.

Chapter 3

THE STRONGEST MEN

A round the time Barry Goldwater was planning his run for the presidency, a talented and ruthless con man glided into Phoenix in a white Lincoln Continental. He had $800 in cash, a ring on each pinkie finger, a mistress in the front seat, and a wife in the back. Arizona was still recumbent in the glow of the 1950s, a place where the enraptured newcomer could reach up and pluck a fresh orange from his own tree. It was cocktail time. It would go on forever.

The newcomer in the Lincoln was Ned Warren, a back-East grifter who within a decade would fight his way close to the center of political power in Phoenix through a series of increasingly bold crimes. A few cops and journalists struggled to bring Warren to account within a state legal system that, when it came people like him, had virtually ceased to function. The end for Warren came only when an embarrassed federal government was forced to intervene. But Warren's crew of arsonists and assassins survived long enough to murder an investigative reporter for *The Arizona Republic*, the state's largest newspaper.

During his fourteen years in Arizona, Warren and other land-fraud artists looted between $500 million to $1.5 billion from the public. They sold thousands of acres that were uninhabitable, belonged to someone else, or had been sold many times over. In what has since become a familiar form of financial fraud, Warren sold fraudulent sales contracts to witting bankers, who bundled them into tranches and sold them to investors. For years, Warren enjoyed virtual immunity from most of law enforcement. By the time the prison gates closed behind Warren in 1975, many Arizonans suspected that other serious crimes had been papered over with political influence.

Warren's fraud victims organized pressure groups and appealed to the state's law enforcement to go after the con man and return their money. For the most part, however, their pleas were ignored, even after a former insider in Warren's operation joined the victims' cause. Richard Frost was a Warren partner who had been shamed or frightened into investigating the fraud machine. When he died, Frost left behind a full-length book manuscript detailing Warren's (and his own) looting of the real-estate market. He amassed thousands of pages of financial records and turned them over to the Office of the Arizona Attorney General, the Arizona Department of Real Estate, and the Maricopa County Attorney's Office. "All of these agencies were kept fully informed" of the progress of his investigation, he wrote.

One of the Warren criminal operations whose records Frost collected was the Arizona Land Company (ALC). He turned them over to the state land department after ALC filed for bankruptcy. "I had spent thousands and thousands of dollars on sorting out these files," Frost later told federal authorities. "And I very carefully protected them. When the thing was finally turned over to a [court-appointed] receiver, they sent a dump truck up and took the file drawers and turned them upside upside-down in the dump truck. And then the files that I'd turned over to the [state] officials, they got lost. There were seven foot of them."

Eventually, a series of investigations by *Arizona Republic* reporter Don Bolles and the Phoenix Police Department pressured the Maricopa County Attorney's Office to act against Warren. Although a grand jury handed up three separate indictments against Warren, they were thrown out of court one by one. Those closest to the case agreed that the county attorney, a Phoenix network insider, intentionally bungled the cases.

Warren's rise to power and wealth as the godfather of Arizona land fraud was made possible with the help of regulators, prosecutors, and judges who saw to it that he would not be brought to justice—that the lid, as the county attorney would say at one point, would be kept firmly *on*.

'THE HYDRAULIC SOCIETY'

In Roman Polanski's 1974 film *Chinatown*, detective Jake Gittes peers curiously at a grizzled Southwestern land king, Noah Cross, after Cross has stolen an entire river from upstream farmers by diverting it to Los Angeles.

> GITTES: I just want to know what you're worth. More than ten million?
> CROSS: Oh my, yes!
> GITTES: Why are you doing it? How much better can you eat? What could you buy that you can't already afford?
> CROSS: The future, Mr. Gittes! The future!

In the Los Angeles of *Chinatown*, as across the American Southwest, the future was expensive because water was scarce, and without it, land was worthless. Even the wealthiest men needed financial help to irrigate their properties, and that usually meant government, preferably one unencumbered with too much democracy.

In 1903, historian Frederick Jackson Turner searched the future and calculated that the prospects for democracy in the arid Southwest were dim because the task of building the dams, reservoirs, and canals of a "hydraulic society" was "too monumental for ordinary people." Its great costs would force Southwesterners "to combine under the leadership of the strongest men." Turner's judgment was vindicated by the appearance of just such men, who represented something new in American life. They would no longer be mere entrepreneurs who commanded free markets by virtue of their will and stores of private capital. They would rise above contradictions, for each would be "both a capitalist and the protégé of the government."

In this phrase, Turner captured a paradox at the center of the emerging Southwestern political culture. It would be dominated by those who made conflicting demands on government. They wanted low taxes and casual regulation even as they lobbied for direct federal subsidies for the enterprises that made possible their private fortunes. For men like Noah Cross, Barry Goldwater, and Kemper Marley, a role for government in financing the hydraulic and electrical infrastructures of the Southwest was necessary because the distances involved were too great for the wealthiest families, or even individual states. On this point, there was unanimity.

As divided as they might be on other issues, when it came to irrigation, Democrats and Republicans came together when the moment demanded to form the Water Party. They usually had their way in Congress, in part through the exceptional talents of generations of politicians. The Arizona congressional delegation exercised so much influence from 1952, when Barry Goldwater entered the US senate, until 1986, when he retired, that its members had reengineered the Sonoran Desert with hydrological projects on a scale rivaling ancient Assyria.

The electrical enterprise was just as ambitious. It represented one of the largest transfers of natural wealth in the history of the western United States by expropriating the energy resources of the Hopi and Navajo people of the Colorado Plateau. The project was known fondly as the "Big Build-Up." It created an electrical-power grid that stretched across the Southwestern deserts from San Diego to Albuquerque and required the cooperation of twenty-three power companies in seven states. Arizona's utilities joined public and private companies in Texas, New Mexico, Colorado, Utah, Nevada, and California in financing and building the grid, which was called the Western Energy and Supply Transmission Association (WEST). The power companies included Arizona Public Service, the Salt River Project, Tucson Gas and Electric, and Southern California Edison, among many other interests, including the federal Bureau of Reclamation. At peak capacity, WEST generated three times more energy than the Tennessee Valley Authority. Along with nuclear energy generated in California, the fuel would come from land owned by the Navajo and Hopi tribes, who were defrauded out of much of the real value of 400 million tons of coal that covered forty thousand acres of Indian land. It was, Thomas Sheridan wrote, "internal colonialism on a colossal scale."

A fellow historian, Andrew Needham, underscored the point. "This creation of the Navajo Reservation as the Southwest's energy hinterland was not simply an economic process connecting production and consumption. It was fundamentally a political project in which metropolitan representatives claimed authority over distant lands and resources." Sociologists described the new business class that grew up to administer the energy project as an urban mercantile machine of "interlocking pro-growth associations and governmental units." Its goals had the support of "newspapers, chambers of commerce, real-estate developers, and corporations that aimed to use metropolitan growth to make great fortunes." Collectively, this class came to be known as "boosters."

At the end of World War II, Phoenix was growing at a rapid pace. The wars of the Pacific, starting with the adventure in the Philippines and continuing through Korea and Vietnam, enriched the city. Phoenix grew from a population of 65,000 covering ten square miles to 440,000 people on 187 square miles by 1960. World War II had transformed Phoenix from a remote western outpost into a center for military aviation and avionics. The land boom that accompanied its rapid increase in population was subsidized in no small part by federal policies aimed at regional development. The city's growth could not have happened without funding from the Pentagon, the Veterans Administration, the Federal Housing Authority, the Federal Transportation Administration, and the Social Security Administration, whose payments to retirees provided the financial cornerstone for Sun City and other Del Webb retirement enterprises. Even the low- and sometimes no-tax policies for business and industry were possible in part because of postwar federal subsidies for state and municipal social programs.

Throughout this period, booster policies for stimulating radical growth had one great and peculiar advantage: supporters possessed a commanding influence over the labor force, whose unions were suppressed by the adoption of the first right-to-work law in the nation. In this as in most other areas of the economy, the boosters enjoyed a social control that was the envy of comparable elites elsewhere in the country. By the end of the century, boosters could look back and see that, in a land scarce in essential resources, they had built one of the largest engines for wealth creation in the West.

Throughout most of its history, Arizona was a one-party state, first Democratic, then Republican. The familiar struggles among parties and ideologies that framed politics elsewhere played out among factions of a single dominant party. Historical sociologist Daniel J. Elazar believed that in

Arizona factions arose as part of the state's "traditionalistic" political culture, which he characterized as "an older attitude that accepts a substantially hierarchical society as part of the ordered nature of things." In the traditionalistic structure, "political competition is expressed through factions, an extension of the personal politics characteristic of the system. Hence, political systems within the culture tend to have loose one-party systems if they have political parties at all."

"Personal politics" was a politer version of Turner's "strongest men." The factional struggles of the single-party system took place within a hierarchy in which power was concentrated in a few hands. Government in Arizona, Elazar concluded, was confined to "a relatively small and self-perpetuating group drawn from an established elite who often inherit their right to govern through family ties or social position."

In the 1950s, banker Walter Bimson, at one time the state's most influential booster, commissioned a study that recommended the wholesale revision of federal statutes to allow large Anglo corporations access to Indian lands on terms so favorable that they amounted to "a wholesale transformation in Indian leasing policy." The legislation passed Congress under the influence of its principal sponsor, Barry Goldwater. He introduced the bill in 1955, the same year he broke from his long support for Hopi traditional government in favor of the new "progressive" tribal council whose main purpose was to sign contracts with Anglo energy companies. It marked Goldwater's turn from supporting self-determination for the Hopi to his new role as intercessor for energy companies, notably Peabody Coal and El Paso Natural Gas. As we will see, because of his unique role in the senate, whose members regarded him as a spokesman for the Southwestern Indian tribes, the legislative success of WEST and the Indian-energy project would come to depend on Goldwater's leadership.

Goldwater and his immediate circle and its allies provided most of the leadership of the booster class. They exercised their influence from within a smaller group that can be called, borrowing the usage of William Chambliss, the Phoenix network. Many were descendants of the old pioneer families, that is, those who settled in Arizona before statehood. Some in the innermost circle of the Phoenix network were on intimate but discreet terms with the higher echelons of organized crime. Often, it could be difficult to distinguish between the pioneers and the boosters on the one hand and the more discreet associations among members of the network and the underworld.

By the 1970s, the Phoenix network and some elements of the legitimate business world had begun to overlap with the criminal underworld. A federal expert on organized crime observed three years before the Don Bolles assassination that in Arizona, "corruption includes judges and police departments, as well as state and local government officials in a position to aid the criminal element." Another knowledgeable observer said "one hundred of the state's community leaders get their major source of income from organized crime." A former president of the Valley National Bank confirmed this estimate and expanded it. "If you took the Arizona Academy list, selected five hundred names to come to a meeting in Phoenix, of those five hundred, you would meet at least one hundred who would be directly involved with organized crime and at least a hundred more whose livelihood depended on organized-crime activities." Taken together, the membership of the Phoenix network fit the definition of a "shadow government" as described by Block and Chambliss. The legitimate businessmen who formed the greater part of the booster class but were not part of the network tended to be professionals active in retail, construction, defense, and related industries, executives who possessed an ambition matched by their often-extraordinary individual abilities. The same could be said of the talents of some of the criminal executives as well.

While scholars have studied the influence of the Phoenix booster class in recent years, its less visible and sometimes more influential constituent groups have gone largely unexamined, including the descendants of the pioneer families, members of the older and newer versions of the Phoenix network, and the upper ranks of the criminal underworld. A close look became possible only after the Bolles assassination and the thousands of investigative documents it produced. Those records force attention on the career of a criminal of rare talent, who in the early 1960s and early 1970s set in motion many of the events described in these pages.

THE POLITICS OF LAND FRAUD

In 1914, Ned Warren was born Nathan Waxman to a wealthy Boston family. He was a child of privilege who as a youth attended elite prep schools and a prominent military academy. But he preferred the con to the legitimate life, he once confessed, because he took a secret pleasure in outwitting others. And it came easily to him. In one of his earliest scams, Warren hired a boiler room of telephone salesmen to sell tickets to a charity concert for blind musicians. The concert was never held; he kept the proceeds.

The future King Ned and a lifelong confederate, William Steuer, moved on to a more-imaginative crime with the same show-business theme. In New York after World War II, they extracted $39,000 from Broadway investors. They persuaded noted Stork Club press agent Chic Farmer to plant a news story in *The New York Daily News* about their invention of a new method for financing stage productions. The scheme offered some insight into Warren's criminal skills. Instead of joining a limited partnership, investors would make a "loan" to a production company. The loan would be repaid from the first profits, after which investors would receive "interest" totaling 50 percent of their initial outlay. The musical was to be titled *The Happiest Days* and follow the personal and artistic crisis of a young couple, a composer of art music and a ballet star, after the banks were shut down during the Depression. It was never produced or, for that matter, written. One year after the first *Daily News* story appeared, the paper ran a small item explaining that Warren and Steuer, then ages thirty-four and thirty, respectively, had been sentenced to prison for fifteen months apiece for grand larceny. The headline writer called the pair "Angel Pluckers."

After prison, there were other youthful adventures, none of which showed the imagination Warren had displayed in New York. One was a phony chinchilla operation in Florida. By the time he arrived in Arizona, he was forty-seven years old and had spent time in the federal prison in Danbury, Connecticut, and another stretch in Sing Sing. In Phoenix, he quickly talked his way into a job selling real estate. He adopted the salesman's uniform of the day: white shoes, white belt, a white tie set off by a dark-colored shirt, and golf slacks. He ate in the best restaurants along Central Avenue and Camelback Road and was always ready with a disarming crack. When asked why he had come to Arizona, he would reply, "For my wife's hay fever. She *loves* hay." It was the kind of joke he would tell over a Dry Sack on the rocks, holding the drink in one hand and clapping the other on his victim's shoulder. He had a slender build, slightly hunched. He wore a habitual five o'clock shadow and maintained a meticulous manicure.

Warren's idea for seducing the business and political class was inspired a few months after his arrival in September 1961, when he picked up a copy of *The Saturday Evening Post* and read a photo essay, "The New Millionaires of Phoenix." He fastened on one new millionaire in particular: the handsome, forty-year-old Leopold (Lee) Ackerman, a fellow New Englander and, like Warren, the product of an Eastern military academy.

Warren learned that during World War II, Ackerman flew DC-3s throughout the Middle East for the US Army Air Corps and after the war acted as the pilot for a group of New England governors as they toured the country. At the Phoenix stop, he met and was impressed by the state's famous progressive governor, Sidney P. Osborn. Within months, the young pilot returned to Phoenix for good, in 1948 landing a job as a reporter and then aviation columnist at *The Arizona Republic*. But the ambitious Ackerman soon left the newspaper to take a job with an advertising agency and joined a number of civic organizations. He accepted the job of state recruiting officer for the Air Force Reserve and led the swearing-in ceremony that inducted into its ranks Colonel (later Major General) Barry Goldwater.

In 1950, Ackerman began a political career with a successful run for the Arizona House as a Democrat. In 1960, he ran for governor and lost but was consoled by John F. Kennedy's election to the presidency. Ackerman was one of Arizona's rare New Frontiersmen. A photo of him with Jack and Jackie taken at the president's inaugural ball took a prominent spot in his Phoenix office. Before long, Ackerman was an Arizona member of the national steering committee of the Democratic Party, its highest unelected position.

Warren found a way to meet Ackerman. He enlisted the help of his mother, who was then married to a prominent New York physician, to wangle an introduction to John Roeder, a Republican state representative to the Arizona House from the bluestocking district in northeast Phoenix. Roeder, a former New

Yorker, had moved to Arizona to take a job with the Snell & Wilmer law firm, then left the firm to work as a researcher for the Arizona Supreme Court. At some point, he was taken under the wing of Sally Goldwater (Bob Goldwater's wife and Barry Goldwater's sister-in-law), who introduced him to the Scottsdale social scene. He became a favorite of John Pritzlaff, father of Ann Olin Priztlaff, an heiress of the Olin family fortune.

Warren asked Roeder to host a party at his home and to invite Ackerman, whose Western Growth Corp. was then bringing in revenues of $8 million a year. During the party, Warren cornered Ackerman and turned on the charm. At one point he mentioned that he had "spent time with Uncle Sam," which Ackerman later said he understood to mean that Warren had done time for income-tax evasion.

By 1963, the friendship between the two men ripened into a partnership. Using Western Growth, Ackerman invested in Warren's principal business of the moment, the Diamond Valley subdivision near Prescott, and Warren in turn hired Ackerman as a "financial advisor" at an annual salary of $150,000. Warren paid the salary in land contracts, his standard practice. In a fatal step for Ackerman, Warren joined Western Growth as operations manager.

For the next three years, the two former Bostonians made money together. In February 1966, an opportunity arose for Warren to take another step up the ladder. A prominent Democrat, Dr. John Kruglick, whose wife was a member of the Phoenix City Council, approached Warren and said he wanted Ackerman's seat on the Democratic National Committee. If Warren found a way to force Ackerman's resignation, Kruglick said, he would invest a half million dollars in Diamond Valley land contracts. Warren did not hesitate. Using his authority as operations manager, he cleaned out the cupboards in Western Growth. He transferred assets and stopped interest payments to investors. Within four months, Western Growth was failing. At its meeting in June 1966, Ackerman swallowed hard and resigned from the DNC, then recommended Kruglick as his successor. In early 1967, unpaid creditors forced Western Growth into involuntary bankruptcy. Days after the bankruptcy filing, Kruglick wrote a check to a Phoenix bank to buy $200,000 in Diamond Valley land contracts.

When IRE reporters interviewed Ackerman as part of their investigation into the Bolles murder nine years later, he was a repentant and ruined man. He confessed that he knew Warren was a crook and regretted helping him to launder his reputation. It was Ackerman who took Warren to see the Phoenix chief of police, who registered him as an ex-con. It was also Ackerman who introduced Warren to state Real Estate Commissioner J. Fred Talley, who at the time was accepting bribes from real-estate developers amounting to $10,000 a month. For introducing Warren to Ackerman in 1963, Roeder was rewarded with a lot in Diamond Valley.

If during all of this Ned Warren was careful to protect himself by paying off important politicians and regulators, he was not beyond the reach of a few prying journalists and cops. The public learned of the details of Warren's rise to power and influence in an eight-part series bannered in *The Arizona Republic* in April 1967. The reporter was Don Bolles, and the series established his reputation as the leading investigative journalist in the state. Bolles's reporting on Warren and Ackerman was the first public exploration of land fraud in Arizona. The paper had generally ignored gangster celebrities in the state, but Warren presented a tempting target. The editors of the conservative newspaper had an additional incentive to run the series. It had the virtue of causing embarrassment to Democrats in a presidential election year. An editor's note on Ackerman's loss of influence was inserted in a text box on page one. It asked, "Was his high post in the Democratic Party bartered?"

After Bolles's series ran, Warren continued to operate undisturbed. Law enforcement waited five years to open a formal investigation. The opportunity came in 1972, when Warren forced one of his many corporate legal entities into voluntary bankruptcy after using it to cheat buyers and investors out of $5 million. As he had with Ackerman, Warren left a hand-picked executive holding the bag. He was James Cornwall, nominal president of the Great Southwest Land and Cattle Co. (the *cattle* was Warren's romantic indulgence). This time, however, a paper trail led directly back to Warren, who had signed a personal guarantee on a corporate loan.

Soon, Warren had a cop on his trail, a bulldog with a bad case of ulcers.

A COP PRIES THE LID OFF

Lonzo McCracken was a lead detective in the Phoenix police-intelligence unit known as the I-Squad. He'd been gathering evidence on Great Southwest's internal operations in the hope of opening a grand-jury investigation. He found enough fraud in the Great Southwest bankruptcy filings to justify a formal investigation of its corporate officers, including Cornwall and Dick Frost, with Warren as his ultimate target. Cornwall was not difficult to crack, or so it seemed. He agreed to talk to investigators in exchange for a plea agreement for a reduced sentence and round-the-clock police protection. If he and most of the witnesses against Warren feared for their lives, they had good reason. After the bankruptcy filing, people close to Warren began to disappear or turn up dead. At least a dozen potential witnesses died in airplane accidents, car crashes, closed garages and, a little later, from the effects of car bombs, stabbings and beatings. One was killed with a handful of .22-caliber bullets.

McCracken had started to investigate Warren informally in January 1971. He developed leads on his own time to avoid attracting the attention of the politically connected police hierarchy.

The detective was in his late forties. A newspaper photo of McCracken published in 1978, when the worst was over, showed a mouth clamped tight, both ends curving downward. His eyes were tough, perhaps flinching from the pain of his stomach ulcers.

One day that January, still on his own time, McCracken and another cop dropped by an office in the 1000 block of East Camelback Road to see Tony Serra. He was not in. The cops left word with his secretary that they wanted to talk to Serra, then drove to the Pullman Pie, a nearby coffee shop, and waited. Serra was president of Western World Investment at the Camelback address on the west side of Central Avenue. He had been a longtime McCracken informant on mob activity in Phoenix. Serra was a minor Missouri gangster, the personal emissary to Ned Warren from Saint Louis mob boss Anthony Giordano, who became famous for shedding Capone-style pinstriped suits in favor of a plumber's khaki work uniform. He had placed a rather large bet on Warren's ability to make large profits in land fraud and sent Serra to Arizona to keep an eye on his investment.

As McCracken and his fellow cop, a member of the state Department of Public Safety, sat waiting, Serra pulled up in front of the coffee shop in a white Rolls Royce driven by "a huge bodyguard with a pistol stuck in his belt," as McCracken later described him. Serra and the bodyguard sat down. The bodyguard ordered a cup of hot chocolate. Serra was wary because his secretary had told him that the two men looking for him were packing guns. When he realized he was dealing with a pair of cops, Serra relaxed and told the bodyguard to get lost, which he did, complaining that he hadn't gotten his hot chocolate.

Serra told the detectives that Cornwall, the president of Great Southwest, was mixed up in land fraud, that Warren was "the godfather of land fraud in Arizona." The conversation rambled on for a time. As he stood up, Serra asked McCracken to pick up the tab. It was the formal start of the investigation of Warren.

More than a year later, on March 10, 1972, at another coffee shop in downtown Phoenix, McCracken met an informant who had worked as a salesman for the newly bankrupt Great Southwest. His story was much the same as Serra's but more detailed and filled with leads. Cornwall was putting out large amounts of "bad paper," meaning fraudulent land contracts, as collateral to secure bank loans in a Great Southwest project called Beaver Valley.

The salesman told McCracken that Warren's practice in selling lots was to send James Tancill, one of his sales managers, to cruise Phoenix dives for pimps, prostitutes, and drug dealers. In exchange for a signature on a land-purchase agreement, each would receive a small cash payment, usually fifty dollars. The contracts were bundled and turned over to a bank for sale to private investors or used as collateral in bank loans. The proceeds were diverted to one of Warren's personal accounts or used to pay off older investments.

Warren had been using this scheme, the heart of his method, for a decade. It had worked for so long, the salesman said, because Warren was protected. When he intentionally ruined one of his companies, he could rely on the federal bankruptcy courts to relieve him of personal liability. In the Beaver Valley deal, however, there was a complication. Warren had signed a personal guarantee on some of the loans raised on bad paper from Great Southwest and Beaver Valley. The error created an opening for Serra, who managed to get a list of most of the Beaver Valley contracts and used it to blackmail Cornwall into turning control of the company over to him.

A few days after hearing this story, McCracken got back in touch with Serra and asked him to confirm what the salesman had told him. Yes, both Great Southwest and Beaver Valley had issued a lot of bad paper, Serra said. Moreover, Warren was unhappy about Cornwall's performance as president of Great Southwest. Serra offered to tell Warren that McCracken was investigating Cornwall in the hope that a resulting shake-up would create an opening for Serra inside the Warren organization. If Warren turned on Cornwall and others, McCracken might be able to turn them into witnesses. McCracken agreed.

Two days later, Serra told the detective he had alerted Warren that McCracken was on his trail. An alarmed Warren was proposing a deal. He wanted sixty days to pull $35,000 out of Great Southwest. If McCracken would give him that much time, Warren would give up not only Cornwall but Howard Woodall, president of another Warren land fraud called the Del Rio Springs project.

Before the end of March 1972, McCracken sat down with Warren at Navarre's Restaurant on Central Avenue. Warren was smooth but visibly uneasy. Sitting next to him throughout the conversation was an unlikely companion: George Brooks, an investigator for Maricopa County Attorney Moise Berger.

Warren told McCracken he was concerned about the detective's investigation into Great Southwest. He admitted that Cornwall and Serra as well had issued bad paper, but he described their sales practices as "stupid." Warren said he had nothing to do with the seamy side of the operation, although he admitted that he had enough money in the corporation that an investigation, if it were made public, would hurt him. Brooks said nothing.

Soon afterward, McCracken confronted Cornwall with Warren's accusations and advised him of his rights. A nervous Cornwall blamed the bad paper on unscrupulous sales crews. He asked for time to clean them up. McCracken responded that he wanted copies of all the contracts. "If I give you all of that," Cornwall replied, "you would have me by the balls." Again, he asked for time.

At that very moment, his brother was in New York, he said, trying to borrow $3 million so that Cornwall could pay everyone off.

On April 10, a Monday, McCracken got a phone call. Great Southwest's holding company had just filed in federal bankruptcy court. Cornwall had lit out for Europe. No one knew where he was.

McCracken's phone rang again. Without informing Phoenix police, an official of the Arizona Department of Real Estate had gone into the Great Southwest offices and impounded all of the company's records.

McCracken exploded. He got a search warrant and took it to the real-estate department, where he served it on the commissioner, J. Fred Talley. The first words out of Talley's mouth were, "Do I need my lawyer?"

'HE JUST ABOUT FAINTED'

McCracken's anger was understandable. By asking for time, Warren had played him for a fool. Without Cornwall, he had no witness against Warren. The evidence he needed was under Talley's control. And he lost jurisdiction when Warren put Great Southwest into federal bankruptcy court.

As he had done before, McCracken hunkered down to wait for another opening. In the summer of 1973, he got it. A tipster informed him that Cornwall had returned home to Salem, Oregon, from his hiding places in Germany and Switzerland. As a young man, Cornwall had attended Bible college in Salem, then moved to Eugene to learn the land-development business.

On July 25, McCracken knocked on Cornwall's front door in Salem. "He just about fainted when he saw me," McCracken told IRE reporter Jerry Uhrhammer, who interviewed the detective in 1977. Uhrhammer had an interest in the Cornwall story. He worked as a reporter for *The Register-Guard* in Eugene before joining the Arizona Project.

Cornwall decided to cooperate. With a tape recorder running, Cornwall told McCracken about Warren's operation, the view from inside the operation. He told how he made monthly payoffs to Fred Talley and George Brooks, who had been assigned to Talley's office by the state attorney general to investigate land fraud.

The Salem interview "was where we found out about Talley," McCracken told Uhrhammer.

Cornwall's confession was the first real breakthrough in the case against Warren. Talley was a big fish, at least in Arizona. In 1963, NBC's *Huntley-Brinkley Report* interviewed Talley on air after he made national headlines with testimony before the US Senate Special Committee on Aging about fraud in real-estate subdivisions. He was considered prominent enough to be included in the anthology of expensive (and paid for) biographies of prominent Arizonans, *Men of Achievement*, which cited his "battle for honesty in real-estate promotion."

McCracken returned to Phoenix with Cornwall's tape-recorded confession while Cornwall left Oregon for Newport News, Virginia, to assume his duties as pastor of the Peninsula Rock Church and Proclaim Center. In April 1974, a Maricopa County grand jury indicted Cornwall and seven other Great Southwest officers on sixty-five counts of securities fraud and eight counts of conspiracy. The indictments added up to $5 million in connection with a single firm, Great Southwest. Cornwall was indicted on each of the counts of securities fraud and one count of conspiracy. Warren was not among the men who were indicted.

On June 4, 1974, the *Republic* wrote about the political scandal behind the indictments. Based on Cornwall's confession to McCracken, the state Attorney Attorney General's Office was investigating accusations of bribery in the form of monthly cash payments to Talley. He took the bribes in exchange for refusing to act on consumer complaints against Warren, and the complaints stretched back to 1962. In 1968, the entire stack of complaints was thrown into a state incinerator on the order of James Kieffer, a Talley assistant.

The destruction of the complaints remained a secret until the *Republic*'s June 1974 story, which aroused great public interest. But no one knew who had authorized Kieffer's incineration. Two men were in a position to know. One was Attorney General Gary Nelson. The other was Robert Corbin, a former county attorney and a future state attorney general who in 1968 was working for Nelson as a special prosecutor. Corbin had been hired to investigate charges of payoffs and bribery against Talley. But when Nelson asked Corbin to find out who authorized Kieffer to destroy the complaints against Warren, Corbin took no action.

WARREN TURNS TO THE REPUBLICANS

At some point in Warren's rapid rise in Phoenix, he realized it had been a mistake to cultivate Democrats like Ackermann and Kruglick, whose party was just beginning a long period of minority status. Warren devised a plan to meet Barry Goldwater. He was circumspect in his approach, which he executed in a series of small deals and adept political contributions. His first move was to get to know William Worthington, a young and struggling GOP businessman.

A native of Barrington, Illinois, Worthington had left the wealthy little country-club community to study business administration at the University of Arizona in Tucson. After graduation in 1955, he set up a small public-relations and advertising firm and got involved in politics. The year he finished college, he was elected president of Tucson's East Side Young Republicans Club. In 1964, Worthington organized a Goldwater for President Committee in Tucson, which quickly led to the chairmanship of the Arizona Young Republicans.

In 1965, a few months after the debacle of Goldwater's presidential campaign, Harry Rosenzweig was promoted from finance chairman to the chairmanship of the Arizona Republican State Central Committee, a post he would hold for a decade. Looking for a fresh face as executive director, Rosenzweig hired Worthington, who promptly moved to Paradise Valley, a wealthy Phoenix suburb, and established himself as a Rosenzweig loyalist. He reopened his advertising and PR business for local Republican campaigns and on the side dabbled in lobbying at the legislature.

One day early in 1968, Worthington dropped in at Navarre's to meet a friend for lunch. Worthington's brother-in-law spotted him and beckoned him to join the group at Warren's table. The land-fraud king expressed an interest in Worthington's advertising firm and offered him some work for his Prescott Valley land-development project. Worthington later told a reporter, "I was scared to death of him. By that time, Don's series had run," that is, Don Bolles's April 1967 series exposing Warren's criminal past.

Soon after the lunch at Navarre's, Worthington said, he fell ill and was hospitalized. By the time he was discharged, his business and his bank account were both flat, and when Warren offered him a piece of his business, Worthington jumped. Warren dangled a deal in a company with a familiar ring, the Queen

Creek Land & Cattle Co., in which Warren held all of the stock. As incentives, he offered a 10 percent share of the stock to Worthington and 20 percent to Worthington's sidekick, Richard Stenz, a Midwesterner from a comfortable background (Elm Grove, Wisconsin). The tall, lean Worthington and the shorter Stenz had social and political connections that were valuable in land promotions.

Worthington's relationship with Warren followed the familiar route traveled by Ackerman and others—socially prominent men accept the nominal leadership of a Warren land operation and find investors. If the pattern had held, the Worthington-Stenz operation would have started leaking money within eighteen months and headed to bankruptcy court. But Warren was restrained. The two men needed a full year to make their first sale for Queen Creek, and more sales followed quickly. After another six months, they felt confident enough to offer to buy out Warren. He accepted. It took them until 1975, but eventually, they paid Warren $625,000.

In 1978, the *Republic* reviewed the records of the Worthington-Stenz purchase of Queen Creek and reported that a young lawyer named William Rehnquist had handled the legal work.

In the end, Warren got what he wanted. Worthington arranged an introduction to Harry Rosenzweig. It was the beginning of a relationship that lasted through many lunches and included frequent requests from Rosenzweig for political donations, which Warren honored.

It was as close to Barry Goldwater that Warren would ever get. As it turned out, it was close enough.

THE NETWORK PROTECTS WARREN

Before Berger ran for county attorney, his friends regarded him as an able young attorney who was something of an idealist about the law. His former admirers watched with disbelief as Berger handled the first case against Warren—Great Southwest—by assigning to the case and then replacing, in quick succession, twelve prosecutors over fourteen months. Each replacement was more inexperienced than the last, and each was given less time to prepare for the case. It was not a matter of incompetent case management. Phoenix police had been prepared for trial since February 1974, five months before Berger was ready. McCracken began to assume that the county attorney was merely playacting at the role of bumbler. The detective believed Berger was acting on behalf of someone who did not want Great Southwest prosecuted or, if the public would not stand for that, someone who did not want Warren prosecuted successfully.

The police had few doubts that it was Harry Rosenzweig who was protecting Warren. Berger was obliged to Rosenzweig after he'd given the younger man a campaign contribution of $15,000 and locked in the support of the Phoenix network. And it was Rosenzweig who ran the county and the city and held the political reins to the Phoenix Police Department. It was understood that Rosenzweig could pick up the telephone and within hours have any troublesome beat patrolman or motorcycle cop reassigned.

By the time the Great Southwest case was ready to go to trial, Berger still had not turned over to defense attorneys any evidence they were owed under the rules of disclosure. He had also run through most of his deputy county attorneys and was down to the last few names. One June 10, nearly three months after Cornwall's arraignment, Berger asked for another delay to change prosecutors again.

Judge Rufus C. Coulter gave Berger's office forty-eight hours to produce and distribute to defense attorneys seven sets of documents, or fourteen thousand pages of evidence, including police reports and Great Southwest company records. At 9:00 a.m. on June 12, with six hours left on the clock and the lone prosecutor assigned to the case still buried in paper at the photocopier, a furious McCracken burst into Berger's office. Shouting obscenities, he banged his fist on the county attorney's desk. He picked up Berger's phone and called his own supervisor at the Phoenix Police Department, Lt. Glenn Sparks, ranting that the county attorney was ignoring Coulter's order and intentionally blowing the case against Great Southwest.

Berger, now angry as well, was forced into action. He commandeered every copy machine in the county building and met Coulter's 3:00 p.m. deadline with minutes to spare.

McCracken was raising the stakes in his match with the chief prosecutor. In the middle of June, after the first stories about Warren's bribe to Brooks appeared in the *Republic*, Berger called a meeting of the principals in the case. Present were several of his prosecutors, including Sydney Mitchell, his chief deputy and confidant; Cornwall and his lawyer, M. Richard Remender; and two members of the Phoenix Police Department, one of whom was Sparks. Berger excluded McCracken from the meeting. Several uniformed officers waited outside the door. They were Cornwall's security unit.

Remender later described the meeting as an excuse for Berger to discover how much Cornwall knew about the involvement of other public officials in the Talley bribery ring. He also believed that Berger wanted to know whether Cornwall had anything damaging on him.

During the meeting, someone—Remender did not see who it was—produced a list of names of twelve people, each of whom was under investigation by Phoenix police in connection with Great Southwest or a related fraud. Berger questioned Cornwall on what he knew about each of the names. Those familiar with Cornwall's testimony said they were surprised to find two names missing: Talley and Joe Patrick, the latter a man whose name later appeared in cases that led to the top of the network. Cornwall had hired Patrick, a well-known broadcaster on Phoenix radio and television, to handle public relations for Great Southwest.

Before he went to work for Warren, Patrick acted as the liaison between Congressman Sam Steiger and Barry Goldwater. He worked on Steiger's 1966 congressional campaign and after the election stayed on as home press secretary. Patrick was also a friend of Goldwater. They met as fellow pilots in the Arizona Air National Guard. Because Patrick was close to Goldwater, Warren insisted that he be offered the Great Southwest job

Remender believed that the omission of Talley and Patrick from the list after Cornwall had already testified about them at length in depositions was a tip that Cornwall would not be asked questions about either and that he would be wise not to bring them up.

After the meeting, the police guard whisked Cornwall away to what was supposed to be a secret location: a hotel near the airport. In less than an hour, there was a knock on the door. It was Robert Storrs, one of Cornwall's defense attorneys, who was not supposed to know where the cops had hidden the witness.

Storrs nervously informed his client that he had learned of Cornwall's whereabouts from a conversation he overheard between Tony Serra and Serra's lawyer.

If Cornwall felt a chill, it might have been a premonition. Nearly two years later, not long after Cornwall entered the state prison in Florence, a gang of hired inmates threw a firebomb into his cell and nearly killed him. The man who arranged for the firebomb was another inmate: Tony Serra.

A LAND FRAUD EMBARRASSES GOLDWATER

The trial of the men responsible for the Great Southwest Land and Cattle Co., excluding Warren, opened in the July heat of Phoenix in 1974. The trial ground through the preliminaries until, in late September, a Maricopa grand jury surprised everyone by indicting Warren on thirteen counts of perjury. For the first time in years, it appeared that Warren would be forced to testify about his business operation. Hope was quickly throttled. Berger knew the perjury indictments were based on statements Warren made in a deposition for federal court, and a superior court judge ruled, as expected, that a federal deposition was inadmissible in a state court. The judge threw out the indictments.

Berger was pursuing an awkward strategy. He wanted to appease the Phoenix network by protecting Warren and at the same time pacify the public and police investigators by making it appear he was conducting a serious prosecution. So he slowed the trial to a procedural crawl. For a time, it seemed to work. Witnesses against Warren began to die off, some from natural causes. In November, Talley died of what might have been a heart attack. When he could drag it out no longer, Berger settled on a final gamble. At the end of 1974, he formed a second grand jury to run concurrently with the first. He made a display of calling witnesses who were hostile to Warren and knowledgeable about his operation, some of them the same people Berger had once tried to keep out of the case.

Two days before Christmas, a county grand jury indicted Warren and three other men. One was Jay Lippard, the Warren front man who handed the $2,000 Warren loan to George Brooks. The second was Brooks. The third—a surprise—was Joe Patrick. A larger surprise was one of the witnesses summoned to the new grand jury. He was Edward Lazar, who had worked as an accountant for Warren since 1970. Warren named Lazar a partner in one of his companies, Consolidated Mortgage, Inc. (CMI), which specialized in selling land parcels to US servicemen in Asia. Warren instructed Lazar to approach Harry Rosenzweig for help in promoting CMI. Rosenzweig agreed. He asked the two politicians to whom he was closest, US representative Sam Steiger and Barry Goldwater, to sign promotional letters for CMI. When the letters were made public, they created one of the biggest public scandals in Goldwater's congressional career.

Lazar had offered to cooperate with prosecutors if they would grant him broad immunity. The first investigator to interview him was McCracken. Lazar and the detective spent all day on January 8, 1975, preparing for the accountant's initial appearance before the second grand jury. He told McCracken about Warren's payoffs to Talley, the accounting structure of the land fraud, and how it worked. Most of it McCracken already knew. But Lazar broke some new ground. He told McCracken about a company, Educational Computer Systems, Inc., that was organized in 1968 to market a new test-scoring machine for schools. The moving force behind ECS was Rosenzweig, a director and active promoter. ECS was a bust. It had not sold a single machine. When Warren learned of Rosenzweig's problem, he saw a way to ingratiate himself with the most powerful man in the Phoenix network. He proposed that ECS buy Warren's Great Southwest Land & Cattle Co. The reasoning was impeccable. ECS needed Great Southwest, Warren told Rosenzweig, because it had legal authority to sell stock and ECS did not. Rosenzweig could raise enough capital to make ECS ready for sale. Rosenweig took the deal.

There was a hitch, however. Great Southwest had ceased operations, and ECS filed for bankruptcy. Any sales of ECS stock would be illegal. It was not clear who was playing whom.

When IRE reporters later reviewed the last days of ECS, they discovered it had filed for bankruptcy on April 7, 1972, and that hours before the filing, Rosenzweig quietly sold $75,000 worth of shares in the worthless company to a buyer in New York. The reporters also discovered that the trade was handled by a Phoenix firm, First Security Transfer, owned by a socially prominent businessman with ties to Frank Bompensiero, head of organized crime in San Diego. In its final report in March 1977, the IRE hinted that the transaction required discretion, not only because of its apparent illegality but because it might have represented a Warren straw purchase of ECS.

The business tie between Warren and Rosenzweig went unnoticed until IRE reported on it in 1977. The out-of-town journalists discovered that Warren tipped off Rosenzweig that Great Southwest was about to file for bankruptcy, and Rosenzweig had immediately sold $75,000 of what was about to become worthless ECS stock. Warren's silence would be required to keep his partner out of legal trouble, providing at least one motive for Rosenzweig to use all of his considerable influence to protect Warren from prosecution.

The grand jury scheduled Lazar to appear a week after his interview with McCracken. The two men continued to prepare for his appearance when Berger suddenly dismissed the second grand jury, citing concern over a law governing how long a grand jury could sit. As a new grand jury was assembled, Deputy County Attorney Joe Howe took over the task of interviewing Lazar for the county. Howe told McCracken he was getting information from the accountant that confirmed Cornwall's version of events in considerable detail.

Then came another surprise. On Monday, February 10, Howe gave notice that he intended to resign from the county attorney's office to take a job as a public defender. Howe told McCracken that he felt overwhelmed. The press was watching him closely. Meanwhile, someone in the county attorney's office was leaking his every move to reporters. On the day Howe hand-carried a subpoena to Joe Patrick requiring him to appear before the new grand jury, Patrick laughed. He'd been expecting Howe, Patrick said. He had read in *The Phoenix Gazette* just an hour earlier that he was going to be subpoenaed that very day. Berger did not wait for Howe's resignation to take effect. He removed Howe from the case, citing his "ethical conflict of interest."

McCracken spent most of the morning of February 19, 1975, working on a list of questions he wanted Lazar to answer at his appearance before the grand jury. At 11:30 a.m., he called Lazar's office to arrange a meeting. Lazar was out, his secretary said.

McCracken called Beverly Paprisi, secretary to the grand jury, and asked that a subpoena be issued for Lazar. At three thirty in the afternoon, Paprisi called McCracken and said she had the subpoena in hand, but it was too late to serve it. She had walked into Berger's office to inform him and Chief Deputy Mitchell that she had prepared the Lazar subpoena at McCracken's request. "Sidney Mitchell laughed like an idiot," Paprisi told McCracken.

After Mitchell calmed down, Paprisi said, he informed her that Lazar was dead. He had been shot five times and died where he fell, in the stairwell of the parking lot next to his office, at exactly 2:00 p.m., an hour and a half before she'd walked in the door with McCracken's subpoena.

AN ACCOUNTANT'S MURDER RAISES THE STAKES

Edward Lazar's death was a turning point in the increasingly bitter struggle between the political bosses and public opinion to influence the outcome of the Great Southwest trial. The *Republic* headline on the morning of February 20 read in large type: "Grand Jury Witness in Probe of Warren Is Slain Gang Style." Next to it was a three-column-wide photo by the paper's John Willard showing a cop examining the body, with the back of the accountant's head resting on a stair step, his face framed by a handrail. A sightless left eye stared vacantly at the cop's knee. The caption referred to the "bullet-riddled body of Edward L. Lazar, former business associate of land-fraud figure Ned Warren."

The murder charged the news environment. The struggle between Berger and McCracken for control of the Warren trial had to end, or there would be no witnesses left.

On the Friday after Lazar's murder, Moise Berger and Sidney Mitchell called in the lone remaining witness against Warren, the man who had been given the title of president of Great Southwest and knew the operation's most sensitive secrets. Cornwall was understandably jittery when he showed up with his personal bodyguard, Officer Rudy Santa Cruz of the Phoenix police Intelligence I-Squad. Santa Cruz objected when the two prosecutors said they were going to take Cornwall somewhere private to have a talk. "If Mr. Cornwall goes, I go," Santa Cruz said. The county officials steered Cornwall down the hallway to a small and little-used conference room on the third floor, where Santa Cruz took his post outside the door.

Once inside, sitting knee to knee with Cornwall and speaking in a whisper, Berger asked Cornwall to help "set a trap" for McCracken. He was a crooked cop, Berger confided. Berger promised Cornwall that he would ask the court to dismiss charges of land fraud against Cornwall if he told McCracken a lie designed to "test" his honesty—that is, whether McCracken would report the information back to Berger. Cornwall was to inform McCracken that he was so nervous about the killing of Lazar two days earlier that he refused to testify to the grand jury. After worrying aloud about the consequences of lying to a police officer, Cornwall agreed.

Cornwall understood that Berger's plan was absurd. Not only did Cornwall's safety rest in the hands of the very people Berger wanted him to deceive, it was obvious that McCracken would conclude that Cornwall had been frightened into silence by Lazar's murder.

The next day, a Saturday, Cornwall called his lawyer and told him about Berger's proposal. On Monday morning, Remender hauled his client down to the police station and laid out Berger's plan to "test" McCracken to the detective himself, Sparks, and two other men, including a sergeant named Jack Weaver. The cops asked Cornwall to repeat everything Berger had said for a tape recorder. They wanted Police Chief Larry Wetzel to listen to the tape. Remender insisted on meeting with Wetzel face-to-face, and the group reassembled in the chief's office later that afternoon. Wetzel listened. Then he asked Cornwall to repeat his allegations on tape and to take a lie-detector test. Cornwall agreed and passed the polygraph exam. The tape recording and test results were turned over to the court.

Judge Charles Hardy, who was presiding in *State v. Warren*, ordered that the evidence not be used in any way or referred to in Warren's upcoming trial. Berger asked Hardy to put his order into writing.

On Tuesday, March 4, Hardy threw out the case against Warren. "I find this conduct by the county attorney [Berger] deplorable," Hardy said. Warren walked again.

The police were not about to let the matter drop, however. The day after Hardy dismissed the case against Warren, the police presented themselves at the county attorney's office for a showdown. The meeting lasted, off and on, nearly two days. Berger admitted that he had attempted to use Cornwall to test McCracken's honesty, but he would not divulge what he found suspicious in McCracken's conduct. He denied Cornwall's claim that he had promised to dismiss the fraud indictments against him if he lied to McCracken. By the time the marathon session was over, Berger declared that he no longer had any doubts about McCracken's honesty. To prove it, Berger ordered that new complaints be drawn up against Warren on six counts of bribery. He said he would invite McCracken to sign the complaints personally.

McCracken had missed the two-day talks between cops and prosecutors because he was laid up with a serious case of stomach ulcers. On the third day, he rose from his sick bed and in the early afternoon arrived at the county attorney's office to affix his signature. He was informed that the complaints had been made out to the wrong precinct of jurisdiction. He would have to wait until 6:00 p.m. for the corrected versions.

Warren was arraigned in East Phoenix Precinct No. 2 Justice Court on March 12, 1975. He was immediately released on his own recognizance. When Berger's office again forced McCracken out of his sick bed to sign new complaints, this time against Joe Patrick, these documents, too, were found to be defective; he would have to wait for these to be fixed as well. The acting police chief wrote a stiff letter to Berger, noting that it was the county attorney's incompetence that had given McCracken ulcers in the first place, and this new round of abuse "may well cause him to be unavailable for trial on doctor's orders." McCracken might have to have surgery on his abdomen to close his bleeding sores, the chief warned.

On March 24, Justice of the Peace Mulford Winsor IV accepted a motion from Warren's lawyers to bar the press and the public from attending the upcoming preliminary hearing in Precinct No. 2. Winsor agreed with Warren's lawyers that a public hearing would create unfair and prejudicial publicity against Warren and that a closed hearing would protect Warren in case the state attempted to introduce evidence that was inadmissible.

The *Republic* sued. Three days later, the Arizona Supreme Court ruled that Winsor had "abused his discretion." On appeal, a federal judge accepted the constitutional argument that permitting the public and the news media to observe the preliminary hearing before a justice of the peace would violate Warren's civil rights. The champion of this argument was US District Judge Walter Craig, a close political and personal associate of Rosenzweig and Goldwater. Craig wrote in his opinion countermanding the Arizona Supreme Court, "It would appear altogether appropriate that the decision in this case be appealed to the Ninth Circuit Court of Appeals."

The day after Warren's secret preliminary hearing in justice court, on March 25, Cornwall returned to Phoenix to appear before Superior Court Judge Rufus Coulter Jr. and pleaded guilty to thirty-three counts of fraud in the Great Southwest case. At the hearing, with Berger in the courtroom, a plea bargain was announced. For his cooperation as a witness, Cornwall would be placed on probation and serve no time in prison. In exchange for the guilty plea, the court, on the day of sentencing, would remove the remaining thirty-two fraud counts and the conspiracy charge.

A SECURITY LEAK TO WARREN

By April, events were moving toward a trial for Warren, Joe Patrick, Jay Lippard, and George Brooks, all of whom had been indicted once again. This time, Berger dug deeper into his bag of prosecutors and put in charge of the new Warren case Deputy County Attorney Larry Cantor, an affable fifty year old with a reputation as an expert at courtroom strategy but someone who was frequently absentminded and late for meetings. He was friendly, almost chatty, forever smoking or chewing on a large cigar.

On April 4, 1975, Warren appeared before Winsor in a preliminary hearing cleared of reporters and citizens. A police report later surfaced that described the scene. Cantor was reeking of alcohol, the report said, and at one point, when Winsor stepped out of the courtroom, Cantor reportedly used a stage whisper to inform Warren's attorney, John Flynn, sitting just a few chairs away, that Cornwall's mother was seriously ill and that Cornwall would soon be flying to Oregon to visit her. The police were outraged. They had kept Cornwall's plan to visit his mother a closely held secret. When Cornwall boarded the flight to Portland at the Phoenix Sky Harbor airport, Warren was sitting among the other passengers. One of Cornwall's guards spotted Warren, sitting far forward. The cops whisked Cornwall off the plane. One officer later wrote, "I believe Warren was on the same flight only by use of information supplied by Cantor."

The confrontation between Berger and the police came to a head in late April. Apparently on their own authority, officers of the I-Squad summoned Berger to a meeting in their office to confront him with additional evidence they'd uncovered during the Warren investigations. In the room were Berger, McCracken, Sparks, and Sgt. Oscar Long. When he sat down at the conference table in the squad room, Berger was confronted with a reel-to-reel tape turning at a steady 7.5 inches per second. He asked that it be turned off.

Why—the cops asked Berger—had he done nothing about George Brooks when he was told as early as 1968 that Brooks was on Warren's payroll? Why had Brooks' original investigation of Warren never been shown to a grand jury? How had Berger managed to lose a stack of forged land contracts from Warren operations said to be "four feet high" after Dick Frost, a Warren front man turned antifraud activist, turned them over to Berger?

How could Berger act as an impartial prosecutor when, according to police information, he was having relations with a woman who worked as a secretary for Warren's land-development companies?

Berger responded that the allegations were lies and accused the cops of coming up with "bullshit" to force him off the case.

A PROSECUTOR'S CONFESSION

As the Warren trial approached in mid-August, Berger and McCracken decided to sit down and have it out. It's not clear who called the meeting, but because it was held in McCracken's office, it seems likely it was he who wanted the parley. That's where he could tape-record Berger clandestinely. Afterward, McCracken typed up most of the conversation, quoting Berger at length, and added comments in the margins, perhaps to make sure that their meaning would not elude even the dullest newspaper reporter.

Berger and McCracken pulled up their chairs at a quarter to four on the afternoon of August 4, 1975, three and half months after the murder of Ed Lazar. McCracken brought up comments in a news story from two of Berger's deputies who complained that Phoenix police lacked the expertise to investigate white-collar crime involving corporate fraud. McCracken had found the comments objectionable. Exactly what did Berger find lacking, he demanded, then softened and handed the county attorney an opening. Did he mean "that we need more men?"

BERGER: There's some big cases that you could be investigating—you know which ones. One is Valley National Bank; another is...[trailing off]. I may be wrong on this, but just from what I saw in the Great Southwest thing, it should be investigated, like Rosenzweig, probably...although in his case, I don't know if you would find a hell of lot. I know that he and his pals need to be investigated.

MCCRACKEN: OK.

BERGER: I don't know if you would really find anything but, still on Rosenzweig, I feel that there's a guy who—Standard Land and Title, Educational Computer Systems. He's a promoter in the thing. There's two cases, there's probably others; there's probably any number of other cases if I would sit down and think that should be pushed. Now, you guys have a problem because you do not have the manpower to do it. I think, this is my own personal belief and it's not professionally, I think you guys are being held back.

MCCRACKEN: Like a city council or a—

BERGER: Yeah, I think they are secretly keeping you from getting the people you need, and I think—for the reason they know real well, if you have a large-enough staff—some of the people you would get, I think this is true over on our side, too. I think those guys on the Board of Supervisors feel the same way, that if we had the people they would be afraid of what we would be doing.

MCCRACKEN: Yeah, I thought about that. I wondered why the state, even at the state level, why they didn't put twenty investigators on it.

BERGER: Yeah, you have been frustrated a lot of times on cases, and I've been frustrated the same way. See, I know these bastards are out to get me.

In McCracken's office, Berger continued with a description of the enemies who were out to get him. The detective egged him on.

MCCRACKEN: You mean the Board of Supervisors or a—

BERGER: It's not just the board. You know, I feel like there's a coalition out there of people. It starts with Rosenzweig, who's pissed off first of all because I didn't do some favors for them. They wanted me to drop some cases, reduce some charges—and I wouldn't do it. OK, that put me in bad with them. The next thing that happened was [US senator Paul] Fannin, [I didn't] prosecute him for drunk driving, he's of that power structure. They all do favors for each other, you know.

MCCRACKEN: Yeah.

BERGER: So he's down on me, so it's easy for him to get [to the] head of the Board of Supervisors and say, 'Don't give the county attorney anything because he doesn't play ball.' It's just that simple. The same way with Rosenzweig. He calls up the board and tells these guys, 'Don't give the county attorney anything because he's not playing ball.' OK, so that's the way that goes. Then we start finding out that Rosenzweig has got himself involved in some of this.

MCCRACKEN: Yeah, involved.

McCracken remained quiet watched as Berger took a long step into the abyss.

BERGER: Yeah, prostitution. I feel that prostitution in this state is being allowed. Now, I'm not a moralist, you know what I mean? You know, probably in a lot of respects, prostitution is in some ways a good thing.

MCCRACKEN: Yeah.

BERGER: But on the other hand, we do have it on our books as against the law, and we have—and a lot of it going on involves some very prominent people. Some of these people are guys like Rosenzweig, who's been involved in it. And I don't think these things are by accident. I think everybody in power, back there behind the scenes, are working together. Now, there is a power structure out there. People on that thing are people we are talking about here. The Valley Bank is heavily represented.

In a digression, Berger expressed his resentment against efforts by some members of the Phoenix Forty, a powerful civic-reform group, to have an outside commission appointed to investigate land fraud, circumventing him. Then:

BERGER: It wouldn't work, anyway. You find you can't get the cases filed. You can't get the work done. Now, cases get thrown out of court, and you don't understand why, you know?

MCCRACKEN: Yeah.

BERGER: And the reason is very simple. The goddamn lid is on the son of a bitch all the way from the very top.

Chapter 4

Origins of the Phoenix Network

M oise Berger's disregard for his professional reputation had a simpler explanation than anyone could have known at the time. When he con-fided to McCracken, "See, I know these bastards are out to get me," the chief prosecutor for Maricopa County was pleading with McCracken to understand that he had been forced to throw the case. What he did not say was that the pressure was coming from Harry Rosenzweig, who had compromising photographs of Berger. But McCracken did not need the explanation. He had copies of the same photos in his desk.

The honey trap that sealed Berger's fate was a house in suburban Mesa where encounters between marks and hookers could be filmed through two-way mirrors. Herb Applegate, a Detroit transplant who owned an English pub and a hamburger chain called Hobo Joe's, ran the brothel. It was so elaborate that its weekly operations budget was $4,000. Its more distinctive flourishes included phallus-shaped doorknobs and towel hooks. One bed-room closet concealed a passageway to a house next door. Applegate owned that house, too.

One of Hobo Joe's executives told IRE reporters that the filming for the blackmail operations took place in "a secret room" that "contained two-way mirrors, one looking out on the main bedroom's large, circular bed; the other facing the living room. Also inside the hidden room was expensive moviemaking equipment...You wouldn't believe who some of their guests were. They were judges, lawyers, businessmen, and some pretty prominent politicians."

Roy Elson, a prominent Democrat, had a brush with the blackmail operation. "Harry set me up, and I fell for it," he said in an interview in 2010. Elson ran for the US Senate in 1964 against Paul Fannin, a member of Barry Goldwater's inner circle. In 1968, he ran for the seat vacated by his former boss, Carl Hayden, and lost both times.

While he was having a drink at the bar in Durant's, a restaurant built by Gus Greenbaum lieutenant Jack Durant, a lawyer friend introduced Elson to an attractive woman. In the course of the evening, the woman invited him to spend the night with her. Elson recalled the early 1960s with relish as the swinging, hard-drinking Sinatra era, when he was in his thirties. The woman took him to the Del Webb Suite at the Ramada Inn downtown, across the street from the loading docks of *The Arizona Republic*. The bed in the suite was nearly as large as a standard hotel room, Elson said.

A few weeks later, Elson was having cocktails in a different lounge when he ran into a network lawyer. "I understand you've been playing around with one of Harry's girls," the lawyer said. There was no doubt who "Harry" was, or that Elson's chances of beating Fannin in the general election had evaporated. Elson poked the lawyer in the chest and told him to inform Rosenzweig that if he tried to use the hooker against him, he would reveal the identities of several gay staffers then working for two powerful Arizona Republican congressmen. Nothing more came of it.

Powerful men dabbling in prostitution was not unusual at the time. Even Kemper Marley, at the time the state's wealthiest man, had a hand in the business. On April 29, 1954, Phoenix Chief of Police Charles Thomas filed a pair of civil lawsuits against Marley and padlocked two concrete-block brothels the rancher owned near the railroad tracks in downtown Phoenix. Both buildings were located in the old warehouse district around the corner from the American Bottle Exchange at Seventh Street and Jackson, the "bottle works" that served as the headquarters of United Liquor and other Marley operations. Perhaps because the municipal code on prostitution was vague and rarely enforced, Thomas invoked a state nuisance law passed by the 1917 legislature that banned the use of buildings for "lewdness, assignation, and prostitution," but he made no arrests.

The courts entered a judgment of guilt against Marley on June 1. Thomas had to wait five months for the rancher to post bonds totaling $2,500 and sign a pledge not to reopen the businesses. News of the Marley brothels appeared on an inside section of *The Phoenix Gazette* in 1954 but was otherwise forgotten until 1980, when the *Republic* rewrote the story in the context of a libel suit Marley had filed against IRE. It ran under the headline, "Marley Expected to Face Questioning on Two Brothels." The lawyer representing Marley in the 1954 case was William Hubbs Rehnquist, a young man at the time, but when the new headline appeared twenty-six years later, he had been sitting on the US Supreme Court for nearly a decade.

In the heyday of the Phoenix network, blackmail was only one way of keeping enemies at bay and associates in line. Others were less extreme. After 1962, when the GOP was consolidating electoral power, Rosenzweig kept a careful eye on the selection of Republican candidates for judgeships, and his campaign fund was a match for Greenbaum's among the Democrats twenty years earlier. Through his virtually handpicked candidates for the courts, Rosenzweig exercised the power to bury inconvenient investigations.

Arizona Attorney General Bob Corbin described to a US Senate committee the procedure he had to follow as the chief prosecutor for Maricopa County if he wanted to take a criminal investigation to a grand jury. "The way we had to operate, we'd have to investigate a case, then I would have to take the case to all the judges in Maricopa County at a luncheon, and then they would tell me which case I could take to the grand jury. That is a very difficult way to operate, because these same judges may have to sit and try the case, and that bothered me quite a bit, but that was the only way I could get a grand jury."

Control of investigations at the state level was more indirect but no less effective. William J. Schafer III, a state prosecutor, told the same Senate hearing that until 1972, state prosecutors had no separate unit devoted to organized crime. It had just three employees, and the unit was considerably less organized than the criminals they were investigating. "There was little understanding of what it had to do, and the direction it had to take," Schafer told the chairman,

US senator Dennis DeConcini, an Arizona Democrat, in 1980. "It was really pushed out to sea to sink or swim on its own. Well, it sank within two years, really."

There was also occasional confusion at the Phoenix FBI about its investigative function in relation to organized crime. In 1964, during Goldwater's run for the presidency, the FBI obtained an advance copy of *The Green Felt Jungle* (1963), by two of the leading organized-crime reporters of the day, Ed Reid and Ovid Demaris. It contained details of Barry Goldwater's relationship with Gus Greenbaum. The bureau contacted the senator and warned him about what to expect, giving him time to prepare a response.

DECLINE OF THE PHOENIX SALOON CULTURE

The struggle to control prostitution in Phoenix had its origins in an incident early in World War II. On Thanksgiving night in 1942, soldiers of the 364th infantry regiment, which had distinguished itself at the Battle of Argonne in World War I, were celebrating the holiday in a row of bars scattered a few miles west of the regiment's barracks in Phoenix. The bars lined both sides of Washington Avenue at Seventeenth Street, the heart of what was then called the "colored neighborhood." The soldiers were black, as were the military police who patrolled the streets in jeeps to keep order.

In one of the bars, a fight broke out. When several MPs walked in and confronted the brawling soldiers, a knife suddenly appeared. One MP shot and wounded the man with the knife. Other soldiers protested, and the noise attracted curious drinkers from nearby saloons. Within minutes, about one hundred and fifty soldiers surrounded the bar. The MPs inside were trapped but managed to extricate themselves from the crowd long enough to radio back to the base at nearby Papago Park for buses to pick up the soldiers and return them to camp. The MPs managed to get the men lined up and ready to board, but as they stepped into the buses, a jeep full of soldiers from the base pulled up with brakes screeching. From all accounts, the men in the jeep had managed to return to the barracks at Papago, load up on sidearms, and return to Washington Street. One of them fired a shot. The soldiers broke from their file next to the buses and scattered into the surrounding neighborhood as handheld weapons "snapped and barked" in the confusion.

When word of the gunfire reached them, city authorities declared an emergency. They ordered police to cordon off about twenty-eight blocks of the near-east side of Phoenix and search for the soldiers, many of whom were hiding in the homes of friends.

Military authorities joined the search by turning over to the MPs eight armored personnel carriers, each equipped with a loudspeaker and a .50-caliber machine gun. When orders delivered through the loudspeakers failed to persuade the soldiers to give themselves up, the armored carriers fired on some of the houses with the machine guns, leaving holes "the size of tennis balls."

Before the night was over, three men were dead and eleven more wounded. Some one hundred and eighty men were arrested, among them a few identified as the shooters who had startled the soldiers into their flight through the neighborhood. They were court-martialed and eventually shipped off under guard to military prisons. Long before that happened, though, civilian authorities conducted their own inquiry. Remarkably, the investigators had little interest in the military's use of the heavy weapons to shoot into the homes of Phoenix civilians. Their interest was to discover how it was possible for black soldiers to "obtain firearms to carry on the pitched battle with police."

When responding to civilian inquiries, army brass changed the subject. They revived an old concern about the rate of sexually transmitted diseases contracted by soldiers who visited the bars and brothels along Washington Avenue. Three days after the shooting, Col. Ross Hoyt, commander of the sprawling US Army Air Corps training field on the city's far west side, announced that he was designating all of Phoenix off-limits to his troops because of the STD problem. When asked whether the move had anything to do with the Thanksgiving incident, he denied it. But when other commanders in the area followed Hoyt's lead and restricted their troops to base, the message was clear to civilian authorities. Prostitution in Phoenix had to go, or the city would be placed off-limits for good.

A military boycott threatened disaster for many businesses in Phoenix, not just saloon owners and pimps in the red-light district. This was a state, after all, whose white citizens had learned in its days as a frontier territory that they could not survive economically without the US Army. Many of the earliest pioneer families, including provisioners like the Goldwaters, had come to Arizona because of the extraordinary sums the US government was spending on the Apache wars.

The Phoenix Chamber of Commerce grasped the threat of the army's boycott and demanded that a grand jury investigate the STD problem. A minority on the city council sympathetic to the army and the merchants demanded the resignation of the majority bloc, which was controlled by urban Democrats in the Gus Greenbaum faction. The majority refused. As the November 1942 elections approached, according to the memoirs of one Phoenix cop, "vice detectives were making the rounds of madams, bookies, drug users, and drug dealers and instructing them to cool it until after the elections."

Because the elections did not change power relations on the council, an impatient chamber leadership broke the stalemate. On December 15, 1942, lawyer Frank Snell and Wesley Knorpp, an executive at *The Arizona Republic*, called a meeting of the chamber's board of directors in the card room of the Hotel Adams. They crafted a demand that the top city office-holders resign and the city council replace them with three "nonpolitical" appointees who would be given "free rein" to clean up the city.

That holiday season witnessed the birth of a reform movement and the end of official tolerance for a wide-open saloon culture. The movement would soon become identified with Barry Goldwater. As in the familiar "town-taming" narrative of the Hollywood Westerns, the old saloon bosses met their match in the forces of virtue. The twist was that virtue was no longer represented as schoolmarms and brides newly arrived from back East. It was the US Army and the chamber of commerce.

When the city council met the day after "the Card Room Putsch," as Snell called it, members voted to fire the city manager. The new manager fired the chief of police. Five days later, Hoyt lifted the boycott, and the city relaxed in time for the Christmas holidays.

But the reform fell apart within weeks. With the pressure off, the resurgent old majority of the city council voted to reinstate the city manager and police chief. The *Republic* editorial columns warned that a disgusted Hoyt was threatening to reinstate the army boycott of the city.

Chamber directors voted to take the fight to clean up the city directly to the voters. They organized the Citizens Good Government Council and put up a slate of candidates for the city election in March 1943 that won without difficulty and took office in May. By mid-November, the *Republic* was confidently reporting that STDs in Phoenix were under control. Until the end of the war and a few months thereafter, the reform slate governed the city.

The saloon culture was not about to accept the defeat without a fight, however. In 1946, a paint-store owner by the name of Ray Busey assembled the Greater Phoenix Ticket to challenge the reformers. Supporters of the GPT charged that a small, unrepresentative elite had seized control of the city through the pages of the *Republic* and the self-appointed civic do-gooders in the Citizens Good Government Council. The argument worked. Busey was elected mayor, and his candidates for city council were voted into office over the *Republic's* warnings that a Busey administration would mean a return to prewar "slot machines, gambling, prostitution, and city bossism." It was the newspaper's last campaign under the leadership of Knorpp; the *Republic* announced in October that the paper had been sold to Indianapolis publisher Eugene C. Pulliam.

With his election in January 1946, Busey announced his determination to restore saloon life to its former status. *The Arizona News* reported early in the Busey administration that the new mayor set the tone by gathering members of the vice squad and other police and city officials in the office of Police Chief Rufus Coulter. There, Busey reminded them that notions of reform would not be tolerated. That is, Gus Greenbaum was not to be disturbed. "You will not molest any of the horse-race bookie places. I want you men to understand I am not collecting anything. Those boys...are friends of mine." The statement, apparently leaked to the *News* by reform-friendly cops at the meeting, was immediately followed by this explanation from the reporter: "The bookie joints all assertedly are controlled by Gus Greenbaum," who "resumed operations in Phoenix after the Busey administration came into control of city hall."

Busey could not have won the mayor's race without making a few concessions. One had lasting significance. During the campaign, he promised to create a Charter Revision Committee to study the structure of city government. In October 1947, he delivered on the promise by appointing Barry Goldwater and thirty-nine other businessmen and professionals to the committee. It formed the nucleus of a continuing organization devoted to public policy that would come to be known informally as "the Phoenix Forty." For the moment, however, the Charter Revision Committee was essentially an updated version of the Citizens Good Government Council.

Despite his appointment of the reform committee, Busey had no intention of cooperating with it. He got rid of Coulter and in his place appointed the pliable Earl O'Clair, who had direct ties to gambling and saloon interests. In response, reformers turned to the county government for help. In Maricopa County Attorney Edward Beauchamp, they found a man willing to take on the vice kingpins.

In late summer of 1946, a few weeks after James Ragan died of mercury poisoning in Chicago while Greenbaum cheered on the killers from his post at the Flamingo, Beauchamp began arresting low-level members and hangers-on of the old network and turning them into informers. He extracted a signed confession from a pimp who gave up the names of madams and bookmakers and criminals and cops who were involved in making or taking payoffs. Particular attention was paid to members of the police department's vice squad, whose officers, the pimp said, were taking collections from brothel owners. The pimp swore that he regularly collected fifty dollars from each of the leading madams in town and turned over the money to one R. D. Linville. *The Arizona News* described Linville as a friend of Greenbaum's and "a wealthy ex-convict" whose job was to make sure the vice squad was paid off in a timely manner.

Linville was reportedly good at his duties, with one notable failure. The madam of a small bagnio called The Cozy refused to pay. Linville turned over her collection account to a city vice detective who arrested the madam three times before she gave up and sold The Cozy to a man described as a mutual friend of Linville and Greenbaum.

Another knowledgeable observer, Harry Rosenzweig, reported slightly different numbers. The madams "would be arrested once a month, and all the girls would be arrested, and they just automatically went down and paid the fine, only the fines went in a bag, and every month the [city] council cut it up....Each girl was fined twenty-five dollars a month into the pot, and the madams—say, forty of them—that's another couple thousand, so there was five, six, seven thousand to divide among five or six guys every month. And they had a bagman. He'd go down and do the collecting."

On occasion, O'Clair made a gesture toward reform. Early in 1948, he assembled a squad of officers and raided the Western News Exchange, Gus Greenbaum's former racing book, which he had instructed Teak Baldwin, Mike Newman, and Jimmy Aaron to reopen in late 1945. Somehow, Western News survived. Cynics noted that the highly publicized raid at the Saint James occurred on the same day that a guest at a Phoenix resort hotel won more than $6,000 on a bet at Western News. The wire service did not say whether the timely intervention of the police rescued Greenbaum from paying off the winner.

The immediate postwar period, then, was a time of seesaw victories and defeats for Greenbaum and his associates. It was a struggle to keep or regain control of city government and, along with it, the protection of law enforcement for their various illegal enterprises. City council reformers kept the pressure on with accusations that vice squad officers were taking bribes. O'Clair continued his denials, at one point telling the council that there was "no organized vice in the City of Phoenix." Council reformers responded by producing a survey taken by "a bunch of Phoenix 'do-gooders' that found fifteen brothels operating openly and notoriously within easy walking distance of police headquarters," a police officer later recalled.

The political struggle to rid the city of the Greenbaum-Busey network occupied most of 1949 and ended with the victory of the Charter Government reform movement and the beginning of the gradual eclipse of the Democratic Party.

Barry Goldwater's younger brother, Bob Goldwater, was interviewed in 1999 for a television documentary. In an cheerful broadcast about Phoenix in the 1940s, the narrator posed a darker question. "The city itself was not so clean, and worse, the city government had its own tarnish?" "We had corruption in government," Goldwater replied. "At the time, it seemed to go together."

THE MURDER OF KATHRYN WICKSON

As the failed prosecution of Ned Warren and Great Southwest Land and Cattle Co. demonstrated, blackmail and the official cover-up were the two most effective methods used by the Phoenix network to keep the lid on dangerous information. Its bosses even had the power to make sure that murders went unsolved, as in the cold-blooded killing in 1945 of a young victim from Yuma, Kathryn Wickson. They could also drive an insider to suicide if he posed a danger as a witness, as in the messy and very public example of Jimmy Aaron in 1959.

One of the most public faces of the criminal network in Phoenix was a former associate of Gus Greenbaum and Kemper Marley. He was a particularly ruthless gambler and clip-joint operator named Clarence E. "Teak" Baldwin.

Teak Baldwin and his gang ran the Steak House, a restaurant and nightclub on North Central Avenue that offered card and dice games. After World War II, the Steak House was one of the last homes of the horse wire in Phoenix. Baldwin also ran a nearby nightclub called the Gilded Cage, remembered by some as a "high class strip joint" that offered stiff drinks and friendly prostitutes. Baldwin nominally owned both clubs, but Marley controlled the former and an influential ex-Chicagoan, Herb Lieb, ran the latter with participation behind the scenes from influential friends. Lieb was probably the single most influential friend of the Chicago mob in Phoenix because of his ties to the outfit's treasurer and accountant, Irwin Weiner, and to Allen Dorfman, the investment banker for the Teamsters' pension funds.

At the Steak House, Baldwin's card and dice games catered to farmers and small businessmen, including plumbers, road contractors, and auto dealers, men who had ready access to large sums of cash. The Steak House clientele is known because men from each of these occupations filed complaints with Phoenix police about Baldwin from 1945 to 1952. He was accused of slipping a hypnotic into a gamblers' drinks, thought to be chloral hydrate (also known as the Mickey Finn after its greenish color). Winners would soon start to lose and eventually pass out. Sometimes they would wake up in a back room with empty wallets, an IOU pinned to their jackets, with no memory of what happened.

Ten days before Christmas 1945, a wholesale-produce dealer from Yuma showed up at the Steak House looking for action. At the side of the older man was an attractive twenty-three-year-old woman, also from Yuma. They had been dating for more than a year. Kathryn Ann Wickson was a bookkeeper for a Yuma bus company and estranged from her husband, a worker on the Imperial Dam project on the lower Colorado River. She had graduated from El Paso High School in 1938 and bore two children, both boys, soon after.

Baldwin was at the bar when the produce dealer, who was already drunk, pulled out a roll of bills that a witness estimated to be worth between $2,000 and $3,000. He slapped the money on the bar.

Pete Abbey was the bartender on duty at the time, but when the produce man pulled out the fistful of bills, Baldwin shoved Abbey aside. He poured drinks for the couple and suggested a friendly game of craps on the bar. Wickson put her hand on her boyfriend's arm as though to restrain him and told him he was in no condition to gamble. He reluctantly obeyed. He put the money back in his pocket and returned to his drink.

What neither the boyfriend nor Wickson realized at that moment was how much Wickson's gesture had enraged Baldwin. "I'll fix that son of a bitch," he muttered, apparently in reference to Wickson but out of the couple's hearing. Baldwin was within earshot of a Steak House waiter, the original informant in the case.

The waiter said Baldwin left the Steak House to go to a nearby drugstore. He was not gone long. When he returned, he told Abbey to pour fresh drinks for the couple and to bring Wickson's to him first. Baldwin "poured a substance from a small bottle" into Wickson's drink, and Abbey served them at the bar.

Wickson took a sip from the drink. She put it down and told Abbey "it tasted funny," the waiter said. Abbey mixed another drink and gave it to her.

The waiter's shift ended soon after that, and he left. When he returned to work the next day, Abbey informed him that Kathryn Wickson was dead. He told the waiter to keep his mouth shut. The waiter asked Baldwin what happened. She died of an enlarged heart, Baldwin said. He had nothing more to say.

And there the matter rested for six years.

They were good years for Baldwin. Now and then a news story about him appeared. In April 1950, for instance, an itinerant artist named Charles Picow, who made a living by drawing portraits of customers in bars for three dollars a sketch, was thrown out of the Gilded Cage. Baldwin and two other men beat him so badly that he was disfigured.

Meanwhile, complaints to Phoenix police piled up from victims who complained that Baldwin had drugged them and taken their money.

Among the authentic reformers who followed in the footsteps of Edwin Beauchamp were two county attorneys who succeeded him. In October 1951, Maricopa County Attorney Warren McCarthy organized the unusual Arizona institution of the one-man grand jury, with himself as the jury, for the specific purpose of investigating the activities of Teak Baldwin. The supervising magistrate was Francis Donofrio, who at that moment was a judge of the Superior Court. Between 1947 and 1949, Donofrio held the office of county attorney, separating the terms of Beauchamp and McCarthy.

Disturbed at Baldwin's impunity from arrest and prosecution, McCarthy and Donofrio opened an investigation. After learning of the waiter's account of the Wickson murder, they subpoenaed Pete Abbey. By this time, Abbey was a well-known figure in Phoenix. He was running Kemper Marley's Cowmen's Club, a gambling operation near the cattle stockyards on Washington Avenue, where he managed a monthly betting handle of $300,000.

Abbey confirmed the waiter's account and added more details from a bartender's perspective. When he returned from the drugstore, Baldwin poured a green liquid into Wickson's drink, a crème de menthe with soda. As Baldwin started to add a little more of the liquid, Abbey protested "that he would kill her with that much." Before handing Wickson the drink, Abbey poured off a bit and added an ice cube. After she took a few sips, Wickson became violently ill and staggered to the women's restroom. When she returned to the bar, she found a fresh crème de menthe and soda waiting for her, prepared by Baldwin.

Abbey did not know what happened next. Another waiter who was still working for Baldwin was called to testify but refused to cooperate and afterward warned anyone else who might be called as a witness not to cooperate. For the moment, McCarthy was working only from a sketchy police report on the incident in 1947 and the Wickson death certificate from 1945. The police report, written by Gordon Selby, summed up the crime in two sentences: "A woman had died as a result of receiving poisoned drinks at the Steak House. However, at that time the officer was unable to develop any further information."

The man who filled out the death certificate was the Maricopa County medical examiner, O.C. West. He was told that after Wickson left the Steak House, she went to a room at the San Carlos Hotel, where she died between three and four in the morning. West was called to the hotel, where he examined her and ordered her body removed to the county morgue. He performed an autopsy and entered the cause of death as "coronary thrombosis with marked fatty infiltration of the myocardium" (heart muscle). When asked whether he had examined the contents of Wickson's stomach at autopsy, West said he had not.

Frustrated at nearly every turn, McCarthy decided to recover whatever physical evidence might still exist. On December 18, 1951, he filled out an application for the exhumation and disinterment of Wickson's remains. Donofrio approved the application.

It can only have been a solemn posse of lawmen who drove to Yuma the following day, December 19, a Wednesday. They included Daniel Gordon, the new county medical examiner; Harry Stewart, an assistant county attorney representing McCarthy; and George U. Young Jr., a captain of detectives in the Phoenix Police Department. After a three-hour drive, they arrived at the city on the Mexican border and put up for the night.

The next day the group drove to Resort Lawn (now Desert Lawn) Cemetery and pulled up at Space 12, which resembled not so much a resting place as a construction site. Pieces of building materials, some in pieces, lay scattered around the gravesite. Cemetery workers explained that when they dug into the soil, they discovered not the casket they had expected but a large wooden crate. After they pried the crate open, they discovered a concrete vault. They sent for a jackhammer to break up the concrete but found that it was reinforced with a cage of iron rebar. Visible through the rebar was a casket. The concrete had been poured through the rebar to fill up the crate, encasing the casket from bottom to top. Only after they removed large chunks of concrete and pried back the rebar could cemetery workers retrieve the casket. It was made of steel.

The cemetery workers managed to open the casket and move the remains of Wickson to a local morgue, where Gordon conducted an autopsy. He gathered specimens of her hair, fingernails from the right hand, a sample of embalming compound found in the lungs, and portions of her heart, throat, liver, stomach, and bowels, both large and small. He also collected samples of embalming compound from the lower abdomen, pelvis, and bladder. McCarthy ordered specimens to be taken to a forensic laboratory in Los Angeles run by the noted police chemist Bay Pinker, who spent several months trying to establish what agent had been used to knock out and ultimately kill Wickson. It was all for naught. "Due to the length of time the remains had been in the ground and the fact that the embalming agents are very similar to those thought to have been used by Baldwin (chloral hydrate), Mr. Pinker was never able to arrive at any definite conclusion after distilling each and every specimen submitted."

Not a word about the case appeared in print. Baldwin walked away from the murder unscathed and continued to drug and rob customers until 1952, when McCarthy indicted him and several of his financial backers. The charges were thrown out of court by a judge, not identified in news accounts, "who ruled that the victims had voluntarily accepted the drinks and paid the gambling debts."

The cover-up of Kathryn Wickson's murder—so elaborate that it involved several tons of wood, soil, concrete, rebar, and plate steel—was a brand of justice in which private interests were able to protect a man who committed an act of ferocious violence by frustrating dutiful officers at every turn.

In 1952, a California man named Edwin E. Warwick won a large but undisclosed money judgment against Baldwin in a civil case heard by a federal jury. Warwick described how Baldwin cheated him out of $4,500 after doping his drinks and inducing him to sign checks. The jury believed him. Again in 1952, the Internal Revenue Service filed a federal-tax lien against Baldwin for $147,400 for the period 1948 to 1951. In a Los Angeles courtroom, Baldwin defended his lax accounting by explaining that the statutes against gambling were rarely enforced in Arizona.

Teak Baldwin remained a member of Marley's operation until he faded into the background and was replaced by younger, up-and-coming gangsters. The public record provides a glimpse of him sitting at a table in the back of a hotel café, nodding familiarly to John Harvey Adamson and construction heir Stan Tanner as they stopped to refresh themselves after delivering a savage beating to a Tanner enemy in one of the hotel's rooms. It was a late glimpse of Baldwin, but not the last one.

In 1980, Marley called Baldwin as a character witness at the rancher's libel trial against IRE, where he denied that Marley had ever been a gambler. Baldwin told the court, "As far as I know," he said, "he can't even play cards."

THE AGONY OF JIMMY AARON

On the morning of June 16, 1953, before the sun rose over the city at the hottest time of the year, a pair of Phoenix police detectives cruising east on Van Buren Street, the main east-west corridor in the downtown, spotted an open window at the Dependable Used Car Lot. They got out of the car and investigated a building at the back of the lot. They poked their flashlights into what appeared to be a storage room and saw a shipping crate with a covering of paper torn open. The detectives drove to the police station for a search warrant. When they returned with the warrant, Captain of Detectives George U. Young (a member of the Wickson posse), was with them, along with Police Sergeant Virgil Lehman from the vice squad. Behind them was a truck. Sitting in the back were enough jail trustees to haul away the contents of the storage room.

As the detectives got out of their car, two men confronted them. One was Herman Matz, owner of the business. The other was Jimmy Aaron, a citizen prominent enough to be a member of the Arizona Club. Aaron owned the car lot along with his sister, Fannie Aaron Matz, Herman's wife. Matz and Aaron tried to talk the cops out of hauling away what turned out to be a suite of expensive and illegal gambling equipment, including tables for poker, craps, and roulette. One of the tables held a thirty-two-inch wheel crafted by J. W. Snead of Long Beach. Attached to one crate was a C.O.D. claim for $600 from a Los Angeles shipper.

After an hour of haggling, Young ordered Lehman to arrest Matz and take him to police court. The trustees hauled off five large crates of gambling equipment, which Young estimated had a value of about $9,000 in contemporary dollars. Matz paid a $300 bond and was told to appear at an initial hearing the next day.

That evening's edition of *The Phoenix Gazette* contained comments from Matz and Aaron that rattled nerves up and down the Phoenix network, whose members were not accustomed to seeing their gambling operations mentioned in the city's daily papers.

Police officials did not explain how they knew from one peek through a window that it was contraband or that it would require a truck and a moving crew to cart it off. The convenient presence of a *Gazette* reporter at the second police visit gave the morning's events the flavor of a publicity bust, meaning Young likely was already aware that Matz had been running a small racing handbook on his lot for several years and that Aaron, a wealthy owner of rental properties, was a partner with Gus Greenbaum and Teak Baldwin in the racing handbook called the Western News Exchange.

"We've had that stuff back there for the past eight years, and it has never been opened," Matz told Young before his arrest. He pleaded with the captain to allow him to call County Attorney William P. Mahoney, a Democrat, "to see if we can't get this thing straightened out without so much fuss." He asked Young, "Why didn't the police let me know they wanted the stuff? I would have brought it over in my own truck. You don't have to make all this stink about it. I've been here thirty-five years, and I have a business to think about. You can do what you want with the equipment. Smash it right here if you want to."

Aaron joined in. He said that sometime in the previous year (1952), he had told former County Attorney Warren McCarthy and former Police Chief Earl O'Clair about the crates, and they had said it would be all right to store the gambling equipment at the car lot. "I think it's a dirty deal to tell a man he can keep the stuff and then arrest him," Aaron added. The next day he changed his story. "I had been advised by an attorney that nothing would be done if we kept the equipment in storage."

By this time, O'Clair had been relieved of his post by the 1949 election. And he was furious at Aaron. "Such a report is absolutely false," he said, "in view of my record of having seized more gambling equipment, during my time in office, than any other police chief in the city's history."

In his new private life, O'Clair, like Matz, was a car salesman, but the former chief of police had gone into another line of work as well. In June of 1952, he took over the operation of a nightclub on East Washington Avenue called the Black and Tan, known to members of the Phoenix police vice squad as well as reporters like Don Bolles as the gateway to a brothel in nearby apartments. Black and Tan's license had been pulled that month after a bar fight and a few weeks later was turned over to one Harry Sodikoff. An ex-cop, Sodikoff had been kicked off the Phoenix Police Department for a series of indiscretions, including assault and contributing to the delinquency of a minor. Not long after that, Sodikoff lost the Black and Tan license for fighting with customers, and O'Clair was brought in to operate the bar. Perhaps coincidentally, Black and Tan sat on land co-owned by Sodikoff and Harry Rosenzweig.

The raid on Herman Matz's Dependable lot was a landmark not only in police work but in the cautiously evolving news coverage of the Phoenix network after World War II; it was important not for the crime but for the details that began to emerge about the network membership, high and low. In 1955, after the murder of Willie Bioff, mentions of organized crime began to emerge in police reports. The Bioff killing gave reporters a news context for items from police reports that once might have been considered too obscure for a closer look. Because of the Dependable raid, the detail that Bioff had spent his last evening socializing with Matz at Mike Newman's house acquired some context and news value. Even so, coverage remained discreet.

As the 1950s drew to a close, it was becoming clear that some powerful enemies were organizing against the Phoenix network. The federal government, in the form of the Internal Revenue Service, was the first to move. On Nov. 29, 1957, a group of men from the IRS intelligence squad, led by its chief, Jack G. Williams, walked into the famed Phoenix Billiard Academy, knocked on the locked door to the phone room, and arrested Mike Newman. The IRS charged him with running a horse book and failing to pay federal taxes on the income. The arrest was a shock. Newman had been given a pass from the law during his twenty years as a Greenbaum protégé, perhaps because of his childhood friendship with Harry Rosenzweig and Barry Goldwater. Why had Newman's immunity expired?

The mystery deepened as the new year approached. Shortly after noon on December 30, unknown assailants attacked Newman and his older brother, sixty-one-year-old Isadore Newman, in the bungalow they shared on the city's near-east side. The crime went unreported until January 16, 1958, when the *Republic* printed three brief paragraphs keying on the fact that Newman's beating was severe enough for him to ask that his arraignment on the gambling charge in federal court be postponed. The reporter described Newman as "a Phoenix bookie suspect, asserted kingpin of that fraternity here." *Kingpin* was a winking acknowledgment of the fact that Newman had taken over what remained of Greenbaum's old handbook. It could not have referred to the size of his business. Federal authorities announced that Newman's handle, or gross, was a modest $250,000 a year.

Newman was found guilty and sentenced to six months in Florence State Prison. On the day of sentencing, Harry Rosenzweig sat in the courtroom. Six months was considered a light term, and federal court officials later admitted that both Rosenzweig and Goldwater had intervened to ask for leniency. In any event, Newman did not serve the full six months. It was cut to three, and he was released from Florence in June after federal judge Walter Craig intervened.

The IRS move against Newman was part of a broader federal crackdown on gambling that in an election year was convenient for the Democrats and embarrassing to Goldwater. The Senate race in 1958 cast an incumbent Goldwater against former US senator Ernest McFarland, who was trying to regain the seat from which the upstart had dislodged him in 1952. Democratic strategists hoped to use Newman as a counterexample to the national GOP plans to emphasize the scandals of the Truman administration as evidence of Democratic corruption in Washington. If that was the plan, it failed. In a year in which registered

Democrats statewide still outnumbered Republicans and the national GOP lost twelve US Senate seats, Goldwater's popularity was insurmountable. He won reelection by more than thirty-five thousand votes. No political obstacles remained at home as he prepared his run for the presidency.

On January 21, 1959, a federal grand jury called a number of Phoenicians to testify about what they knew of bookmaking in Phoenix. They summoned Newman, Herman Matz, Jimmy Aaron, and Harry Rosenzweig. The grand jury called Rosenzweig because he owned the parcel of land at 30 West Jefferson, the site of the billiard academy where Greenbaum and Newman had operated their horse book for decades. In the news story about his testimony, the *Republic* referred to Rosenzweig as a "Phoenix jeweler."

After his rescue from state prison, Mike Newman began to spend much of his time in Las Vegas working at the Riviera. The question of why Newman would agree go to work for the Riviera after the murder of his mentor, Greenbaum, was at least partially cleared up in mid-February, when the federal grand jury took testimony from a surprise witness. He was Sid Wyman, a co-owner of the Dunes, who had employed Newman as a coordinator for Phoenicians who booked gambling junkets to his casino. The colorful Wyman, an associate of the Saint Louis mob who one day would be inducted into the Poker Hall of Fame, was also a co-owner of the Riviera. Wyman told reporters the grand jury asked him about Newman's duties at the casino. Whatever he told them seemed to satisfy the grand jury, which dissolved after handing up one indictment. It charged Jimmy Aaron with failure to pay $5,000 in excise taxes on a less-than-modest handle of $55,000 from his handbook in the back of Matz's car lot.

The Aaron case dragged on, with the prosecution in no apparent hurry to put him on trial. On a Sunday night in late October 1959, a year after his alleged crime, a distraught Aaron hailed a cab on the near-east side and asked to be taken to a rental-car agency on Central Avenue. Aaron climbed into the backseat. When the cab arrived at the car rental, Aaron handed cabbie James Reagan a ten-dollar bill for the dollar-fifty fare and told him to keep the change. He told Reagan to go into the rental agency and order a vehicle for him, then abruptly changed his mind. "Let's go," he told Reagan.

Aaron and Reagan drove east to First Street and Fillmore. Aaron pulled out a pistol, a Spanish make, and pressed it against the back of Reagan's head. "Do as I say, and you won't get hurt," he said. "Keep your hands on the wheel. Don't smoke." It was just a few minutes before 7:00 p.m.

Aaron asked the cabbie where he lived and where he kept his personal car. They drove to Reagan's apartment on North Fourth Avenue, parked the cab, and got out. With Aaron holding his pistol on Reagan, they walked west to Sixth Avenue and Jefferson, where Reagan had left his car. They drove east out of town on McDowell Road, stopping once for gas and cigarettes. At the Beeline Highway, they turned north and followed the incline of a cliff that led to the Mogollan Rim, the Arizona high country and its Ponderosa pines. Ten miles outside Payson, Aaron ordered Reagan to stop at the side of the cliff. He stared down into the darkness below. "This is not the place," he told Reagan, and ordered the cabbie to turn around and head back toward Phoenix.

"Every five or ten miles, he would tell me to stop," Reagan told police. "Then he would say, 'This is not the place,' and I would drive on."

As they approached the outskirts of Phoenix, Reagan saw a Maricopa County sheriff's cruiser approaching in the distance. It was 10:40 p.m. He slowed his car to a crawl—about three miles per hour—and steered the car erratically to attract the cop's attention. Aaron did not seem to notice.

In the distance, Deputy Lloyd Watkins noticed Reagan's maneuver, stopped his cruiser and got out. He waited for the slow-moving car to reach him. He waved Reagan to a stop and walked toward the car. The cabbie jumped out of the car and warned him, "He's got a gun."

As Watkins stepped toward the car, Aaron put the pistol under his chin and pulled the trigger. He slumped backward. The bullet exited from the top of his head and lodged in the roof.

Police examined the Spanish pistol and discovered that Aaron had loaded a single round. In the backseat, they found a small cardboard box with six live rounds and a suicide note addressed to Fannie Matz, his sister. When he woke up that morning, Aaron wrote to Fannie that he found himself "hopelessly insane." He was afraid that he would have to "spend the rest of my life in an institution and be a drag on you."

"I realize this is the only way out," Aaron wrote. "I go to a peace that I must have. You must realize the terrible tortures I have gone through the past few weeks."

What were the "terrible tortures" Aaron endured? One can only imagine the corner he found himself in. The IRS sweep in 1959 against the remaining gamblers in the old Greenbaum network had produced a single indictment— against him. If there were to be more indictments, he would be the informer. If he didn't cooperate with the IRS, they had only Aaron to prosecute. He took his secrets to the grave.

Aaron left these few last words to his sister. "I am sorry, so sorry. You will never know. I go with nothing but love, love for you."

GOLDWATER AND THE DEL RIO SPRINGS FRAUD

In 1971, business for the Phoenix network was proceeding at a placid but profitable pace when a scandal rattled through the news pages. The *Republic* reported that Barry Goldwater and his protégé in the House of Representatives, Sam Steiger, signed letters on official US Senate and House stationery that endorsed a land fraud aimed at enticing homesick active-service enlisted men in Asia to buy, sight unseen, worthless land in the Chino Valley north of Prescott. In a few cases, the land was almost vertical, which is to say, on a cliff face. Del Rio Springs was one of the most-notorious land crimes in Ned Warren's sizeable portfolio and reached into every corner of the Phoenix network, including federal and state politicians and bureaucrats and a convicted killer who would play a major role as an informant in the Bolles investigation.

The Del Rio Springs scandal was kicked off unintentionally by Warren's accountant, Ed Lazar, when he drew up drafts of the letters signed by Goldwater and Steiger and dated them. It was August 18, 1971. Lazar gave them to Warren, who passed them up the line to Harry Rosenzweig, who presented them to the politicians for their signatures. The signed letters were returned to Warren, who hand-carried both of them to interested parties in the state of Washington.

Awaiting the letters in Washington was a group of former salesmen for Investors Overseas Service, the pyramid scheme built by the notorious Bernard Cornfeld, a nervous international swindler with a stutter who was a close associate of Robert Vesco until Vesco robbed him of $250 million. Cornfeld's salesmen showed Goldwater's letter to American soldiers dreaming of home in the bars of Okinawa and the Philippines, which was helpful in selling Warren's worthless land.

In Phoenix, little of the Del Rio Springs scam was known when the Goldwater-Steiger letters were discovered and reported. Publicity over the letters was brief but intense, with great attention paid to the congressional letterhead. Al Sitter, a *Republic* reporter, called Goldwater to ask who had requested the letter. The senator was patient with Sitter but foggy in his responses. In private, however, he was furious with Sitter and the *Republic*. He wrote to a close friend, "I have been as close to the *Republic*'s efforts to destroy people as you have, in fact, maybe a little closer, so I am well aware of everything that has been going on. Frankly, the letter written supposedly by my office or by me relative to the land north of Prescott is something that is of a mystery...to us also." He added that he had written "a very, very strong letter to the publisher of the paper" complaining that the letter had "gotten out."

Who prompted Lazar to draft the Goldwater letter for Warren? That remained a mystery until 2005, when archivists at the Arizona Historical Foundation found an unusual memo in a box of Barry Goldwater's papers. The author was John P. Frank, a legal historian and an intellectual leader and former chairman of the Arizona Democratic Party. Frank titled the memo *Confidential Material for Senator Goldwater*. Attached were several pages from a statement made by Howard N. Woodall, a close associate of Warren.

Of the many con men who orbited Warren, none was more effective or more ruthless than Woodall. He arrived in Arizona in 1968, attracted by the easy money made in criminal land sales. His talent won him a job as a salesman with a flourishing Tucson operation run by Joseph S. Agers. When federal authorities charged Agers with cheating some twelve hundred investors out of $7 million, Woodall joined a Warren fraud then flourishing near Yuma, the

New Life Trust. Before long, New Life and other Warren schemes in the area collapsed under the weight of ten federal indictments, and Woodall moved to Phoenix to work as a salesman for Del Rio Springs.

Warren's original head of the Chino Valley operation was William Carson, but by the time Woodall appeared on the scene, Carson was dead. A less confident grifter than Woodall might have had second thoughts about joining Del Rio after studying the circumstances of Carson's death. It happened after the federal prosecutors indicted Carson as part of the Yuma cases. Carson testified about Warren before the US Securities and Exchange Commission, then fled with his wife to Texas in the company plane. In midair over New Mexico, an explosion ripped the plane apart, killing the Carsons. Although murder was suspected, it was never proven.

Woodall suddenly found himself president of Del Rio. He demonstrated his skill from the start. When he discovered that some Del Rio construction equipment was registered in Carson's name, Woodall coolly reregistered it under his own, and then forged the signature of Carson's dead wife on the release.

Del Rio's major obstacle to sales was that its real estate lacked any kind of development, even the most basic utilities. Woodall was able to clear that hurdle by hiring flexible lawyers to pay off municipal and state regulators. But his true innovation was bribing field employees of the utility companies. Woodall confessed that he had slipped anywhere from "couple of hundred dollars to a couple thousand" to utility workers in exchange for signed written statements asserting that Del Rio had contracted with the utilities to extend power, water, and telephone lines to the subdivisions in question. The statements omitted any mention of burdensome costs. For example, the phone company estimated that in some cases it would cost as much as $62,000 to string and install a phone line from the main trunk to some of the properties. Under questioning, Woodall said he'd made good-faith efforts to acquire utility services but had been forced to use up too much of the improvement funds to pay off blackmailers.

Woodall's fraud was uncovered when the federal government discovered that neither he nor Warren owned the land they were selling as Del Rio Springs,

Inc. The FBI had little difficulty rounding up the evidence. In 1977, Woodall was convicted and sentenced to ten years in prison for mail fraud and other crimes.

Woodall's intimate knowledge of Warren's business methods made him a useful witness to federal authorities and to the Arizona House of Representatives. When he testified to the Arizona House Government Operations Committee in November 1977, armed federal marshals and officers from the state highway patrol ringed the hearing room. Legislators' questions focused on Del Rio Springs: who owned the real estate he'd been peddling? Woodall told lawmakers that of the two large tracts he had subdivided for sale, one still belonged to rancher Stan Tanner. Ownership of the other parcel was clouded. It had been acquired through a federal-state land exchange, the details of which were a secret.

Woodall knew a few details. "The heads of the Republican Party" struck the deal for the land exchange, he testified, but the GOP leaders and the amount of money involved was unknown to him and remained a closely held secret. He said it was legal for him to proceed with sales on the second subdivision because it had been approved by the unnamed GOP leaders. They even named the price they expected to be paid as their share in arranging it, Woodall said.

When a Republican legislator asked Woodall to name the party officials and the price, an assistant US attorney sitting next to Woodall instructed him not to answer the question. When Woodall's candid mood persisted, as in his description of how he kept the Del Rio fraud rolling by handing out bribes to county, state, and federal officials as well as lawyers and title companies, he was shushed again. The matter was dropped for good.

Early in the following year, when he testified in one the trials related to the death of Don Bolles, Woodall was permitted to give the names of a few people he had bribed, but none was a federal official or a politician. He named J. Fred Talley, who was dead; Moise Berger, who had left office and moved out of state; and a minor functionary in the state real-estate department in Tucson. When Woodall appeared in court again a year later to tell what he knew about a plot to kill Stan Tanner, the judge ejected the press and public "while Woodall testified about a public official, whose name was not revealed."

However, a partial record of Woodall's statement to federal prosecutors in October 1977 is preserved in John Frank's confidential memo to Barry Goldwater. A federal court had just convicted Woodall for attempted murder, and he agreed to act as a cooperating witness for federal authorities in the hope that he could reduce his twenty-year sentence to fifteen and be accepted into the FBI's witness-protection program.

Among the subjects raised in chambers was the Goldwater letter promoting Del Rio Springs. "At one point," said lawyer David G. Derickson, "he [Woodall] and Frank La Sota, who is one of his lieutenants in the organization, talked to Harry Rosenzweig about getting Barry Goldwater and Sam Steiger to sign letters recommending the value of the property in Del Rio Springs..."

Rosenzweig agreed to the promotion, Woodall said, and assigned the drafting of the letter to Lazar. Within hours after Rosenzweig arranged for the two politicians' signatures, Warren was on his way to the state of Washington, where he parlayed the letters into a business relationship with the former IOS salesmen, now reorganized as CMS. Warren proved himself their master by cheating them out of several million dollars. By the time CMS sued Warren, it was too late, for most of his properties had already gone into bankruptcy court. And thanks to another former Warren associate, Dennis Kelley, Warren, too, would soon be on his way to prison.

The Woodall promotion displayed an uncommon organizing talent. He combined the skills of specialists from the highest and lowest ranks of the Phoenix network. Run-of-the mill mobsters cooperated with legal and financial specialists in land fraud; international swindlers rubbed shoulders with legitimate businessmen, politicians, and statesmen. It was organized criminality of an advanced sort.

None of the most experienced political hands involved in the scheme, including Harry Rosenzweig, seem to have considered that getting Goldwater and Steiger involved in the Del Rio Springs fraud might carry unusual risks for the politicians as well as themselves. After all, the enterprise, in the normal Warren stratagem, not only failed; it was *designed* to fail. The expected date for its bankruptcy was penciled into his day planner on the day Del Rio Springs was incorporated. As with most Warren properties, and as Woodall would later tell the Arizona legislature, the purpose of incorporation was to strip lot buyers and investors of their assets, hide the money, then dump the rubble into the legal and financial landfill of the federal bankruptcy courts. By the time Del Rio filed for bankruptcy in 1973, it had extracted from its victims $10 million in less than two years. But the political gentry who made Del Rio possible walked away clean.

'A CALLOUS DISREGARD FOR JUSTICE'

To the very end, Moise Berger was obedient to the people he had complained about on the tape recording made by his enemy, police Detective Lonzo McCracken. On August 19, 1975, Berger filed a third motion to dismiss charges against Ned Warren. Berger told the court that James Cornwall, the only remaining witness to Warren's crimes, had lied on a significant point that called into question his credibility as a witness against his old boss. During the nearly year-long trial, Cornwall testified that he had cashed a check for $200 on a Friday early in March 1971 and on the same day delivered the money to Warren. But bank records showed that in fact the check was deposited on Tuesday, March 9.

Berger said he recoiled in shock when he discovered the three-day disparity in dates. "This constitutes conclusive evidence that Mr. Cornwall was not being truthful," Berger told the court. Judge Charles Hardy granted the motion to dismiss the charges against Warren because Cornwall could no longer be regarded as credible in any other matter. Hardy, a Democrat known for his devotion to civil liberties, was effusive in remarks to the press. "Mr. Berger had an ethical duty to dismiss," he said. "Considering the widespread publicity given to the charges against Warren, I feel that Mr. Berger's decision evidences a great deal of courage."

Although Berger had approved a plea agreement with Cornwall promising him probation rather than prison if he testified against Warren, Berger remained silent when Judge Rufus C. Coulter, who was handling the issue separately, announced that he was throwing the plea agreement out of court. As a basis for his decision, Coulter cited a recommendation from the state probation department. It recommended that the plea agreement not be honored and that Cornwall be given a maximum sentence. That would have amounted to three hundred thirty years. Coulter accepted the recommendation against the plea agreement but not the maximum sentence. On September 16, 1975, as Warren relaxed in the freedom of his mansion on Camelback Mountain, Coulter sentenced Cornwall to thirty-three years in the Arizona State Prison in Florence.

If the sentence created the impression that someone was trying to get Cornwall to shut up, it was reinforced a few months after his cell door closed behind him in Florence. Someone threw into the cell a Molotov cocktail that came close to killing him.

Coulter's sentence astonished everyone and enraged some. Among them was Don Bolles. He wrote a letter to Coulter.

Dear Rufus:

The following views are my own and not those of the paper. Since you went on the bench, I have had a healthy respect for your ability and judgment.

On the Cornwall sentencing, you really blew it.

I have extensive personal knowledge of all facts of this case. Since I first investigated Ned Warren in 1966–67, I have been amazed at how he was allowed to operate so openly in Arizona without one successful prosecution for bleeding millions of dollars from investors. He did, in fact, let front men take the fall for him, but it is much deeper than that.

Cornwall is no saint, and he did have knowledge of what was going on, but he was clearly the puppet at the end of a string, he did turn state's evidence, he did cooperate fully with law-enforcement authorities over fourteen months, during which time he was literally bankrupted.

Your stiff sentence tells me, and everyone else who has knowledge of the facts, that bargains with the county attorney and courts in Maricopa County are totally valueless. If anybody asks me in the future if he should rely on promises made to him, I'll advise him to plead innocent and get John Flynn [Warren's personal attorney].

Shame on you. This is the worst example of a travesty of justice since Judge Myers gave probation to the Mesa dentist who slashed two people to death.

Don Bolles
Sept. 17, 1975

Coulter was unmoved by Bolles's complaint. "I agree with you, 'Cornwall is no saint,'" he responded two days later, "and I truly believe that he deserved to be punished for the crimes that he committed...Perhaps it will have some deterrent effect on future land fraud in Arizona."

Bolles was not alone in his despair. Early in the next year, a little more than two months before Bolles was killed, McCracken sat down to write a consolation for the police officers and journalists who had tried and failed to bring Warren to justice. An untitled memo prepared for his own files had the tone of a man writing for history.

"The ruthlessness, the boldness, the complete disregard for the thousands of victims that lost their life savings, the family without a father, the complete disregard for the honest people's rights, including the cops and juries doing their duty, and the callous disregard for the American justice system. The alternative: disregard it and go on—become a part of it by your silence. At times the sins of omission are greater than the sins of commission. This would be brought home with devastating clarity if you were to sit in my office and watch an older man and his wife crying because their life savings from the sale of their home, their farm, was gone, all that [was] left represented in a stack of worthless documents."

On August 4, 1976, the one-year anniversary of the interview between McCracken and Berger, and two months after Bolles's murder, the *Republic* published the contents of a "confidential law-enforcement memorandum." It was the transcript of the interview with Berger that McCracken had recorded, typed, and annotated.

The following day, Berger announced that he intended to resign his post to teach at the Western State University College of Law in California. He refused to answer questions about the transcript.

Within days, Berger was gone. He never returned. And the lid stayed on.

Chapter 5

COLLAPSE OF THE LAND FRAUD

B y the middle of the 1970s, Ned Warren was sitting on an empire. He had made millions of dollars in an operation that ran on intimidation, payoffs, and as much protection as political influence could buy. It was also the moment when everything started to change. He could shrug off as a mere inconvenience his indictment for perjury from a county grand jury in September 1974. A federal grand-jury indictment of his son-in-law for extortion a few weeks later would have been more troubling. But when the grand jury called his accountant, Edward Lazar, to testify against him in February 1975, Warren was worried enough to hire professional hit men to kill Lazar. But the pros from Chicago Heights botched the job by turning it into a flamboyant message murder.

Unlike the earlier Warren business partners and witnesses whose killings were camouflaged as plane crashes, heart attacks, and suicides, the Chicago hit men, in the tradition of their city, insisted on leaving a calling card. After shooting Lazar in the head with a .22-caliber pistol equipped with a silencer, they scattered a few coins over his body as a warning to anyone else who might want to "drop a dime" on Warren.

Warren's aura of invulnerability did not last long after that. Some prosecutors and cops took message murders personally. In June 1975, federal prosecutors expanded the extortion charges already filed against Warren's son-in-law, Gale Nace, to include Warren himself. After a summer jury trial, Nace and

Warren were convicted in federal district court in Phoenix and sentenced to twelve years in federal prison. Warren remained free on bail for another two years as his appeals moseyed through the back canyons of the legal system. But he remained under surveillance, which made it difficult for him to manage his business. During this period, day-to-day control of his criminal gang fell to the wildly unqualified John Harvey Adamson.

It had been two years since Warren rescued Adamson from his role as a skulking shakedown artist and part-time repo man. In the meantime, thanks to his friendship with Carl Verive, Adamson had become well connected; Carl and his brother, Louis, even played a supporting role in the Bolles murder. "It was through Carl and Lou Verive that Mr. Adamson met Jimmy Robison," the triggerman in the Bolles car bombing, police noted.

Adamson cinched his reputation when he lined up the two contract killers in the Lazar hit. It was arranged at Applegate's Old English Pub in Phoenix, a mob hangout. Adamson and Warren met there and took a table together. Carl Verive arrived, walked to the far end of the bar, out of earshot, and ordered a drink. Warren and Adamson went over the details of the package-murder deal and the price. Adamson asked Warren why he had come to him to arrange the hits. "I thought you might know somebody," Warren said. Adamson replied, "No, I don't know anybody."

Warren ignored the remark and motioned to Verive at the bar. After getting Verive's attention, he pointed a finger at Adamson. Then Warren got up and walked toward the bathroom at the back of the bar. As he walked past Verive, he muttered something inaudible to Adamson. A moment later, Verive followed Warren into the bathroom.

The deal took fifteen minutes. Lazar would soon be dead. One of the assassins later told police that he and his partner made the accountant kneel before they shot him.

Adamson later said that Warren originally had asked him to arrange for three contract killings. "He wanted to know how much I would charge for three murders, or could I arrange for them to be done," Adamson told police. Real Estate Commissioner J. Fred Talley was one, Lazar was another, but he could not recall the name of the third. But he knew it was not Bolles, he said.

For fourteen months after Lazar's murder, Adamson, now boss of the street crew, expanded his professional brief. Over those months, he provided three different clients with criminal services that required the manufacture of dynamite bombs. All three bombs were fiascos. Two failed to explode, and one left its victim alive and conscious long enough to name Adamson as his killer.

A question that hung over Adamson's cumulative carnage like so much smoke was why experienced gangsters like Warren and Verive would risk their credibility on a man whose crimes nearly always blew up in his face.

THE MAN IN THE WHITE FISHNET SHIRT

The man who made possible the federal investigation that brought down Ned Warren was neither a cop nor a journalist. He was a businessman who favored turquoise jewelry and white fishnet shirts. He owned Little Hughie's, a downtown nightspot popular with blacks and Latinos.

As an owner and manager of successful gay bars, Dennis Kelley was comfortable in the Phoenix demimonde. But he was also a member of the privileged world of Phoenicians who lived north of Camelback Road, where Barry Goldwater lived. His parents moved in Goldwater's social circles. When he was still a boy, they took Dennis to the senator's home in Paradise Valley where he handled memorabilia on the great man's desk and poked at the film projectors recessed in the walls. Kelley was a member of what in Phoenix was society, and he had a sense of entitlement not so different from the senator's. Underworld characters like Adamson, who liked to bait Kelley by calling him *honey* or *sweetheart* to his face, badly underestimated him.

Kelley first met Warren at a party in the spring of 1973 in the home of friends who lived on the grounds of the Phoenix Country Club. It was a mix of advertising people, bankers, lawyers, and politicians. Warren accompanied his wife, Barbara, known for her poise. Their fiercely loyal daughter, Nancy Nace, attended, along with her husband, Gale, who would later be cuffed to his father-in-law in a Seattle courtroom. Nace was then in his forties, tall and skinny, groomed, tanned, and pugnacious, with a distinctive Miami accent.

In early June, Warren invited Kelley to his office. He had a proposition. Earlier in the year, through Investor's Realty, one of his many companies, he'd bought an aging cocktail lounge and realty company and gave them to his son, Junior, to run under his own name. But Junior was a terrible manager, Warren confided, and the place was losing money. So Warren proposed that Kelley sign a management contract and turn Junior's into another of his successful gay bars. He and Warren would split the profits fifty-fifty and, if it did well, they would either sell it at a profit or expand by finding another bar to buy. Kelley agreed. He was glad to be in business with Warren, Kelley later admitted. He was wary of Warren's reputation as a tough guy but tempted by his skill at making money.

Junior's turned out to be a hit with the gay crowd, and money poured in all through the summer of 1973. Then Warren suggested a closer business arrangement. Kelley would be promoted from manager of Junior's to full partner. An equal division of profits from income or a sale would still be part of the deal. In return, Kelley would sign over to Warren 50 percent of Little Hughie's, with Warren reassigning his interest to one of his corporations. Kelley would be named president of Investor's Realty, replacing Junior.

And that's how Kelley stuck his neck through the noose—with his eyes open.

In a matter of days, the partners set up several two-signature checking accounts and merged the accounting records for Junior's and Little Hughie's. Meanwhile, Kelley began negotiating for the purchase of a bar called Roman Gates that was to be modeled on the success of Junior's. It would be redecorated to the taste of a lesbian clientele and renamed Happy Gardens. Warren insisted that a new management corporation be formed to handle all three bars and advanced the new corporation enough money to buy the lease for Happy Gardens and fund its remodeling and start-up operations.

Warren tied the last knot in the agreement by insisting that Kelley record with the state certain license restrictions that would prevent him from selling anything without Warren's approval or without satisfying any attached mortgage. From that moment on, Warren controlled the outcome of any sale and—a provision noted when it was too late—any proceeds from fire insurance.

Much more paperwork followed, all to the same end. Warren was tightening his legal control over all the properties while assigning responsibility to a figurehead (Kelley) who was now head of a corporation over which he had no control. It was the same method Warren used routinely to denude partners in his land frauds.

The tempo of events picked up as the summer waned. After Kelley filed the license restrictions, Warren started coming up with new demands. As soon as a buyer was found for Junior's, the bar's monthly receipts mysteriously collapsed. Warren said they needed to buy time. He told Kelley to close any existing two-signature accounts and open new ones at different banks to gain a two-week float on outgoing checks. Warren created new corporations and closed others. Corporate officers jumped across companies and from one title to another in a pattern only Warren seemed to understand. He typed up his instructions in rapid fire and in detail on a typewriter next to his desk. When the paperwork required a lawyer, he would bark at Kelley, "Get this to Mickey Clifton."

On September 17, 1973, the point of it all became clear. The moment was memorialized later on John Adamson's "Activity List," a handful of index cards on which he had recorded in chronological order his own crimes and those of others in which law enforcement had expressed an interest. This was Adamson's first, scrawled entry: *09/17/73 ARSON LITTLE HUEY'S BAR.*

The next morning, September 18, as Kelley crane-legged through the ashes of his first business, he saw that the entire stock of liquor in the back room had been stolen. The vending machines were broken into, their cash boxes removed, emptied, and discarded.

ADAMSON RISES TO THE TOP

Ned Warren's gang modeled itself in some recognizable way on the Italian mob but possessed none of its traditions and very little of its discipline. Most of its members or hangers-on were heavy drinkers or drug enthusiasts or both and, apart from Carl Verive, incapable of performing steady work. They preferred the uncertain but less-demanding employments of the drug economy and prostitution. The Warren empire was sustained in part by hookers, dealers, addicts, and barflies on Van Buren Street who wrote their names on meaningless documents for a fee of fifty dollars apiece. The documents were real-estate contracts committing the signatories to decades or years of monthly payments. Warren presented the signed contracts to local bankers as collateral for cash loans. He put a specialist, James Tancill, in charge of the street crew that collected the signatures, and Adamson and other enforcers were expected to help out during busy periods. Before they went to the bankers, the contracts went through Mickey Clifton, who was the closest thing Warren had to an in-house attorney. It was to Clifton that Adamson turned for legal representation in the hours after his arrest for killing Bolles.

In the Phoenix gang, most of the men were expected to be handy at a variety of tasks, such as driving for the bosses and their girlfriends, bouncing drunks out of Warren's bars, beating witnesses, collecting real or claimed debts, and torching buildings in which Warren had an insured interest. On their own time, they were free to engage in thievery and fencing of a general sort, often the contents of semitrailer trucks hijacked on the interstate highway. Carl Verive worked off and on at local plumbing outlets.

Not all of the members of the Warren crew were generalists. Junior Warren and Fred Green, for example, concentrated on the arsenal, which included the automatic weapons Junior bought and sold. Green was a professional gunrunner who organized shipments of guns to Mexico. Junior handled the financial transactions, sometimes in cash, sometimes in drugs.

If Adamson was the loudest and most aggressive member of Warren's crew, his behavior was amplified by his daily consumption of a quart of vodka and whatever cocaine he managed to find. It was because of his recklessness that Warren decided to hire him in the first place. Adamson started out as little more than a bum drinking behind the bushes that lined commercial parking lots on Camelback Road. To survive, he ran a scam that netted enough money for him to get by. He jumped from behind the bushes to demand that motorists give him as much as forty dollars after they returned to their cars and found that someone had chained a thirty-pound concrete block to one of their tire rims. After he performed this trick on Ned Warren one night when the crime boss returned to his Cadillac from Le Continental restaurant, Warren was so amused that he hired Adamson on the spot as a bouncer and debt collector.

Once he was inside the gang, Adamson began to spend a lot of time with Carl Verive. He and Adamson had their own lives and their own scams, such as supplying a small store in downtown Mesa with goods stolen from trucks, mostly clothes. In March 1973, according to his own list of crimes, Adamson stole a group of paintings from the nationally known Sombrero Playhouse in Phoenix. From time to time, he and Verive performed odd jobs together. One of Verive's occasional tasks was to drive customers' cars to and from the Mesa auto-sales lots of Jack Ross, a Goldwater family in-law. He and Adamson installed fencing around a swimming pool for Howard Woodall, one of two Warren partners in the land-fraud operation who had his own independent contacts in national organized crime. (Tony Serra was the other.)

When Adamson and Verive were not working for Warren as bouncers or fixers, they cruised the city. They hit the dog and horse tracks, scouted for action in their network of familiar bars and restaurants, anywhere they could pick up gossip. When the opportunity arose, they turned to more customary mob work, like burglary.

On these street cruises, Adamson once told the Phoenix cops, he sometimes drove around from morning until night. One evening, the police found him alone in a bar on Central Avenue and bought him drinks as they pumped him for information about Verive. They found Adamson to be a good source of information about the Italian gang members in town. It would not be too much to call Adamson a police informer, especially when he was drunk.

Verive's nickname, "Big Carl," referred not to his status in the mob but to his size. An Illinois state's attorney's report in 1972 described Verive as a "syndicate muscleman." When police took his mug shot in 1972, he was forty-one years old, stood an inch under six feet, and weighed 235 pounds. He was built like a wrestler across the chest and shoulders. His eyes were set wide apart and fixed in a pinhole stare. A broad nose might have been broken and reset in several places. A brief biography included a charge of assault with a deadly weapon in 1959 in Wheaton, Illinois; mail fraud in Milwaukee six years later; a citation for being drunk and disorderly in Phoenix in May of 1970; and a theft in Chicago that September.

Carl left Chicago to elude an indictment for "a fraudulent scheme against the Chicago Title & Trust Co. involving the cashing of an insufficient $2.5 million check." Around the same time, he got a call from his brother, Louis asking for help. Louis needed him as an enforcer in the Phoenix end of a nationwide securities scam known as the Church of Christ Manors, which had victims all over the country, including Phoenix. After that matter was settled, Louis moved on to California, but Carl found that he liked Arizona and spent as much time there as he could.

The Chicago Heights crew came to run a good share of street crime in Phoenix in the 1970s, some of it for Warren. In November 1973, Adamson beat up a witness who had testified in a state case against Howard Woodall, Warren's leading con in the Del Rio Springs land fraud. The next month, Woodall hired Verive to perform the same service in another case. Verive presented himself at the front door of Lee Galvin, who had testified in civil court that Woodall perjured himself in a deposition. Verive's task was to "dissuade [Galvin] from becoming a witness against Woodall," as the Arizona Appeals Court later summarized the incident. To prepare for the confrontation, Verive spent a few hours in a bar. Then he and another man, a "Mr. Baugh" (perhaps Jack Barge, one of Warren's tough guys) showed up at Galvin's home and knocked on the door. "Do you know Howard Woodall? Well, he sent us," Verive told Galvin. Verive and his companion then beat Galvin senseless in front of his family. They stopped only after Galvin's wife started screaming. Verive's payment for the beating was $900 in cash and a used motorcycle.

Few knew just how connected Verive was. An Illinois police report listed Jackie Cerone, a former top boss of the Chicago Outfit, as one of his associates. That meant something to Arizona law enforcement, for it was Cerone who had personally ordered the execution of stool pigeon Louis Bombacino in Tempe.

THE CHICAGO HEIGHTS CREW IN PHOENIX

The Chicago Heights street crew was one of several armed street militias that formed the backbone of that city's crime industry. At its peak, it could claim seven large and active crews, with only two or three remaining by 2011. Historically, Chicago Heights was the least known of the mob crews, perhaps because of its remoteness from the geographic heart of the mob operation. Originally, it was called the 26th Street Crew after its origins in the angle of the city that opened to the southwest between the Stevenson and Dan Ryan expressways. As it expanded southward, it became known to law enforcement in the 1960s as the South Side Crew. Eventually, it merged with earlier operations in the area and extended its influence as far east as the Indiana border and finally to cities in the far West. The crew is now known as the Chicago Heights crew, after the usage of mob historian Matthew J. Luzi. By the early 1960s, the Chicago Heights gangsters owned real estate and businesses in Las Vegas, southern California, and Arizona.

The emergence of the group in Chicago Heights was announced in 1923 by a "terrific explosion" that was apparently an accident. It blew out the front of a downtown building that housed a wholesale confectionary business. The confectioners were running one of the largest bootleg-alcohol operations in the Midwest, with Chicago Heights a kind of regional reservoir for illegal hooch in northern Illinois. They developed a network of distilleries that included neighbors' bathtubs, three-story stills in hollowed-out homes, and warehouses that operated around the clock. Together these operations produced millions of gallons of 160- to 190-proof alcohol every year. The single-family homes contained whiskey stills so large, they occupied a house from top to bottom, from the joists in the attic to the concrete pad in the basement, with holes cut through the floorboards in the first and second stories. In winter, after heavy snowfalls, police could see which houses contained stills by flying small planes over the neighborhood to see which houses had bare, dry roofs.

Chicago Heights mobsters were known for their violence against newspaper reporters and editors. In 1938, they used a baseball bat to deliver a beating to William McCabe, editor of the *Weekly Spectator* in nearby Joliet. In 1957, McCabe's protégée, forty-one-year-old Molly Zelko, disappeared after putting the *Spectator* to bed late one night. Her shoes were found next to her abandoned car. The case was the subject of such intense national interest that US Attorney General Robert F. Kennedy, who was investigating the coin-operated amusement industry in Chicago, personally grabbed a shovel to help open what a mobster had falsely claimed was her grave.

THE TOCCO BROTHERS RUN THE STREETS

In 1971, Don Bolles wrote his first major investigative series on organized crime since his eight-part epic on Ned Warren. The new series focused on the state's other powerful organized-crime figures. In the Cold War style of the day, *Republic* editors labeled the series "The Menace Within." Bolles gathered notes for it during a cross-country research trip that included Detroit and Chicago, where he spent days in newspaper morgues taking notes on any mob figures he could find who had ties to Arizona. The most important story of the series, published on the seventh day, was devoted to the Chicago Heights mob, whose presence in Phoenix was known to the local police but not to the public until Bolles's series ran in the newspaper.

Bolles discovered that the leader of the Chicago Heights crew until the late 1960s was Frank LaPorte (real name: Francisco Liparota). Until he retired to Arizona, where he died in 1973, LaPorte was the boss in Chicago Heights, Joliet, and Calumet City. By the time the Bolles series reached print, LaPorte was ill and his crew was in the hands of his successor, the notorious Albert "Caesar" Tocco.

It was a matter of record in Chicago that Al Tocco personally ordered the murders of at least four people. His men dispatched many more, and they performed their duties so casually that it was said the crew gave seasoned FBI agents sleepless nights. By 1981, a former mobster observed in his memoirs, "Tocco's crew had taken killing to a whole new level, so that watching a guy die didn't mean anything anymore. The Chicago Outfit was out of control." This was the early seventies scene from which the new Phoenix underworld emerged. Its leader was Tocco's younger brother, Joe, owner of a pizza shop in Scottsdale that bore his name, "Papa Joe's." He was the arbiter of internal disputes involving the Chicago Heights mob in Phoenix.

After Bolles's first public references to Chicago Heights in "The Menace Within," the crew was rarely mentioned. It was not until the mid-1980s that the gang's Phoenix ties were brought up. In testimony before the Senate Judiciary Committee, Joe Tocco was identified as "Arizona's most active leader of organized crime." But it was only when a hit man by the name of Robert Douglas Hardin confessed to his role in the murder of Ed Lazar that the Chicago Heights mobsters in Phoenix started to come into focus. Hardin, a young, illiterate killer with a chubby face and frizzy hair, surrendered to police after the body of his partner in the Lazar hit, Nick D'Andrea, was found dead in the trunk of a car in Chicago. After extracting what they needed from a willing and frightened Hardin, the FBI sent him to Phoenix to be grilled by state investigators. They learned that the man who had acted as the broker for Ned Warren in the Lazar hit was Carl Verive in the incident at the Old English Pub.

THE BRAWL AT HAPPY GARDENS

The new joint venture between Ned Warren and Dennis Kelley was a lesbian bar with the seductive name of Happy Gardens. It was an immediate hit. One night soon after the opening, Warren and his wife walked in with another couple to witness Kelley's success. The husband was the owner of a nightclub in the neighborhood who said his wife was tantalized by the idea of a same-sex bar for women. Warren thought it amusing to take a table close to the dancing customers, where from time to time he offered salacious remarks. As the evening wore on and the two husbands grew drunk, Warren turned belligerent. He yelled at passing dancers to come to his table to meet the club owner's wife, making comments about her husband's inability to satisfy her. When the wife left the bar with one of the dancers, the two men began to shout at each other, trading threats and insults.

At some point during the argument, Warren threatened to grab a weapon from behind the bar. Meanwhile, the club owner left the table and stumbled through the back door. Two men climbed out of a car and confronted him, then manhandled him and shoved him back into the bar. When they pulled their victim into the light, Kelley saw that the two men holding the club owner erect were Junior Warren and Fred Green. He heard Junior speak to the man. "What's it going to be?" Junior asked. "Your guts spilled over the floor, or home to Mama where you can hide under the covers with a big fat tit in your mouth?" The man walked wordlessly back inside and melted on a barstool. Warren left the club without another word.

Within moments, Happy Gardens' back door opened and five men strode in: John Adamson, Carl Verive, Hank Landry, Jack Barge, and Rocky Gambino, the roughest guys in Warren's gang. The five men joined Junior Warren and Fred Green and stood in a line off to one side, watching the women moving in pools of light. After a few minutes, Adamson walked up to the table closest to him and said to the people seated there, "OK, folks, this table is ours. It's reserved for me and my friends here." The chairs opened up as their occupants scattered.

Dennis Kelley couldn't bear it. He went up to the table Adamson commandeered. "Look, John," he said. "You can't come in here and muscle the crowd like that."

"So, who's gonna stop me?" Adamson said. "Not you, honey."

Kelley recalled the dialogue in detail because he remembered it as a turning point in his life.

"Look, Warren wouldn't like it if you cost him business…"

"Warren don't like you so much anymore, pretty boy," Adamson said. "Me'n Warren, we're thicker'n sin." Barge and Gambino laughed.

"Hey, honey, I want to tell you something," Adamson continued, motioning Kelley to come closer, as though sharing a confidence. "You know who fired your club? You know who fired Little Hughie's? Well, if there's any arson done around this town—you know, a real professional job—well, honey, you're lookin' at the man who done it."

Barge and Gambino, both of whom had worked at Little Hughie's, taunted Kelley with hints that they knew about the theft of the liquor and coins from the vending machines, something that had not been reported in the press.

Things quieted down. At closing time, Kelley started totting up the night's receipts. Adamson brought a man over to meet him. He was an insurance adjuster looking for a kickback on his approval of the settlement on the fire at Hughie's. Kelley reached into the cash register and pulled out a handful of twenties and counted them out. It was, he realized, the beginning of a shakedown that would never end.

Before he left, Adamson leaned over the bar and leered at Kelley. "Me and the cops are good friends. Now, you can think anything you want to, but it won't do you no good…I'm movin' up, and there ain't no one who can stop me. I've got friends, all the right people, and they know what I can do."

On September 27, ten days after the fire at Little Hughie's, Warren told Kelley he had found buyers for Happy Gardens. Make the arrangements, Warren ordered.

By this time, Kelley's hopes began to erode that he might be one of the few Warren partners who managed to stay healthy and get rich. His life was narrowing to a hard choice: run and lose everything, or stay and get killed.

The sale of Kelley's half of Happy Gardens was his last hope to extract some gain from his dilemma. It could stake him to a new start somewhere outside Phoenix. He was reminded almost daily of the precariousness of his situation in Adamson's sneers, Warren's demands, and escalating threats from Gale Nace, who ordered him to start writing checks to repay the loans and advances Warren gave him to remodel Happy Gardens.

One day in early October, Nace confronted Kelley. This time, the threats were specific and itemized.

"Kelley, if you don't pay up, and soon, we're going to have you all busted up…I've got a friend who'll break one of your arms for fifty dollars. Nice and neat. He'll break two of your arms and a leg for a hundred and fifty dollars. He'll break both your arms and your legs for two hundred dollars…You know what's so funny about that, Dennis? This is what's funny. To get your arms and legs fixed up again, in the hospital, it's going to cost you exactly what you owe us. I figured it up."

On October 15, Warren called Kelley into his office and said he would advance him the cash if he would give up his share of the profits from the Happy Gardens sale. Kelley signed and took the money. Then he drove to a gun shop and bought a .38-caliber snub-nosed revolver.

THE REVOLT AGAINST WARREN

By November 10, 1973, anonymous death threats had begun to supplement Nace's demands for money. Kelley's debt to Warren had reached $100,000, Nace said.

Kelley looked up a lawyer he had known in high school, Tony DiPrima, and laid out his situation. The lawyer explained what kinds of civil actions were available. But that wouldn't help much. Call the police, he said. Better yet, I will call him for you.

DiPrima picked up the phone and dialed the police department. He asked for Lonzo McCracken. When McCracken came on the line, the lawyer handed the phone to Kelley. Haltingly, Kelley told his story again. The detective wanted to talk, wanted to know where Kelley was.

"I'm downtown, five or six blocks from you."

"Can you see me right now?"

"Yes."

"Come on over, and we'll talk."

Kelley agreed. He left the lawyer's office and stepped into his Continental. He squealed out of the lot and turned north, in the opposite direction from McCracken's office, and drove blindly, aimlessly, to get as far away from the police station as he could. As Friday afternoon settled into evening, he found himself driving into South Mountain Park, working his way up the long mountain road to the ridge high above Phoenix and the desert valley.

He pulled into an overlook and watched in the mountain silence until the city lights flickered on in the distance.

On Monday, Kelley called McCracken and apologized for missing the appointment. McCracken agreed to meet him the next morning at a restaurant at McDowell Road and Black Canyon Highway, far removed from downtown.

"I'm one of Ned Warren's front men," Kelley said to the detective as he stuck out his hand. They talked for three hours, with McCracken writing down everything in a small notebook.

McCracken persuaded Kelley to meet with Warren and Nace while wearing a wire in the hope that one of them would repeat the death threats. It could be used as evidence in a federal civil-rights case involving extortionate-credit transactions.

On Wednesday morning, Kelley walked into Warren's office on North Central Avenue. Nace was there, too. Kelley wore a small microphone and a transmitter. McCracken and Joe Boofer, a member of the intelligence squad, were parked discreetly across the street with a police radio receiver plugged into a tape recorder.

Throughout the conversation, Warren played the role of the disappointed mentor, lamenting his poor judgment in trying to help a businessman as lousy as Kelley. Nace demanded a third mortgage on Kelley's home and any cash he might have stashed away, then launched into a series of threats. Kelley tried to get some evidence on tape.

"Why does Gale have to threaten to have me killed?" he asked, speaking to Warren. "The day he threatened to have my arms and legs broken—I came to you about that." Then he added, "That detective—Lonzo McCracken—he called me last night at the house, and he wants to know what I know" about Junior's, about Investor's Realty, about land fraud.

"Don't talk to him," Warren said.

"He gave me his office number and said anything I could pick up to call him and let him know."

"Fuck him. Tell him you don't know anything about it."

The next morning Kelley met McCracken and Boofer for coffee. They asked him to testify against Warren in court. Kelley pointed out that no one had ever testified against Warren and lived.

It was not precisely true that no one had lived after fingering Warren. James Cornwall, McCracken's star witness against Great Southwest, was still alive. On the other hand, he had just been sentenced to prison on a manufactured charge that violated his immunity agreement with the county attorney. There was no point in using it as a contrary example.

Kelley agreed to be a witness against Warren if they could get the land-fraud boss into a courtroom.

On Friday, six days after Kelley walked into lawyer DiPrima's office, McCracken called Clint Brown at the FBI. He had a story for him, McCracken told the FBI agent. McCracken gave Brown everything he had—all of the paperwork and the original tape recordings from Kelley. A transcript of the meeting between McCracken and Brown ran to nineteen pages, single spaced.

Brown followed up. He opened a jacket for an investigation of extortion against Warren and Nace. Over the next three months, Brown and other

FBI agents added investigative updates from McCracken and from searches of records and interviews with people close to Warren's operation. On January 22, Warren called the FBI to complain about their inquiries. He left a phone number. When an agent returned the call, there was no answer.

On February 22, a group of FBI men sat down with Kelley to go over the details of the case.

On March 20, 1974, the Warren investigation was assigned case number #179–69. Its files were sent to J. Edgar Hoover and to the US Attorney's Office in Phoenix. More copies went to the Organized Crime and Racketeering Section of the Criminal Division of the Department of Justice, then under the leadership of Henry E. Peterson, who at that moment was consumed by the Watergate scandal. More promising, a copy was forwarded to Richard P. Crane Jr., the attorney in charge of the Los Angeles Strike Force on Organized Crime, which also reported to the DOJ.

In the report, the FBI referred to Warren as a leader of an organized-crime ring. It was a measure of the FBI's realism that it wanted the LA strike force to take the lead in the federal prosecution. The strike force had jurisdiction over organized-crime investigations in most of the southwestern United States, including Nevada and Arizona, and its prosecutors were often careful not to step on the toes of local US attorneys, who could be loath to prosecute members of the local power structure—the same people who got them their jobs.

The FBI, McCracken, and Kelley did not have to wait long for an answer from the strike force, but when it came, it was disappointing. The evidence submitted was too thin to support a federal charge, their attorney wrote. On the other hand, it seemed promising. Try again, he said.

Meanwhile, Kelley decided to spend a few months out of harm's way in Denver. He stayed in touch with McCracken, who kept working the case and talking with the FBI.

On June 26, 1973, McCracken sent the local FBI bureau fourteen sets of Phoenix police reports. They were transcripts of interviews with state liquor-control officials McCracken believed were on the take from Warren. Also in the stack were documents dealing with the sale of Junior's and three tape recordings from Kelley's meeting with Warren and Nace on November 14, when Kelley wore a wire. The FBI distributed copies of everything but the tape cassettes, which it forwarded to the bureau's audio lab for analysis. The lab reported that there was too much environmental noise to make a clean transcript.

Kelley returned to Arizona at the beginning of August. Waiting for him was an ominous note from a friend in Tucson. Warren was spending a lot of time in Chicago. No one knew why.

By early September, it was clear to Kelley that the pace of the FBI investigation was picking up. He found himself talking to local, state, and federal cops. Among them were McCracken and Clint Brown, as he expected. He also got calls from FBI agents Cecil Eislinger and John Hunt. Investigators on Arizona Attorney General Bruce Babbitt's staff called as well. Finally, Kelley testified before a federal grand jury and afterward responded to requests for interviews from Don Bolles and Al Sitter at *The Arizona Republic.*

THE GRENADE ON THE BARSTOOL

On September 14, 1973, a Saturday, Kelley got a call from John Adamson. Meet me at Durant's restaurant at five thirty, he said.

Kelley might have been feeling a little cocky from his time away from Phoenix and less fretful now that he was surrounded by allies. What could Adamson do to him with half the cops in Arizona developing a case on his boss? He called McCracken, who wasn't in. He left a message: Meet me at Durant's at 5:45 p.m. It's important.

Kelley gave his car keys to a valet in the parking lot in back of Durant's. Don't let anyone touch my car, he said. Kelley walked in through the back door, past the porterhouse steaks whistling on the grill, and into the dining room.

He was already seated in one of the burgundy banquettes when Adamson walked in with Carl Verive. Hank Landry was right behind him. All three made a beeline for the bar and ordered drinks from Tommy, the manager and, at the moment, the bartender as well.

"What have you got for me?" Kelley spoke first as Adamson slid into his booth.

Adamson peered at him through his prescription sunglasses. It was obvious he'd already been drinking. "I don't have anything for you," he said at length, "but you better have something for me."

Kelley peered back. "Like what?"

"Let's start with five thousand dollars," Adamson said. "Let's say you owe me that for having stripes painted on the parking lot at your club once."

Kelley retorted that he had paid for the striping and had a canceled check to prove it. "Sue me," he added.

So the meeting was another shakedown. Kelley was astonished that Adamson could be so reckless. He could be included in the extortion charges. Kelley looked around for McCracken.

Adamson demanded that Kelley, "for starters," hand over the turquoise jewelry he was wearing.

Landry walked up to the booth, grabbed Kelley's wrist, and started to force Kelley to slide over so he could sit down next to him. Verive was a just few steps behind Landry.

Without thinking, Kelley looked up at Verive and gave him a wide, affectionate smile. Reflexively, a surprised Verive smiled back, then recovered. Landry was startled by the almost conspiratorial exchange of smiles and for an instant relaxed his grip. Kelley yanked his arm free and screamed, "Tommy!" as loudly as could, and stood up. As the three men fell over one another trying to grab him, Kelley slipped out of their fingers and ran to the kitchen, grabbed his keys from the valet, dashed to his car, and pointed the Continental toward home.

It had been a close call, and Kelley knew it. When he got home, he was shaking. He went into the bedroom and recovered his .38 snub-nose from the bed stand, poured himself a double shot of whiskey, neat, and lit a cigarette. He called Clint Brown at the FBI. In an unsteady voice, he told Brown what had happened at Durant's and that he was going to drive to the Nu-Towne Saloon on Van Buren Street to find his roommate and warn him not to return to their apartment for a while. He was taking his revolver in case Adamson had gone there to look for him.

Brown tried to talk him out of taking the gun, but when Kelley refused, Brown said he would call McCracken and tell him where Kelley was headed.

The Nu-Towne Saloon is a one-story, flat-roofed, rectangular concrete-block building sometimes painted white. It sits across from the city's main post office and remains famous as the city's oldest gay bar (*Est. 1971*). Kelley had not told the cops that he had an ownership interest in the Nu-Towne.

Kelley pulled around to the back of the bar, fished for his keys, and let himself in. He waited a moment to let his eyes adjust to the dim light. He saw the front door open. Adamson stood in silhouette in the doorway.

Before long, Adamson spotted Kelley in the back and strode directly toward him, one arm swinging free and the other carrying a cloth bag with something heavy in it.

Kelley put his hand on the grip of the .38 in the side pocket of his jacket. Adamson walked up to him, lowered the bag carefully onto a nearby barstool, keeping his grip on the bag.

"Hello again, sport," Adamson said.

Kelley didn't speak. He eyed the bag. He and Adamson were too far from the front of the bar for anyone to hear what they were saying.

Adamson stood next to the barstool, swaying slightly. "I got a little grenade in this sack," he said. "A little bomb. All I got to do is pull a little pin and toss it"—he jerked his free thumb over his shoulder toward the front of the bar— "and the whole place goes up, and all these nice people get bad hurt…Now, why don't you just give me all that ducky jewelry you got on there?"

There was no telling what Adamson had in the sack. Could have been a rock, could have been a baseball. But it could have been a hand grenade.

Kelley motioned to Bob Rabe, the bartender, and asked him how much he had in the till. A few hundred, Rabe said. Let me borrow it, Kelley said. Rabe dug the money out of the cash register and handed the bills to Kelley, who took them with his left hand and held them out to Adamson, keeping his right hand out of sight in his jacket. Adamson kept one hand on the bag and with the other stuffed the bills into a pocket.

Each man regarded the other with what seemed like ancient familiarity.

"Someday you're going to go too far," Kelley said.

"Someday you're going to wish you had the guts to nail me," Adamson said.

At length, Adamson said, "Let me tell you something...This is a tight town. Your cop friends can't help you. We can snatch you off the street any time we want to, and nobody'll know the difference...You get to hustling and pay up. Or you get bombed out."

Adamson held up the bag. "Next on my list—guaranteed," he said. "You pay up and lay off."

"A Sorry Goddamn Mess, this Town"

The next morning, Kelley met McCracken for coffee at the Wagon Wheel, a combination restaurant and bowling alley on the far-east side.

McCracken apologized for missing Kelley's call asking for backup at Durant's and Clint Brown's call warning him about Kelley's trip to the Nu-Towne.

"I'm just sorry I wasn't around when the FBI called," McCracken said. "Adamson would have been in jail now, or dead—his choice. I told Bolles just an hour ago, it seems like our luck is running out. We've got those bastards all set for prosecution, but nobody'll prosecute yet. Everybody's scared shitless, or owing them favors. A sorry goddamn mess, this town."

McCracken looked drawn and weary.

"Can't you come down on him for extortion? I can testify. I've got nothing to lose."

"It won't do no good, Kelley. We've tried time and again. We can't make a case against Adamson. The city and county just won't touch him. He's got too many legal friends, too much protection from all the people he does dirty work for."

'Restructure your Memory'

On a Wednesday soon after his talk with McCracken, Kelley's phone rang. It was Harry Rosenzweig. Come down to my office right now, Rosenzweig said. I want to talk to you. It was September 25, 1974.

Kelley paced up and down his apartment. What in God's name could Rosenzweig want with him? He had met the man when he worked as a volunteer on Barry Goldwater's second US senate campaign. He'd hauled campaign literature in the trunk of his car, and like thousands of other Phoenicians, he had attended the occasional Republican fundraiser. He was too afraid of Rosenzweig to go and much too curious about what the boss would say not to go.

Kelley jumped in his car and headed downtown to Rosenzweig Jewelers to take his turn among the glass cases filled with diamonds and watches that filled the sales floor. On one side, a flight of open stairs led up to an office mezzanine. Supplicants had to walk through the merchandise until they were summoned because there was no place to sit.

Rosenzweig appeared at the top of the stairs and beckoned Kelley to ascend to his office. Its walls were covered in photos of Rosenzweig in the company of Goldwater and other famous men. A "Man of the Year" award from a Phoenix advertising association hung on one wall.

Rosenzweig had a distinguished head of silver hair, wore tailored suits and a pinkie ring. He chose his words with a casual precision. "I don't believe I've seen you around for a while, Dennis," he said, nodding to an empty chair in front of his desk. Both sat.

"I think it was the, uh, last big fundraiser over at the hotel."

Rosenzweig nodded and sat silently for a moment.

"I think perhaps I should get right to the point. I see no need to discuss peripheral matters. I would like you to think seriously on what I am about to tell you, Dennis." He looked at Kelley.

"Yes, sir?"

"I would think that you would have gotten the message by now." Rosenzweig's gaze narrowed.

"I don't understand."

Rosenzweig enunciated carefully.

"I want you to restructure your memory as regards your business dealings with Mr. Ned Warren Senior, and his many friends, of whom I am one."

Kelley remained silent.

"Need I repeat myself, Mr. Kelley?"

Kelley shook his head.

"All right. Then we understand each other. The gentleman I speak of and his many business associates will be so informed. And I will hold you accountable."

THE FBI SETS A TRAP

US Attorney for the District of Arizona William Smitherman had, according to his many admirers, had an almost Calvinistic sense of duty, and few were surprised when he took Kelley's knowledge of Warren's crimes to the federal grand jury. Smitherman laid the groundwork in September 1974, when he ordered federal investigators to drive up and down East Camelback Road and hand out subpoenas to bank managers ordering them to produce account records of the known eighty-seven corporations held by Ned Warren. By November 10, federal agents had identified in a single bank thirty-two accounts holding a combined $552,791 in cash.

With the federal grand jury preparing to take testimony in the Warren case in early October, the FBI was working overtime. Clint Brown and another agent interviewed Adamson on the last Sunday in September, asking him about the confrontation with Kelley at Durant's and the Nu-Towne Saloon on September 14. They met at La Strada, near Warren's office on North Central Avenue. McCracken showed up for part of the interview.

The agents went over Adamson's story with him again and again. Nearly all of his answers could be summarized under two main points: "It was mostly a misunderstanding," and "I can't remember much of it because I was drunk."

Asked whether he'd made threats to Kelley, Adamson "strongly denied" it, agents wrote, "stating that he wished to take a lie-detector test and for [Kelley] also to do so to establish his innocence."

Asking for a polygraph was a mistake. Before he could say another word, Adamson was handed a subpoena to appear before the federal grand jury.

Warren's extortion trial was held in Seattle in 1978 after a change of venue. He was sentenced to twelve years in prison. Under an unusual arrangement, he was permitted to serve the first eight months at home. In exchange, he promised to cooperate with a state investigation into his land-fraud operations.

When he lied to investigators, the state won a conviction for land fraud and bribery that resulted in a sentence of fifty-four to sixty years in state prison, but Warren's health declined rapidly after that, triggered by triple-bypass surgery on his heart, and on October 9, 1979, he died of congestive-heart failure in the prisoners' ward of Maricopa County Hospital.

Chapter 6

THE PHOENIX UNDERWORLD

E arly in the fateful year of 1976, John Harvey Adamson was a kind of walking explosive, half-drunk on vodka mixed with Valium and further intoxicated by his power as the new street boss of Ned Warren's old crew. He was ready to take any kind of job. That included murder. By this time, he no longer needed Carl Verive to find contracts among the professional killers in the Chicago Heights crew. He would take the fees for himself.

Within a little more than a year, Adamson picked up three commissions calling on his skill, such as it was, at making bombs.

The first of the three big jobs came early in 1976. Barry Goldwater was searching for a solution to a nettlesome political problem whose solution required the utmost discretion and use of force. Either Goldwater or someone in his political operation enlisted attorney Neal T. Roberts to organize a covert solution. To that end, Roberts called a meeting for late January at his home that was attended by Adamson and three other men. One of the men was Joe Patrick, whom Roberts introduced to Adamson as Goldwater's "spy" on the Navajo reservation. The purpose of the meeting was to find a way to remove from office by any means necessary the incumbent Navajo president, Peter MacDonald, who was a nettlesome problem. Adamson offered to create a hoax bomb whose "discovery" could be blamed on MacDonald to discredit him among his supporters. Roberts approved the plan for the hoax bomb, and Adamson was hired to execute it.

The second job was more ordinary. Not long after the meeting at Roberts's home to discuss the Navajo job, the lawyer asked Adamson to use a real fire-bomb big enough to blow up a building in Phoenix that housed the Indian Health Service. Roberts had an ownership stake in the building and was to collect his share of the insurance money.

The third job was the one that made Adamson famous. This one, too, came through Roberts. Adamson testified that the contract on Don Bolles came from one of the wealthiest and most powerful men in the state. Like Warren, rancher and liquor wholesaler Kemper Marley was in urgent need of criminal services. He wanted Bolles dead because he believed the *Arizona Republic* reporter was only weeks away from exposing his role in an illegal Las Vegas casino-skim operation. For the Marley job, Roberts took a direct hand. He set Adamson's fee, devised his alibi, and arranged for his escape to a hideout on the Colorado River.

Questions about Roberts's role in the killing of Don Bolles have remained unanswered for forty years, but needn't have. Police records show that the essential facts about Roberts' role in the contract killing were known within days or weeks after the murder. The deeper mystery, then, was why the Bolles murder remained only half-solved for four decades and who had the power to freeze the investigation. Solving that mystery would require an understanding of the relationship between Adamson and Roberts, on the one hand, and between Roberts and Goldwater on the other, both illuminated by a long-forgotten political crime against the Navajo people.

'SIMPLE BOMB MANUFACTURING'

What struck people about Neal Roberts was his height. Those who met him often remarked on his six-foot, four-inch frame and a self-confidence that verged on narcissism.

One day in January 1976, while Roberts and John Adamson took their posts along the rail at the Ivanhoe to go over plans for the arson, Roberts pulled out a copy of his insurance policy. He held it up, waved it at the Ivanhoe patrons, and asked whether any of them could tell him whether the policy would pay off if a firebomb destroyed the property. Adamson spotted an insurance agent named

Earl and waved him over. Roberts asked the agent to look at the policy to see whether it "covered bomb explosions." Neal Roberts was not a man who felt he had to watch his tongue.

By the mid-1970s, as Ned Warren was languishing at home under court supervision, the Warren gang became the Adamson gang, an amateur imitation of the Chicago Heights crew. Adamson was then in his early thirties, with a six-foot frame that carried 200 pounds. Like Roberts and Max Dunlap he was a graduate of North High School, but unlike the lawyer and the real-estate developer, he struggled through life, a flop at nearly everything. He attended Arizona State University for a few years but dropped out because of bad grades. He married his high-school sweetheart, but the couple separated after four years because Adamson could not keep a job. A turn as an ambulance driver left him $4,000 in debt. Finally, he acquired a tow truck and became a repo man, a profession that brought him in contact with the Phoenix underworld and, eventually, after four years, land-fraud king Ned Warren.

After Warren was sentenced to prison, leaving his criminal gang rudderless, Adamson stepped forward to take over the duties of crew boss but struggled with the new job. Meanwhile, Roberts's role expanded. He did have skills to offer. When called upon, Roberts could smuggle almost anything into prison, including a murder contract. In the fall of 1976, four months after Bolles's murder, Warren turned to Roberts to arrange for the death of an inmate in the Arizona State Prison in Florence: Tony Serra, the Saint Louis mobster who was the first member of the Warren fraud to become a police informant. Roberts arranged to smuggle a letter into Florence to Gary Tison, who would soon become notorious nationwide for a violent prison break. Warren said he would pay $25,000 for the hit, and in January, it was done. Four men in the prison machine shop attacked Serra, who fought back. It took fifteen stab wounds, many blows from heavy pipes, and an electric drill to the skull to finish the job.

As events would later prove, Roberts also knew how to arrange for a getaway plane, a hideout, and a cover story. Because of his nearly lifelong ties to the old Phoenix network, Roberts enjoyed even more protection than Warren. Unlike Warren, however, Roberts never had to bribe anyone in authority. On the contrary, they paid him.

The year Don Bolles was killed, Roberts was forty-five years old. He was born in Houston, Texas, and soon afterward, the family moved to Pine Bluff, Arkansas. In 1935, they resettled in Phoenix in a comfortable bungalow on Palm Lane, less than a block from Encanto Park. In 1948, a week before Thanksgiving, when he was seventeen years old, Roberts was awakened before dawn by gunshots and found both of his parents dead. His father had shot his mother in the face, put the barrel in his mouth, and pulled the trigger again. The effect of this gruesome experience on the young man can only be imagined. There is no record that Roberts spoke of it in later years.

Roberts graduated from North High School just six months earlier in the same class that elected Max Dunlap president. After the Thanksgiving trauma, he recovered enough to take up his undergraduate studies at Phoenix College, then finished them at the University of Arkansas at Fayetteville. After graduation and just before he entered law school at the University of Arizona in Tucson, he married. In 1955, he won his law degree and, in the same year, passed the Arizona bar exam.

In 1959, Roberts landed a job as an assistant attorney general on the staff of Attorney General Wade Church, the last of the state's liberal New Deal politicians. That same year, he was elected president of the Phoenix 20—30 Club, the local chapter of a service organization for ambitious young professional men. It was a heady time for Roberts, who was eager to make a mark. On a Saturday in July 1959, Roberts was one of a group of eight young men who attracted public attention for pranking the press. They loudly let it be known that Governor Earl Long of Louisiana, who had just announced a visit to Arizona, reserved a room at the Adams Hotel. The pranksters pulled up in front of the hotel in a limousine. As reporters and photographers captured the moment, a man emerged wearing slipper socks, gray pants, a long blue coat, and a white pillowcase over his head. In the crook of one arm, he balanced a watermelon, which slipped and smashed on the sidewalk before he was ushered through the hotel doors. Reporters quickly established by phone that Long was in El Paso, and they reported the highjinks in good spirits the next day.

The first sign that something was going wrong in Roberts's life came when he abruptly left the Attorney General's Office after one year on the job. Within another year, his wife sued him for divorce in a battle that lasted six years. Two years after the divorce, he married a German model, Antje Bianca Samter. Both brought children to the marriage.

For several years, their new family was to all appearances successfully blended and living in a large home in Paradise Valley. After a few years, Roberts decided to move downtown. He remodeled a five-unit apartment house at 90 West Virginia Avenue, within walking distance of his favorite bars on Central Avenue. Between them, the couple had six children, all teenagers. The family was "a sort of mini Brady Bunch," the Associated Press reported. Antje said, "Neal has been in love with this place since he was a little boy." The house had its own parking lot and a swimming pool. He set up his law office in an annex just steps from the pool.

Neal and Antje used their new living arrangement to entertain visitors. Among those who joined their social circle at the compound were John Adamson and his wife, Mary. In September 1974, Adamson devoted a dinner conversation to his literary ambitions. Antje said later he told her he had "authored a book on simple bomb manufacturing" for which he was trying to find a publisher. He proudly showed her the manuscript. "You can walk into any drugstore and get home remedies containing enough to blow up a car until there's nothing left," Antje said Adamson told her.

The evening salons did not last long. After a year of bitter arguments, Neal and Antje separated, then divorced. Antje explained that she could no longer put up with Neal's boozing and the thugs who hung around the law office. She was sick of his cynical charm and the other women in his life, and she was tired of being helpless to change him. When she begged him to go back to the way things were when they first married, he laughed at her.

Friends and former clients said Roberts's decline accelerated after Antje left him. The compound on Virginia Avenue turned into a meeting place for Adamson, Carl Verive, and their associates. Antje said of her former husband, "Somehow he seem[ed] to attract people who are scum, leeches." Max Dunlap, who was later convicted for a role in the Bolles murder, used similar language. He told a courtroom that same year that although he "liked Neal," the people around him were "the scum of the earth." His former classmate at North High had "a mind like a snake," Dunlap said. "I don't know one thing in the world that Neal loves."

A Slush Fund for Dirty Tricks

On January 6, 1976, a light plane carrying two members of the Navajo Tribal Council and an official from the Bureau of Indian Affairs crashed in a box canyon, killing everyone on board. The Piper air taxi took off from Albuquerque and went down near Grants, New Mexico, while flying at a normal cruising speed but at a dangerously low altitude in poor visibility. It was five months before the murder of Don Bolles.

Investigators concluded that the plane crash was caused by pilot error and winter weather. But members of Barry Goldwater's political operation in Window Rock saw it as an opportunity to exploit what they regarded as a Navajo predisposition to think of accidental deaths as the work of hostile spirits.

The Goldwater operatives met in the offices of the Navajo Area School Board Association (NASBA) in Window Rock. Among them was Joe Patrick, a Goldwater operative who called himself the senator's "spy." NASBA was a semi-private group organized in 1973 "to activate direct parental participation in the education of Navajo children," but it was widely understood on the reservation that NASBA's main purpose was to serve as a Goldwater listening post. A former lawyer for the Navajo Tribal Council called NASBA "a slush fund for political dirty tricks" in part because it accepted funds from the National Right to Work Committee, a prominent antiunion organization close to Goldwater. The subject of discussion at the NASBA meeting was how to turn to political advantage the anxiety created among tribal members by the accidental deaths of the two council members in the plane crash. Specifically, how could it be used to help remove Navajo President Peter MacDonald from power?

For Goldwater, MacDonald's growing control over Indian energy resources was creating a problem. By January 1976, it was coming to a head.

For decades, large energy corporations interested in deposits of coal, natural gas, and uranium on Hopi and Navajo land had followed a well-trodden path.

They started at the Bureau of Indian Affairs (BIA) at the Department of Interior. The companies would present their contract proposals for mineral extraction to white officials at the BIA, who would pass them on to the white tribal lawyers, who turned over the contracts to the tribal council with a recommendation for approval. The tribal councils, trusting their lawyers, would vote as they were advised, even though the contracts often badly underpriced the value of the minerals and contained little or no protection for tribal water, land, or air.

Over the years, reports piled up of multinational companies making scandalously and sometimes criminally unfair profits from Indian energy contracts. In the case of Hopi coal, suspicion came to rest on John Boyden, a lawyer for the Hopi Tribal Council. Boyden, a Salt Lake City attorney, represented the Hopi during negotiations with Peabody Coal over a massive open-pit mine at Black Mesa. Under his urging, the Hopi Tribal Council signed the Peabody contract in 1966. (The Navajo had signed two years earlier.) What the Indians did not know was that while Boyden was being paid by the Hopi council, he also was working for Peabody and taking a fee. The arrangement was discovered in 1994, when a researcher going through Boyden's posthumously donated private papers found correspondence and billing records proving that he had been on the Peabody payroll all through the negotiations. Under his urging, the Hopi government approved the contract without public hearings or notice to Hopi tribal members.

This was the situation in 1970, when Peter MacDonald was sworn in as president of the Navajo Nation. He made energy policy a priority and organized an association of native owners of mineral resources in the American West called the Council of Energy Resource Tribes (CERT). Collectively, the member tribes could claim at least nominal control over some of the most valuable energy reserves in the western United States, including half the uranium, 30 percent of the low-sulfur coal, and about 4 percent of the oil and natural gas.

MacDonald's opponents began to refer to him as "the Indian Shah," and it was true that he sometimes displayed a monarchical disposition. In 1975, the El Paso Natural Gas Company and the Consolidated Coal Company proposed a lease allowing the two firms to mine eight hundred million tons of Navajo coal over thirty years, with proposed payments to the Navajo of some $450 million. MacDonald handled the negotiations himself. Without consulting the Navajo Council or the BIA, MacDonald signed the deal. Goldwater and other white politicians were cut out of the loop. A year later, Exxon, the world's largest energy company, asked for uranium-exploration rights over four hundred thousand acres of Navajo land on the New Mexico side of the reservation. Many believed that it was the secrecy around the proposed Exxon deal that provoked Goldwater's decision to remove MacDonald.

THE GOLDWATER-MACDONALD WAR

MacDonald was a Navajo success story. He left the reservation at the age of fifteen to join the Marine Corps. After serving four years, he earned an engineering degree and in 1957 took a job with Hughes Aircraft in California, where he earned a reputation for his advanced design for a submarine gyroscope. By his own account, by 1963, MacDonald was living in a suburban ranch house with a swimming pool and a growing discomfort over the contrast between his life and conditions on the reservation. One night, after his mother pleaded with him to leave the world of the *billigaana* and come home, he asked for a one-year leave of absence from Hughes and returned to the Four Sacred Peaks to accept a job from the newly elected tribal chairman, Raymond Nakai. Nakai wanted to raise the tribe out of its dependence on the BIA and asked MacDonald to head the new Office of Navajo Economic Opportunity (ONEO), an antipoverty program that used non-BIA funds left over from the Kennedy administration. MacDonald accepted and, bypassing the BIA, applied for grants that eventually amounted to $900,000 a year. There were complaints, formalized years later, that MacDonald had been less than accountable in his handling of the money.

Meanwhile, MacDonald plunged into Goldwater's 1964 presidential campaign. Eight years later, he was rewarded with a seat in the Arizona delegation to the Republican National Convention in Miami, where he was singled out for a still-higher honor: Goldwater chose him to be one of the convention speakers who would place Richard Nixon's name in nomination for reelection to the presidency. As the chairman of the largest tribe in the country, both in population and square miles, MacDonald was prized as a representative of the GOP's "new majority."

To MacDonald and some others of his generation, Goldwater's message of self-sufficiency and self-reliance had strong appeal. It promised an end to what they regarded as the suffocating weight of the BIA on the reservation and an ideological alternative to the disaster that was visited on the tribe by the Democrats of the New Deal. In 1934, in reaction to environmental problems created by serious overgrazing and erosion, the BIA ordered the wholesale slaughter of Navajo sheep. The decision was made without regard to the social consequences, which included a serious reduction in the authority of Navajo grandmothers, who by custom were the owners of the sheep. The loss of their sheep reduced their ability to hold together traditional families against urban pressures, including badly paid day labor and alcohol. Goldwater offered self-determination in business as well as politics.

In 1968, while MacDonald was still administering ONEO, he learned that the new Nixon administration was considering him for a post in Washington, a move that plunged him unexpectedly into Washington energy politics. Walter Hickel, the new Secretary of the Interior, told MacDonald he wanted to appoint him Commissioner of Indian Affairs (head of the BIA). Even before he agreed to seek the appointment, MacDonald said he started receiving congratulatory phone calls from Steiger and Goldwater, asking for "some favors they would like from me," including a strong suggestion that he appoint a Hopi as deputy commissioner. There were other calls, including some from pols in the Dakotas who had specific recommendations for Anglo construction companies they wanted to be used for reservation roadwork. Despite support from Nixon aide John Ehrlichman and lawyer Leonard Garment, the MacDonald appointment dragged on into 1970.

In the meantime, MacDonald decided to run for the tribal chairmanship against Nakai, and he won. In Washington, unspecified opposition in the Senate to the MacDonald appointment crystallized after Nixon replaced Hickel. The new Secretary of the Interior was Rogers C. B. Morton, who was also the treasurer of the national Republican Party. Several months after MacDonald was sworn in as Navajo chairman, Nixon budget director Frank Carlucci called him to say that he had two pieces of bad news. The first was that MacDonald had lost the appointment as Commissioner of Indian Affairs. The second bit of news was much worse.

Morton had written a letter formulating White House support for a plan that would forcibly transfer tens of thousands of Navajos from land they had shared with the Hopi for nearly a century. The proposal to partition the land, which happened to be rich in coal and uranium, took legislative shape as the Navajo–Hopi Land Settlement Act. A close Goldwater ally, Representative Sam Steiger of Arizona, was the principal sponsor.

Carlucci's phone call was the first time MacDonald had heard about the land partition. He was thunderstruck. At that moment, he abandoned any hope for federal office and resolved to "go over [Morton's] head to change the official administration position." He placed urgent phone calls to his allies in the administration, Garment and Ehrlichman, and pleaded with them to oppose the idea of a population transfer on the grounds that it violated Nixon's "expressed interest in Indian self-determination." Both men agreed and soon afterward read MacDonald a letter they had written for both Nixon and Morton to sign in support of the Navajo position. Garment said he would carry the letter to a meeting with Nixon and Morton in New York and was confident that he could get both men to sign it. But Garment failed.

Morton was irate when Garment handed him the letter. He threatened to resign if Nixon ordered him to sign it. He was so angry, Garment reported to MacDonald, that he threatened to resign as national treasurer of the GOP. The fate of the Navajo traditionalists was decided by Morton's fury, the cause for which was never made clear. In retrospect, it appeared to be related to Morton's emerging role as the administration's policy-maker on energy development, and he wanted more federal and corporate control over Indian energy assets in the American West. In 1974, during the Arab oil embargo, Morton was named energy czar in the Ford administration.

Morton's support for the transfer of long-established traditional Navajo families was the first blow to the Navajo president. When it was followed by an announcement that Goldwater would appear before a House committee to support the partition, a shocked MacDonald began to rethink the tribe's political relationship with Washington.

In the several months remaining before the US Senate held its hearings on the partition bill, MacDonald approached Goldwater's liberal opposition in the Senate and in the Democratic Party in the hope of finding allies powerful enough to block the partition. He met privately with Senators Ted Kennedy, Walter Mondale, and George McGovern, chairman of the Senate Subcommittee on Indian Affairs. They received him warmly. Among other things, the Democratic senators agreed to use their contacts to ask for newspaper and magazine coverage of the Navajo position. After meeting with the liberal leaders, MacDonald walked into the headquarters of the AFL-CIO to ask for union help in confronting Goldwater. Like many Navajos, MacDonald once wrote, he was inclined to think of unions as enemies: gangs of hostile Anglos, often Teamsters and construction-trade officials who pushed their way around the reservation to take the best energy-related jobs while denying Indians union membership. It's unclear whether MacDonald grasped the political risk he was taking in his new alliance with organized labor. By asking for labor's help, he was committing the one unpardonable act in Arizona politics.

Goldwater's 1974 campaign for reelection to the Senate was a bitter affair. The unions' Committee on Political Education (COPE) organized a voter-registration drive on the reservation, and Navajo voters signed up by the thousands. In response, Goldwater enlisted the help of blue-collar workers at the Union Pacific Railroad, a group led by Burley Blunk of Winslow. "Goldwater established [Blunk] in the bar where the gandy dancers [railroad track-maintenance workers] drank," a former Navajo tribal lawyer, George Vlassis, said in an interview. "When there was a vote, they'd have the gandy dancers go on to the reservation and tell the Navajo to vote the way Goldwater told them." The atmosphere was so tense, Vlassis said, that throughout the election campaign, he carried a sidearm in his briefcase.

For the first time since his name first appeared on a statewide ballot, Goldwater failed to win in a landslide. In the formerly secure Apache and Navajo counties, he was defeated for the first time. Raul Castro, the Democratic candidate for governor, took nine thousand Navajo votes in a record turnout. MacDonald and the AFL-CIO delightedly took the credit for Castro's victory. Goldwater regarded it as an insult.

In a postelection news conference, Goldwater charged that COPE had handed out travel vouchers and beer tickets to Navajos in exchange for their promises to vote for Castro. He called for an immediate investigation by the Justice Department.

Within weeks after the election, US Attorney General William Saxbe dispatched Dennis Ickes, director of the Office of Indian Rights, to meet with Navajo General Council Harold Mott and twenty-six Navajos from around the reservation to testify to acts of voter fraud. Ickes and his assistant director spent several days in Farmington, Window Rock, and Gallup listening to other witnesses, then returned to Washington to persuade Saxbe and FBI Director Clarence Kelley to send a team of eight FBI agents to Arizona "to ferret out specific evidence and information" about voter fraud on the reservation. Privately, Ickes assured Mott that he had compiled enough evidence to take the case to federal court.

Goldwater opened another front as well. "In talking to the administrative assistant of Goldwater," Mott wrote, "it now appears certain that [Arizona US Attorney William C.] Smitherman will reopen the grand jury investigation of MacDonald's alleged misappropriation of money while he was head of the Office of Navajo Economic Opportunity." During all of this time, according to a member of Ickes's team of federal investigators, Joe Patrick made a show of coming around to investigators' offices to find out what they were learning.

MacDonald fought back. "The charge is not only false," he said at a news conference, "it stands as an insult to every Navajo who exercises the right of a citizen to vote…I think [Goldwater] is living in the days of cowboys and Indians and has failed to recognize that Indians are beginning to participate in the voting process." He referred to Goldwater as "Kit" Goldwater, after Kit Carson, whose name is a curse among the Navajo.

GOLDWATER'S THREE-PRONGED STRATEGY
The scale of the Goldwater plan to remove the Navajo leader from office was ambitious in its scope and intensity. It involved a three-part strategy that required the resources of the federal government, the news media, and the new Phoenix underworld.

The first line of attack was economic. Goldwater introduced legislation in the US Senate that had the effect of removing the Navajo tribe's control over its mineral resources. The second was legal, involving a concerted effort by the US Justice Department to charge MacDonald with corruption. Both efforts were aided by front-page coverage in *The New York Times*.

The third pincer was covert. It deployed political dirty tricks to "raise havoc" on the reservation, that is, to incite enough disorder to justify a declaration of martial law or a similar emergency to remove MacDonald, by force, if need be. The model invoked was the suppression of the Lakota rebellion at Wounded Knee in South Dakota three years earlier.

MacDonald made it easy for the Justice Department to implement its part in the removal strategy. A federal grand jury in Phoenix indicted a member of MacDonald's administration after the man diverted $13 million in federal funds intended for low-cost housing to a convicted felon and con man whose role was revealed in *The New York Times* on May 16, 1976. A few days after this story ran, some six hundred Navajo activists organized a loud but peaceful demonstration in Window Rock demanding MacDonald's resignation. It was hardly enough to justify martial law, but in the view of Joe Patrick, it was a good start. Patrick told Navajo legal counsel Claude Keller that he had helped organize the demonstration as a "Walk for Better Government" and said he "was instrumental in the May 16 article."

Goldwater acknowledged to the Associated Press that he triggered the federal investigation by filing a request to the General Accounting Office for an audit of federal programs on the Navajo reservation. In April, the federal probe was given a boost by *The Phoenix Gazette* and the Associated Press when unidentified government sources leaked deposed statements that had been shown to the grand jury. The stories were framed by comments from anonymous sources in the Justice Department.

'HE'S A SPY FOR GOLDWATER'

It was John Adamson who provided the only public glimpse of the third pincer in the Goldwater plan to unseat MacDonald. It came during Adamson's first appearance in an open courtroom after his arrest for the Bolles murder, when anything he said was bound to make headlines. Public interest in events on the Navajo reservation already had been kindled by the federal indictments of MacDonald for corruption. But it was not federal prosecutors who took an interest in Adamson's role in the MacDonald matter. They confined their questions to the federal insurance-fraud case against Neal Roberts in the attempted firebombing of a building in Phoenix. It was his own lawyer who asked Adamson to describe his role in planting a propaganda bomb on the reservation, and it had the desired effect on reporters covering the hearing.

A detailed record of Adamson's role in the MacDonald plot has survived in a more concise account than the one he gave at the federal hearing a few weeks later. He told his lawyer a few weeks earlier that he joined the plot at the second meeting of the group that gathered in Window Rock on January 6 to discuss the crash of the air taxi. Someone in the Goldwater camp had told the Window Rock group to consult with Neal Roberts on how to use the opportunity presented by the plane crash, Adamson said. During the meeting he learned that Roberts was promised the position of chief legal counsel for the Navajo if MacDonald could be removed, and he had already worked out that the position could be worth about $700,000 a year in payoffs. Roberts had Adamson to create the havoc. It was Roberts's idea to invite Adamson to the second meeting, hosted by the lawyer in his Phoenix law office on Virginia Avenue.

Five men were present, Adamson said. In addition to himself and Roberts, there was Raymond Nakai, whom MacDonald had succeeded as Navajo president; Harold Mott, former legal counsel to the Navajo Tribal Council; and Joe Patrick, head of the Goldwater political operation in Window Rock. Adamson and Roberts did most of the talking.

ADAMSON: There was a meeting held in Neal Roberts's home [in January 1976] between Neal Roberts, myself, and Joe Patrick. Neal said, "John, this is Joe Patrick." We met, and he said, "Joe works on the Indian reservation." And I said, "Well, what does Joe do on the Indian reservation?" And he said, "Well, he's a spy." I said, "Well, that's good,

I guess. He's a spy for Senator Goldwater. I guess that makes it even better."

"What does he do for Goldwater?" [Roberts] says, "He watches what goes on, on the reservation, and reports directly back to Goldwater with regard to Peter MacDonald," and that Goldwater wants MacDonald off the reservation, and they were interested in having me go up and create havoc on the Indian reservation about that particular time because it was that time during the year when there was a plane crash, and a couple of Indian officials were killed and they were going to have a funeral or a wake or whatever it is Indians have, and he wanted me to go up there and perhaps plant a bomb, blow up a car, create general havoc up there so that perhaps martial law would be declared, discrediting MacDonald, who Neal Roberts could have replaced through Senator Goldwater...

QUESTION: The position of Peter MacDonald?

ADAMSON: Right, and then Neal Roberts could be appointed as chief counsel for the Indian Nation, and he mentioned to me that he had in fact talked with Goldwater, verifying, I guess, that Goldwater wanted Peter MacDonald off the reservation. Or wasn't cooperating with him or wasn't doing what he was supposed to do or was having problems with him, or anyway, their relationship wasn't the way it should be going between Goldwater and MacDonald.

QUESTION: Now, when you had that conversation with Neal that you were just talking about, was anybody else around?

ADAMSON: No, just Neal and I.

QUESTION: Joe Patrick wasn't there?

ADAMSON: No, the only time Joe was around was when they were figuring out what to do with that guy Peter MacDonald up there. I suggested to Joe, I said, "Hell, I'll go home and make you up a package of dynamite right now, and you just take it up with you to the Indian reservation and stick it in whosever office you want to, or I'll attach a couple of magnets and attach it to someone's car up there, and then call the cops or the feds and let them find it, and you just do it.

QUESTION: What'd he say?

ADAMSON: He turned pretty pale—I don't think he wanted to hear about it. He liked the idea of getting it done, but he didn't like the idea of going out and walking around with dynamite.

QUESTION: Any money mentioned?

ADAMSON: I told them I'd do them a favor—I'd just go up there and *do* it.

For the Navajo job, John Adamson was almost as good as his word. He used his signature six sticks of dynamite, but the blasting cap he inserted into the explosives was intentionally faulty. Adamson drove north with the intention to hide the bomb in the chambers of the Navajo Tribal Council in the bewintered capital city of Window Rock, where they hoped it would be discovered by one of the hundreds of Navajos who gathered at a memorial service for the air-crash victims.

Adamson drove north to the reservation, but soon after entering a land of fifty miles of visibility in all directions, the lone white man with the bomb in his trunk began to feel conspicuous. He drove as far as Tuba City, a Navajo town one hundred fifty miles west of Window Rock just off the north-south highway that connects Flagstaff to southern Utah. He threw the dynamite in a trash bin in a tribal-administration building, then turned around and drove back to Phoenix. News stories about the discovery of the bomb ran in *The Gallup Independent*. They stirred limited interest, and there was no disorder.

At the federal hearing a few weeks after Adamson described these events to his lawyers in private, Flynn, acting for Roberts, called Joe Patrick to the stand. Patrick affirmed that he had attended the meeting at the Roberts compound in January 1976 and that Roberts had introduced him to Adamson. Patrick told the court he worked on the reservation for the Navajo Area School Board Association and, during a trip home to Phoenix for that weekend, happened to drop in to see Roberts. He said Adamson dropped in and soon left with no serious discussion of anything by anyone. "I don't think he [Adamson] was there more than ten minutes," Patrick said. He finished his testimony by declaring, in response to a final question from Flynn, "I was not a spy for Goldwater."

The news ran at the top of the front page of the *Republic* the next day under the headline, "Adamson Describes Plot Against Navajo."

'WHY WOULD HE SAY SUCH A THING?'

The revelation that Adamson had participated in a bomb plot separate from the heavily publicized attack on Bolles and the attempted arson of the Indian Health Service would have been a front-page story on its own merits. But the Goldwater angle pushed it into a larger category than daily news. Goldwater had a reputation as someone with a winking admiration for gangsters, but it was unthinkable that Arizona's "national monument," as he was sometimes called, could be involved in a plot to overthrow the Navajo government. And it was unimaginable that someone on his team might think it wise to make use of Ned Warren's criminal gang for any purpose. The revelation had even greater force by the time of the federal hearing because pulic interest in Adamson, who by this time had already confessed to killing Bolles, was intense.

For a day or two, the coverage of the Bolles case in the *Republic* took on a sense of renewed urgency, for it appeared that state or federal prosecutors might be getting closer to solving the central mystery: who paid for the murder? If the investigation was reaching as high as the Goldwater circle, perhaps authorities were making sure that no one, not even Arizona's most admired man, would be exempt from questioning.

In the excitement of the headlines, it was easy to miss the all-important detail that it was not the prosecutors who had elicited the story of the Navajo plot from Adamson but John Flynn, who was also Roberts's lawyer in his federal arson charge. It was Flynn and his client, not the prosecutors in the US Attorney's Office, who wanted the narrative of the Navajo bomb on the record.

Adamson's testimony about the Tuba City incident was magnified by what appeared to be a remarkable coincidence. On the same day and at virtually the same moment Adamson was holding a federal court spellbound with tales of dynamite and martial law in the land of the Diné, Barry Goldwater was testifying to another federal grand jury down the hall.

Reporters met Goldwater as he emerged from the other grand-jury room. Strangely, he was already armed with the news that Adamson had identified Joe Patrick as one of the men who attended the meeting at Roberts's house to plan the Navajo coup. The senator also possessed the information that several witnesses had identified Patrick as his "spy" on the reservation. He was curt and visibly angry. Rather than respond to questions on the steps of the federal courthouse, he announced, he would hold a news conference the next day at his house in Paradise Valley.

When reporters arrived at the senator's home, Goldwater told them he had been given a copy of a statement Patrick made on February 2 to agents of the federal Bureau of Alcohol, Tobacco and Firearms (ATF). It was a stroke of luck for the senator because it forearmed him with the details of Patrick's account of the meeting that implicated him.

The senator quoted aloud a few lines from the ATF report. Patrick had indeed told the agents he had worked as "an informant for Goldwater" on the Navajo reservation, he read. He then denounced Patrick. The senator told reporters "he did not understand why Patrick would say such a thing. He knew Patrick because they had flown together in the Arizona Air National Guard," but "he's no more informant than if I might say, 'Joe, what happened on your last flight to Germany, or your last flight to Saigon, or how's the National Guard going?'" He said he had not spoken with Patrick for a year and a half.

In 2006, an FBI copy of an ATF report surfaced that might have been the one Goldwater was referring to in his press conference. It included an interview with Patrick about the critical meeting at the Roberts compound. The report, written by agents George W. Kelley and Arbie Odom, was not distributed to the press. It supported Adamson's versions of events. "Mr. Patrick related that he attended a meeting in Neal Roberts's residence in Phoenix, Arizona, where the following topics were discussed: Joe Patrick's association with Senator Goldwater [redacted]. That John Harvey Adamson, Neal Roberts, and Joe Patrick did in fact discuss causing an explosion, fires, and other things [redacted]." However, Patrick added, "this was just conversation and nothing serious at that time."

Patrick had lied either to the ATF agents in the February 2 statement, when he said he was Goldwater's informant, or to the federal court on February 16, when he denied it. Either way, his credibility could be attacked, and it was.

Establishing the truth about the relationships among Goldwater, Roberts, and Patrick was important. Was Roberts working for Goldwater when he invited Adamson to the meeting? Was Patrick working for Goldwater when he attended the meeting? Who approved Adamson's proposal to carry a bundle of dynamite to the reservation? Was Roberts promised the position of chief counsel for the Navajo if MacDonald was replaced?

These were among the questions opened up by Patrick's statement to the ATF. They were the kinds of questions that ordinarily are answered in a formal setting and under oath. When that moment arrived, however, there was no official interest in presenting them.

It is unknown who gave Goldwater a copy of the ATF report. When reporters asked the senator how he had come into possession of Patrick's statement to the ATF, he told them he got it from the FBI. A *Republic* reporter called the FBI to verify Goldwater's claim about his source and reached Roger Young, an assistant to the special agent in charge in Phoenix. Young denied that the FBI had been the source for the document. He said Jim Reeves, head of the Arizona ATF, had told him that his office had not been Goldwater's source, either. Acting US Attorney Joel Sachs said his office had not been Goldwater's source for the document. The ranks closed again.

The question of the political and professional ties between Goldwater and Patrick remained a live one among journalists. In 1979 Jerry Kammer, then a reporter for a New Mexico newspaper, learned that Patrick had indeed helped organize the Window Rock demonstration that called for MacDonald's resignation. Patrick had boasted to Claude Keller, chief counsel for the Navajo tribe, that his duties extended as far as soliciting news coverage for the demonstration. Kammer's four-thousand-word investigation attracted little attention.

Years later, Patrick published on the Internet a photo of himself sitting with Goldwater on a couch, his arm draped behind the senator's shoulder. The photo appeared to have been torn from an album and taped back together. It bore this inscription over Goldwater's signature: *To a valued friend, Joe Patrick.*

WHAT THE NAVAJOS DISCOVERED

The ATF report on the meeting attended by Adamson, Roberts, Patrick, and the others was included as an attachment to an investigation into the Bolles murder. The Navajo Tribal Council ordered its legal department to pursue "an investigation into allegations that unlawful attempts had been made to disrupt the Navajo Tribal government and to impose some form of 'martial law.'" The result was the *Preliminary Report to the Navajo Tribal Council*, written by a member of the tribe's legal staff, Michael V. Stuhff, who submitted his report in February 1980. It is the only official government investigation into John Adamson's role in the MacDonald affair. The report established that Goldwater's political organization used Roberts and Adamson, who later perpetrated the Bolles murder, in an illegal scheme to help supplant the Navajo tribal government.

Stuhff wrote in the report's cover letter, "Plans to 'raise havoc' on the Navajo Reservation are linked to the Goldwater organization and to Goldwater's close associates."

Using its subpoena powers, the Navajo Tribal Council also answered many of the questions about Patrick and his relationships with Goldwater, Roberts, and Adamson. It subpoenaed NASBA's personnel records for Patrick, including his expense reports, calendar of meetings, and telephone conversations with reporters and public officials. Among the people Patrick spoke to from his NASBA office, according to the phone records, was Barry Goldwater.

Patrick's phone logs showed that he made calls to the Capitol Hill switchboard in Washington, DC; to the Department of Justice; to the White House (listed as well as unlisted numbers); and to the National Right to Work Committee in Falls Church, Virginia. The logs for January 9 through January 13, 1976, contained his notes about conversations with Goldwater aide Jack Murphy and with Goldwater himself. The *Preliminary Report* characterized these calls as "frequent and substantial contacts with Murphy and other Goldwater aides...including phone calls to the unlisted Scottsdale number of Judy Eisenhower," Goldwater's chief of staff.

The phone records show unambiguously that Patrick was in direct contact with the senator and his political staff and that Goldwater was not telling the truth when he said he had nothing more than a passing acquaintance with Patrick.

WHAT GOLDWATER TOLD THE GRAND JURY

The loyalty of Arizona authorities to Barry Goldwater would be hard to exaggerate. That included US Attorney William C. Smitherman, who was in charge of the case against John Adamson. Smitherman was a Republican, a Nixon appointee, and a volunteer in Goldwater's reelection campaigns. Even so, his staff admired him for his integrity and his refusal to be intimidated by political power brokers. He had once responded to a detailed set of instructions in a letter from Attorney General John Mitchell by writing, *Thank you for your letter.* No more, no less.

When the State of Arizona announced its plea agreement with John Adamson in January 1977, the court noted that the US Attorney's Office in Arizona had agreed to abide by its terms. After the plea was struck, preparation for the trial against Adamson came to a halt, and the state turned its attention to the Dunlap and Robison trial. The state released Adamson into the custody of the Justice Department for interrogation by the FBI.

What the FBI heard from Adamson caused consternation among federal authorities. An assistant US attorney alerted Smitherman that FBI interviews with Adamson had produced a troubling story that could complicate their case against Neal Roberts in the arson matter. Adamson had told agents about the bomb with a faulty fuse that he left in a trash bin in Tuba City as part of Roberts's role in creating "havoc" on the Navajo reservation. More urgent was the news that Adamson identified the interested party behind the Navajo job as Senator Barry Goldwater. The preliminary hearing at which Adamson would have divulged this information in public was still five weeks in the future. It would be revealed under questioning by a lawyer who represented both Adamson and Roberts, John Flynn. Flynn was famous for arguing the *Miranda* case before the US Supreme Court, based on a brief written by John Frank.

According to the assistant prosecutor, Smitherman took a moment to study what the FBI said they had learned from Adamson about the Navajo plot and Goldwater's role in it. Then he said, "Well, let's go ask him."

A few days later, Smitherman and the assistant US attorney flew to Washington to confront Goldwater in the Senate Office Building. The two prosecutors laid out what Adamson had told the FBI and informed the senator that they would like him to return to Phoenix to tell a federal grand jury what he knew about Neal Roberts and the Navajo bomb.

Goldwater raised his hands with palms forward, as though in mild protest. "Well, you know, you can't subpoena me while Congress is in session," he said.

The assistant US attorney responded, "I understand that, but they're not in session."

Goldwater assented and said, "Yeah, I'd be happy to come back."

This, then, was the original purpose of Barry Goldwater's appearance before the federal grand jury in Phoenix on February 16, the same day that Adamson was testifying a few doors away in the Phoenix federal courthouse.

In his office, Goldwater was read his Miranda rights, a routine procedure for grand-jury witnesses in those days, thanks to John Flynn. According to the assistant US attorney, who led the questioning in front of the grand jury, Goldwater was questioned for between ten and fifteen minutes. The prosecutor declined to discuss Goldwater's testimony in any detail, but when pressed, he acknowledged that he had asked the senator no questions about the plan to force MacDonald out of office and none about the Bolles murder. He confined his questions to the attempted firebombing of the building that housed the Indian Health Service—that is, to the one case against Roberts that had no connection to Goldwater.

The prosecutor stated that he was interested in Goldwater's answers only insofar as they might affect the outcome of the arson case against Roberts and James Robison. "I wanted to make sure that they weren't going to have any ramifications in the then-pending trial against Adamson—or rather [correcting himself] Roberts—in the approaching trial in the Indian Health Service case," he said.

"I was asking [Goldwater] the questions in front of the grand jury, and he was saying, you know, 'I don't know anything about that.' You know—'I know this guy [Roberts]. I mean, it was not a memorial-type thing that I would remember,' and that was the end of him.

"We never—you know, he [Goldwater] was, obviously, never called as a witness in Roberts's trials," the prosecutor concluded.

The grand-jury session with Goldwater was officially ruled "unproductive." But the prosecutor never arrived at the issues that led to Smitherman's request for Goldwater to appear before a grand jury, that is, the plan to remove MacDonald from office and the role, if any, the senator might have played in it. Sometime between the flight to Washington to confront Goldwater and his appearance before the grand jury, it was decided that the US government would confine its questions to the arson case.

Federal prosecutors did go on to try Roberts and Robison for the attempted arson of the Indian Health Service after Adamson agreed to testify against his coconspirators. After a change of venue, Roberts and Robison went to trial in San Diego in February 1978. The case fell apart when a lone juror, the foreman, expressed doubts over Adamson's credibility when he testified that he saw Roberts hold up an insurance policy at the Ivanhoe bar and ask whether it covered arson. Roberts told the trial jury that it was Adamson who brought the insurance policy to the bar. As a favor to Adamson, Roberts said, he showed the policy to an insurance agent sitting nearby and asked his advice on questions unrelated to explosives.

At trial, the agent was identified as Earl Bushley of Phoenix. Bushley backed Roberts's version, saying the questions he had posed about the policy were merely "general." The jury foreman, after first joining in the unanimous guilty judgment, changed his vote, saying there was enough doubt on this point to think Adamson might be lying. "I feel in my own being that Neal Roberts is innocent," the foreman said. The case collapsed in a hung jury and was dismissed. A series of appeals and retrials similarly led nowhere, and Roberts remained free until his death.

A Kilo in a Gucci Bag

After the Bolles murder, Neal Roberts's career slid further into decline, including at least one season as a low-level criminal in a mob-built resort. By the early 1980s, before alcoholism and poverty overtook him, Roberts spent a season as a cocaine dealer at La Costa, near San Clemente. He would buy one kilo at a time and retail it by the gram to resort residents, buying and selling through a group of couriers. He made the buys from the backseat of a black Mercedes bearing California plates. He would hand out through the car window a Gucci bag containing $55,000 in cash and in return take a kilo of cocaine in an identical Gucci bag. One of the couriers who delivered coke to Roberts was Robert Sprouse, an associate of a Scottsdale mobster who was a member of Chicago's North Side crew. Sprouse told Phoenix police that Roberts was working four or five kilos at a time in as many Gucci bags.

Roberts lived out the few remaining years of his increasingly feeble life in the same manner he had for decades, perched on his favorite barstools in downtown Phoenix, a ghost from a nearly forgotten past, bent, aged, and haggard, a figure of no official interest. When he died twenty-three years later, just before Valentine's Day in 1999, *The Arizona Republic* obituary writer called him "the mysterious central figure in the Don Bolles murder."

In 2012, the website of Investigative Reporters and Editors still carried this note as the last entry in its chronology of the Bolles murder: "Jan. 28, 1999: Phoenix attorney Neal Roberts dies in poverty at the age of sixty-six of coronary-artery disease, cirrhosis, and emphysema. His former secretary says Roberts told her he was involved in the Bolles murder at various levels, but investigators say his statements may have been influenced by his heavy drinking and taste for melodrama."

Chapter 7

KILLING THE NEWS—DON BOLLES

If at age forty-six Don Bolles was a little careworn, he'd earned it from a decade and a half of hard investigative reporting. A reassignment to the state capitol pressroom was a demotion of sorts, but there were signs he welcomed the change. He replaced the seersucker suit and tortoiseshell spectacles with aviator glasses, and he let his 1950s crew cut grow out. Sometimes he wore a short sleeve knit polo with an ineffably corny bolo tie. It might have been a sign that he was feeling a little more at home in the desert, a long way from his native New Jersey.

Bolles was the son of an Associated Press editor. After leaving the army, Bolles followed his father's trade and joined the Associated Press, working his way west to Phoenix, where he joined the staff of *The Arizona Republic* in 1962, a critical moment in the newspaper's history. A new managing editor, J. Edward Murray, hired Bolles as part of a team he was assembling to restore the paper's credibility after its gifted but idiosyncratic owner and publisher, Eugene Pulliam, made a costly editorial error. For the editions of May 11, 1959, Pulliam ordered the entire news report yanked from the front page and replaced with an editorial attacking the state's attorney general. It ran under the headline, "Communism and Mr. Church." It was ignited by a speech to the state AFL-CIO convention by Wade Church, Arizona's last prominent New Dealer, who had proposed the creation of a "people's council" of labor, school, religious, and minority groups to keep an eye on the influence of corporate lobbyists in the state capitol. The lobbyists were so powerful, Church argued, that they could be referred to as the legislature's "third house."

An incensed Pulliam, believing he had glimpsed the bayonets of the Red Army above the city gates, called in one of his editorial writers to compose an attack. He was a man Pulliam regarded as an expert on communism because he was an exile from Bulgaria and trustworthy because he was a brother-in-law. "Mr. Church's 'people's council' idea comes straight from the writings of Karl Marx," the full-page editorial stated. It concluded with a few pointed questions: "Does Mr. Church advocate socialism for Arizona? Does he advocate communism?" The editorial reinforced Pulliam's reputation as a newspaper "titan" who had a capacity for recklessness.

Church's libel case required seventeen years to resolve. After winding through two jury trials and several appeals, Church collected $625,000 in damages and interest. Long before that, however, a chagrined Pulliam realized he had overreached. To help rebuild the newspaper's credibility, Pulliam hired Edward Murray, president of the Associated Press Managing Editors Association, who had gained a solid national reputation at *The Los Angeles Times*. Pulliam promised him a free hand. In 1962, Murray assembled the paper's new reporting team, and Don Bolles was part of it.

From the start, Bolles showed considerable skill at turning over rocks. He started by uncovering kickbacks and petty corruption in state agencies but soon moved on to investigate the criminals who were plundering the real-estate markets in Phoenix and Tucson. In 1967, he wrote an eight-part series on the emerging boss of Arizona land fraud, Ned Warren. The series established his reputation as the state's leading investigative reporter. He followed it in 1970 and again in 1973 with two ambitious series on the Mafia in Arizona.

Bolles's interest focused on an old Arizona family, the Funks. Years earlier, they had sold their jewelry stores to buy a minority share in the local greyhound dog-racing tracks, which they managed for the out-of-town Emprise Corp., the majority owner. Bolles investigated the dog tracks at a time when journalists in New York and congressional-committee staffers were looking at connections between Emprise and organized crime. *Newsday* editor and reporter Bob Greene, along with investigators for the State of New York, established that Emprise patriarch Louis Jacobs of Buffalo had close business ties to the old Detroit mob boss, Joseph Zerilli Sr.

Florida Congressman Claude Pepper and his committee, whose members included Arizona Representative Sam Steiger, developed an interest in Emprise after federal prosecutors named the corporation a coconspirator in an illegal Mafia straw purchase of the Frontier Hotel and Casino in Las Vegas. Two younger leaders of Detroit families with land holdings in Arizona, Michael Polizzi and Joseph Zerilli Jr., wanted a casino for the Detroit mob to skim instead of sharing points with other families. After the Las Vegas gambling commission turned down their request for a casino license, they put up the money for what mobsters called a "clean face" (a straw purchaser with no police record) to buy the Frontier. Things ran smoothly until Zerilli and Polizzi attracted attention to the amount of money they were skimming from the Frontier casino—a quarter of a million dollars a month off the top. A federal court in Los Angeles sent them to prison in 1974.

A reporter of Bolles's intensity would naturally want to see how far the Frontier casino case extended into Arizona. Meanwhile, a congressional investigation failed to produce anything conclusive about mob-related Emprise activities into the state. One of the FBI's leading mob investigators concluded that after Louis Jacobs and the old gangsters from the Depression generation retired, Emprise's "ties to organized crime were tenuous." But in his own probe of Emprise and the Funks, Bolles incautiously allowed himself to be drawn into a kind of partnership with Steiger that fed the congressman's considerable appetite for publicity. As a member of Representative Claude Pepper's House Select Committee on Crime, the first congressional committee to take a close look at organized crime in Arizona, Steiger arranged for Bolles to testify about what he had discovered about the Funks and Emprise. Bolles accepted. But the Pepper probe was a fiasco. In January 1973, it collapsed in a scandal for which Steiger was in large part responsible.

As the Pepper committee was wrapping up its investigation, the Emprise attorney who was coordinating the corporation's witnesses surprised a stranger in his hotel room. He turned out to be a member of Steiger's congressional staff who was either planting or removing an illegal eavesdropping device. The Emprise attorney called the police, who arrested the staffer when he confessed he had been acting on orders from Steiger. An account of the arrest ran on the front page of *The New York Times* the next day, hours before the scheduled release of the committee report. The press focused on the arrest and ignored the contents of the report, which contained a long but inconclusive discussion of Emprise and the Arizona greyhound tracks.

Bolles's reporting on the Arizona dog tracks soon deflated as well. The Funks sued him for libel and named Steiger, a frequently quoted source, and the *Republic* as codefendants. The plaintiffs won a settlement in 1974. Its exact terms remain sealed, but an attorney close to the case said the agreement required the *Republic* to remove Bolles from the investigative beat and to promise he would never write another word on the Funk family. The Funks also insisted that Steiger apologize and pay them a dollar. The congressman did both.

At the time, his fellow journalists regarded Bolles's apparent failure as a case of a good reporter allowing an investigation to turn into a personal obsession, as some of his notes later suggested. But events would show that the mob did have a significant involvement in the Phoenix greyhound track. Two years after the collapse of his racetrack investigation, Bolles discovered or was given a document that showed how Kemper Marley was part of a money-laundering scheme at the racetrack.

A FATAL PHONE CALL

Bolles made the best of his reassignment to the legislature. Freed from the stress of the newspaper's toughest reporting job, he shed thirty pounds. In April of 1976, he prowled the new-car showrooms and bought a white, four-speed Datsun 710 that he proudly showed off to other reporters at the statehouse. According to an account written soon after the murder, Bolles was glad to lose at least one artifact of his old life: a battered, 1968 Plymouth with 105,000 miles on the odometer. Veins of gummy residue marked the spot on the Plymouth where he had attached strips of transparent tape connecting the hood to a fender "as a giveaway if anyone rigged the car with explosives."

Not long after he settled into his new beat, on June 2, 1976, Bolles got a call from John Adamson. He told the reporter he had proof of a secret, illegal land deal involving Barry Goldwater, Harry Rosenzweig, Kemper Marley, and Sam Steiger. It was a ruse to entice Bolles into showing up at the Clarendon Hotel and wait in the bar long enough for Adamson to attach a bomb to the undercarriage of his Datsun. Adamson's partner, a scar-faced part-time plumber by the name of James "Jimmy" Robison, trained in radio communications by the US Navy, waited in his truck not far away with an electronic trigger in his hands.

When Adamson failed to show up at the Clarendon bar, Bolles left. He walked through the first-floor corridor to the parking lot in the rear of the hotel. He had parked the new Datsun in the fourth space from the left in the front row, where a bundle of dynamite, fixed with magnets to the bottom of the car, just under the driver's seat, awaited him. Bolles opened the door, slid into the driver's seat, and turned the ignition key. As he backed the car out of the parking space and put it in a forward gear to drive off, Robison, watching from the cab of his pickup, stabbed a button on a remote-control device. It ignited a fuse cap in a bundle of dynamite that blew out the bottom and the door on the driver's side of the car. It was something of a miracle that Bolles remained conscious long enough to name Adamson as one of his killers.

SALOONS OF CENTRAL AVENUE

In January 1977, members of the several agencies of law enforcement claiming jurisdiction over the murder of Don Bolles met with John Adamson in a Tucson courtroom. He'd been in custody since June 14, the day Bolles died of his wounds. On the last day of December 1976, Adamson confessed and signed a plea agreement. The Tucson hearing was a forum for state, Maricopa County, and Phoenix law enforcement to examine Adamson on the details of his confession. Depending on his truthfulness and cooperation, he would be given a sentence of twenty years.

On hand were the state's lead prosecutor in the case, William J. Schafer III; Deputy County Attorney Eugene G. Neil, county liaison with the state; and Adamson's own lawyers. Phoenix Police Detective Jon Sellers questioned the accused killer and made a two-hundred-fifty-page record. Adamson's responses contained references to some sixty characters, many of them in conversations with Adamson in sixteen different bars, each of which he could recall by name.

Many of Adamson's most frequently mentioned characters were part-timers or hangers-on in the outer orbit of the old Warren gang. They were men who cruised the streets and the racetracks with Adamson and Carl Verive, or they were attorneys like Mickey Clifton or "Suitcase Charlie," who worked in the half light of criminal law and whose offices Adamson used occasionally to meet his own criminal clients. They were brown-shoe lawyers attached to politicians who needed a discreet service for a mistress or a favor from a madam, or bartenders who would pass on messages to cops, or owners of plumbing-supply companies prone to arson, or the occasional "degenerate" (offense not named), or the odd uptown business executive who liked the atmosphere of the Phoenix saloon culture that extended up and down Central Avenue and side streets close by and included The Velvet Hammer, The Iron Maiden, Smugglers, The Phone Booth, Chauncey's, Roscoe's Kemo Sabe, Mr. Fat Fingers Cocktail Lounge, Chez Nous, The Garnett Lounge, The Olive, The Island, and—always—The Ivanhoe and Durant's.

But most of Adamson's testimony keyed on three men: Max Dunlap, Jimmy Robison, and Neal Roberts.

Dunlap was an unlikely figure to be caught up in a ragged murder-for-hire scheme. He was good-looking in a squared-off Midwestern sort of way, affable and socially prominent. He had been one of the most popular kids in his high school, a double-letter man in basketball and track in all four years and at one point president of the North High student body. He went on to succeed as a developer. Thanks to his benefactor, the rancher and liquor king Kemper Marley, Dunlap was well off by the time of the Bolles murder, with interests in land development up and down the Arizona side of the booming Colorado River. The Dunlap part of the story in the Bolles case was difficult for some

Phoenicians to accept. Yet this was the man, Adamson said, who had hired him to kill Bolles—and not just Bolles.

Who would accept the testimony of a hard-core boozer like John Adamson over the word of Max Dunlap? To skeptics, the story looked like a cover-up, even after the state tried and convicted Dunlap and sentenced him to prison. The evidence against him was hard to refute. Phoenix police found that Dunlap had been a courier between Roberts and Bolles's killer. Dunlap was said to have delivered payoff money to Adamson's lawyer before the assassination and hush money afterward. Dunlap said he was a patsy who had been doing a favor for someone he had never seen before and could not name. A jury found him guilty and sentenced him to death in January 1978. A sinuous legal history of appeals and retrials kept him in prison until he died in 2009.

THE SILVER INGOT SCAM

It was at Fat Fingers, a neighborhood bar just north of Camelback Road, where Dunlap had threatened him the year before, Adamson said. "I'm going to have you killed," Dunlap told him. He was angry with Adamson for swindling him out of thousands of dollars by failing to deliver a crate of stolen silver bullion. Adamson thought of Dunlap as a rich mark, someone he could tap for at least a few hundred or a thousand dollars for "expenses" in exchange for a credible story. When Dunlap realized Adamson had cheated him in the ingot scam and started making death threats, Adamson refused to take them seriously.

Adamson recalled that Dunlap made his first death threat over the ingots late in the first half of 1975. He said he could recall the general date because Fat Fingers owner Dick Trauzone was at the bar during his conversation with Dunlap, which meant that Trauzone had not yet sold the bar to buy a different tavern. Trauzone was an important landmark in Adamson's mental geography because the new bar was The Ivanhoe, situated a dozen blocks south at the Park Central mall. The Ivanhoe would become the closest thing Adamson had to an office. He often met Neal Roberts there when it was inconvenient to meet in Roberts's in-home law office a couple of blocks west. Adamson had known

Roberts for about three years, he said, which was roughly the time he testified against Ned Warren before the federal grand jury in late 1974.

Adamson's accuracy in the details of his confession was the prosecutors' main weapon in the Bolles case. The promise of a twenty-year sentence for a deliberate, cold-blooded murder was a big spur to candor. Prosecutors often reminded him that any lie could lead them to tear up his plea agreement, and the next stop would be death row.

That didn't settle the question. On the important point of his knowledge of Roberts's role in the bombing, Adamson's responses were terse or prepared with the help of prosecutors, who were careful about confining their interest in what he knew about Roberts's involvement in the Bolles case to his conversation with Dunlap at Roberts's home. There is no record that anyone but federal prosecutors asked Adamson about Roberts's role in the murder.

In his questioning, Detective Sellers carefully established that Roberts's conversation with Dunlap took place outdoors in Roberts's yard, and not indoors in his law office. Adamson neither offered nor was asked anything further about Roberts's role.

On other points, Adamson's testimony was detailed and consistent. His description of the hoax of the silver bars, to take one example, was helpful in understanding the relationships among the key conspirators in the Bolles plot. It started when Adamson met an itinerant con man named Doug Damon, who showed him an ingot of what appeared to be silver and its uses as bait for naïve investors.

Adamson met Dunlap at Roberts's office in the summer of 1975, showed him the ingot, and told him he could get more. Dunlap bit hard. "Max wanted to buy a load of silver," Adamson told the closed Tucson hearing courtroom. "Doug was to pick up half the money for the silver up-front. I was to fly to Denver, Colorado, to pick up the silver, drive it back to Phoenix, deliver it to Max Dunlap, you know, in a warehouse, at which point I was to receive the other half of the money to give to Doug." Max gave Damon about "sixteen to eighteen thousand" dollars as a down payment. Damon had no intention of delivering the silver but took the money. He disappeared with it, cheating not only Dunlap but Adamson as well.

SELLERS: So he [Damon] ripped you off, too?

ADAMSON: Correct. So then comes the big problem of a very irate Max Dunlap, who is, first of all, furious with Neal Roberts.

To avoid Dunlap's wrath, Adamson went to Fat Fingers, where he asked Trauzone to call the Del Webb Townhouse and rent a room for him for several nights. After one night's stay, Adamson grew bored and moved out. He returned to the box-sized apartment in a dingy courtyard on North Eleventh Street that he and Mary called home. Two or three days later, Adamson testified, "In the middle of the night, Neal Roberts calls me and is very upset. And he says, 'John, I want you to talk to Max.' And I figured, 'Well, it's going to come sooner or later.' I said, 'I'll talk to him tomorrow.' He says, 'No, I mean right now.'" Then Roberts uttered a barely disguised threat:

> He [Roberts] says, "Mary—you have a nice wife and family," he says. "This guy [Dunlap] is really upset. He's going to do something. I want you to talk to him right now."

The tone of Roberts's remark was unmistakable. He was issuing an order. The moment dramatized a change in the relationship between the two men. Roberts was taking control of Adamson and his crew because the younger man had been careless in handling Dunlap, whose interests overlapped with Roberts's in Lake Havasu City.

> ADAMSON: "Where am I supposed to meet him or get ahold of him?" He [Roberts] said, "Call him at home." I called Max at home and he said for me to meet him at Fat Fingers, which we did. Max and I met at Fat Fingers. Again, Max was furious at being ripped off for money. He had figured out that I was in on the thing, and he said, "I'm going to have you both killed," meaning Doug and myself, and pulled out a large amount of money. "I'm going to leave this in a car at the airport. There is going to be two guys come in from Chicago." "Well," I said, "that's silly."

Adamson brazened his way out of danger by pointing out that he would hardly have agreed to meet with Dunlap if he had been in on the bullion scam. He was flattering Dunlap by implying that, if he had cheated him, he understood that Dunlap would have killed him on sight.

At this, Dunlap backed down. But there would still be a price to pay.

ADAMSON: "Max says: 'You're going to have to kill Doug when you find him.'"
SELLERS: Whenever you [first] approached Max on the silver deal, did you have some bullion to show him?
ADAMSON: I had one bar.
SELLERS: Was it actual silver or phony?
ADAMSON: Phony.

Of Doug Damon's whereabouts, Adamson had only a few rough leads. "Doug at the time was living in Las Vegas, and he was working—he was working a scam in California with a fellow named Bates," Adamson said. Then, from memory, he added a very specific clue. "And I think if you will check out the telephone credit card, 1715277159Q…which I was told was an FBI credit-card number, you might be able to substantiate what I'm telling you."

'KILL BOLLES NOW'

Tempers eventually cooled over the silver-ingot scam. But it wasn't long before Adamson needed cash again. He called Dunlap and told him someone had spotted Doug Damon in Las Vegas and that he was willing to travel to Vegas to kill Damon but needed $300 in expense money. Dunlap gave him $500. On his return, Adamson told Dunlap he couldn't find Damon. It was another shakedown.

It was around this time that tensions renewed between Roberts and Dunlap. Adamson testified that at one point Neal threw Max out of his office. He didn't know why.

In late spring of 1976, Dunlap started talking about a new project, Adamson said. He told Adamson he wanted to see him about killing Don Bolles.

Sellers asked Adamson when the subject of murder first arose.

ADAMSON: The first time it came up—Don Bolles—the first time 'murder' in quotes was mentioned, Don Bolles's name was not brought up. The conversation took place one morning. We met at Neal Roberts's house, and at that time the meeting was for me to meet Don Aldridge, who was going to run for—What did he run for? What did he run for?"

SELLERS: Councilman or something up in the Kingman area.

ADAMSON: OK. Whatever he was running for, he wanted me to meet Don Aldridge, and Max was there on that occasion. Max and I chatted briefly of nothing in particular until we went outside. Oh, I know what it was. He wanted to know if I could get some clothes that would fit Don Aldridge. He needed a wardrobe. At the time, I had access to clothes I—So I asked Don his size and that sort of thing.

SELLERS: Let me ask you a question, John. Who was at that meeting at Roberts's office, you and Don Aldridge, Max Dunlap?

ADAMSON: And Neal Roberts.

SELLERS: Neal Roberts. Anyone else?

ADAMSON: It seems as though I can recall somebody else being there, but I can't tell you who it was. I can't remember who it was, but it seems in the back of my mind that somebody else was there, but I—I don't know who.

SELLERS: Harry Noye?

ADAMSON: I was going to say Harry Noye, but I'm not sure.

Harry Noye and Don Aldridge were business partners with Roberts in the Lake Havasu City real-estate market. Roberts handled the legal affairs of both men in Lake Havasu and Phoenix. It was Noye who, at Roberts's request, found a place for Adamson to hide after the Bolles murder.

SELLERS: OK, OK. And then—so then this conversation between you and Max came up about getting clothes for Don Aldridge.

ADAMSON: That happened outside as we were leaving. Mr. Aldridge was there, and myself and Neal. I think Neal—Neal and Don Aldridge were going someplace. Anyway, it left Max and I alone in Neal Roberts's yard in front there.

SELLERS: It would be in the front yard, not the backyard?

ADAMSON: The front yard as you enter off of Virginia.

SELLERS: Right.

The state's legal construction of this conversation—whether Dunlap initiated the talk of murder inside or outside of the house, in Roberts's yard—would become central to the prosecution's notion of Roberts's culpability in the murder, or lack of it.

ADAMSON: OK, Max asked at that point how much it would cost to have someone killed. And I told him, I said I didn't know at that point. I said, "Who are you talking about?" And he says, "You can't tell Neal anything about this." I said, "I don't plan on telling anybody anything about it. What—I have got to have information if you want an answer." He says, "Neal is very, very close to this individual and word would be back to him and—it would spoil the whole thing, but it's Bruce Babbitt." I said, "Do you want to hit Bruce Babbitt?" And he said, "Yes." And I said, "I don't know." I said, "I—I don't have any idea. Attorney General?" I said there would be a lot of problems. I said—I don't remember if I asked him why or if he volunteered it, but anyway, the reason was that Bruce Babbitt was either at the time or was in the near future going to either investigate or impose strict limitations and control on the liquor industry, which involved Kemper Marley directly.

SELLERS: Did he mention Marley's name?

ADAMSON: Yes, sir. And that he had—that Max had approached Kemper Marley about getting rid of Bruce Babbitt, and he wanted to know how much it would cost. Then he also mentioned, he said, "And there is another fellow that's given Kemper a bad time, too." And then he mentioned King Alphonse. But at that particular meeting, he wanted a price.

SELLERS: OK, so the two names brought up were Bruce Babbitt and King Alphonse.

ADAMSON: Right. So then I went—I went to Jimmy [Robison], I believe. I can't remember if I went to Jimmy and asked him or if I just told him off the top of my head a price. But somewhere in between there, in between the time of that meeting and the next time I talked to him with a price, Bolles's name had been brought up, and a package deal was arrived at, and I believe the—the price was $50,000, I believe, was the price for the three of them, and expenses. That sort of thing.

SELLERS: OK. Did he [Robison], whenever Bolles's name came up, say, "Why Bolles?"

ADAMSON: At that particular time it was—Kemper's name was brought up. And about the racing commission, that he [Bolles] had given Kemper Marley a bad time and that he ought to be killed, that he wanted—that Kemper wanted him killed.

SELLERS: Now, that was my next question. He indicated to you that Kemper Marley wanted him killed?

ADAMSON: That was my understanding.

SELLERS: Did he indicate to you who was paying the $50,000?

ADAMSON: No. He told me that money would be no problem because Kemper had either vast interests or owned banks in Mexico.

A little later, Sellers returned to the theme:

SELLERS: Did you agree to the package deal?

ADAMSON: No, I—I—To be honest with you, I just—I thought it would be another move with Max. I really didn't think it was serious at first. I—Like I say, it didn't—it didn't—I—It didn't carry a lot of weight at that particular time that it was—it was just something else that he brought up and discussed.

SELLERS: OK. So you had one meeting in Neal Roberts's front yard—
ADAMSON: Yes.
SELLERS: About murder for hire.
ADAMSON: (Witness nods his head.)

In Adamson's account, weeks passed that spring of 1976 with no further talk of murder between Dunlap and Adamson. There was one exception. Adamson once again approached Dunlap and asked him for $1,000 in expenses for the Bolles hit. Adamson took the money but never reported back.

Dunlap tracked him down. He wasn't hard to find.

ADAMSON: Max came up to me one day in The Ivanhoe and he said, "Look," he said. "You're responsible for me spending a lot of money." And he said, "I'm tired of it." He says, "This has got to be done soon"— and he was talking about Bolles. He says, "Bolles is going to do something here pretty quick, and we have to get this done." Now, at this point in time, I realized that something was going to happen. Up until this point, I really hadn't planned that anything was going to happen. I had planned at this point that it was going to be another silver move. At one point in time, I can recall meeting Max at The Ivanhoe and him saying, "When is it going to happen? I want to be out of town." I said, "Well, it's going to happen in two weeks." And then I called him and said, "No, Bolles is going to be out of town for two weeks." At this point, I hadn't even made contact with Don Bolles or attempted to have Gail [Adamson's girlfriend] make contact with Don Bolles. So at that point, I still figured it was another move at this point.

But something happened that accelerated planning for the Bolles assassination. "Look, it's got to happen," Dunlap began to insist. Dunlap told Adamson that Bolles was working on something so damaging to Marley that the reporter had to be killed as soon as possible. The "something" was likely the mob record of a Las Vegas casino skim, written by a casino manager, which implicated Marley directly. It identified the rancher in three separate passages as the person whose approval had to be secured in advance whenever skim money was transported from Las Vegas to Phoenix to be laundered through the betting operation at the Phoenix greyhound track. If the diary was authentic, it meant that Marley was a business partner with men in Las Vegas in the collection, laundering, and distribution of part of the Chicago mob's casino skim.

If there was a moment at which the doors began to close behind the participants in the Bolles drama, this was it.

In his talks with Adamson, Dunlap grew increasingly agitated.

ADAMSON: At the one occasion at The Ivanhoe, [Dunlap] said, "Look, it's got to happen," he said. "I want it to happen. It's got to happen. Bolles is working on something, and it's going to occur in about two weeks. He's got to be killed.". . .I realized that if I didn't do it, it was going to be done and, like Max told me, *I knew about it.* . .I realized that it was going to happen whether I did it or somebody else was going to do it.

Adamson *knew about it,* meaning that even if he refused to go along with the murder, he was so deeply implicated that he could not avoid having the other conspirators pin it on him. And if he went through with it, he could be killed afterward to guarantee his silence. It was every assassin's dilemma.

Adamson made a last, desperate gesture. He called a deputy county attorney, Charles Hyder, an acquaintance from an old murder case, and asked to meet him for a drink. (A year later, Hyder would be elected county attorney.) Hyder asked whether it was urgent. He was going out of town. Could it wait? Adamson said, "We'll wait until you get back." But he never called Hyder again. The last door closed behind him.

ROBISON TRICKED INTO CONFESSING

Among the gangsters who haunted the edges of the old Warren gang was a little-known con man named Howard Woodall. Like Warren and Roberts, Woodall was a criminal who knew the underworld of Phoenix real estate. But unlike Warren, he had independent contacts with powerful men in the Chicago

Outfit. He had run cons in Florida and Colorado before he joined the Arizona land fraud, where he succeeded by staying in the shadows of Warren's operation. Even though it was his idea to solicit the promotional letters from Barry Goldwater and Sam Steiger for the Del Rio Sprfings fraud, to take one example, his name never arose in that scandal.

There was a mystery about Woodall's origins. He understood the proper drape of an expensive suit but talked like a street mope—a "dese an' dose" guy who could never recall that the name of Barry Goldwater's best friend was not "Harry Rosenzweiger," as he pronounced it. Still, only the foolish underestimated Woodall. He could out-con his fellow con men and negotiate with hired killers. And when the time came to save his own skin, he shed his mob loyalty as smoothly as a dinner jacket, as when he cooperated with Arizona legislators in their inquiry into land fraud.

As he sat in federal custody, Woodall quickly evolved from a hardened criminal into a cooperative prisoner. He offered to tell the FBI everything he knew. His knowledge of mob lore and his personal relationships with characters involved in the Bolles case might have been enough to get the FBI's attention. At that moment, the FBI was supporting state prosecutors in the murder trials of Robison and Max Dunlap.

Woodall sent word to the FBI that he wanted to share what he knew about the Bolles case. The bureau was not, at first, impressed. Agents recorded the event laconically in a teletype from Phoenix to Washington. "[In] November 1976, a federal prisoner incarcerated at [redacted by FBI] indicated he was present and overheard [redacted] discuss murder of Don Bolles long before the actual killing took place." Woodall refused to say more unless the government granted him a federal parole and dismissed all outstanding warrants against him. When the FBI showed—or feigned—limited interest, Woodall offered to throw in what he knew about the murder of Teamsters president Jimmy Hoffa.

The FBI was under pressure to solve the Hoffa case and was putting together a case summary, the HOFFEX memo, which named leading suspects and motives in the murder of the former Teamsters president. The bureau was grilling federal prisoners with mob backgrounds to turn up investigative leads. How much

Woodall knew about the Hoffa case and the three or four other crimes the FBI questioned him about is impossible to determine from the redacted FBI files. But someone believed that Woodall was a figure of value because of his contacts in the overlapping worlds of the Chicago Outfit and the Phoenix network.

At the start of 1977, the bureau began to take a closer interest in Woodall's offer to share his knowledge of the mob in Arizona, noting that the approaching trial in the Bolles murder was the subject of "extensive and continuous national media coverage." By this time, the trial of James Robison and Max Dunlap had been postponed several times because of judicial challenges and motions for a change of venue, maneuvers that gave investigators more time to develop information. But the FBI continued to be coy with Woodall. It rejected his first offer and came up with a counter: Woodall would return to Phoenix as an informer and find a way to extract a jailhouse confession from Robison. If he succeeded, the FBI would support his application to the federal witness-protection program after he served a minimum sentence and if he remained cooperative in related cases. Woodall took the deal. In February 1977, he was convicted of mail fraud in federal court and sentenced to a maximum of twenty years in a federal penitentiary. The courts allowed the FBI to return him to Phoenix.

In March, the FBI installed Woodall in the Maricopa County Jail, where Robison was awaiting trial. Woodall required a couple of months to cultivate his old associate. At first, the two men acknowledged each other by exchanging a few words during the jail routine. One evening in mid-June, jailers contrived to position Woodall just outside Robison's cell on the pretext that Woodall was waiting for a phone call from his lawyer. Robison's cell had a steel door, but he could see and hear Woodall through a small opening used for passing meals. Robison spoke to Woodall in a voice phlegmy from a bad head cold, Woodall later testified. For the first time, Robison brought up his role in the Bolles killing, including the bombing itself.

Robison described to Woodall how he watched Bolles walk out the back door of the Clarendon Hotel and climb into his new Datsun in the first row of the parking lot. Robison was sitting in his pickup next to an apartment house a safe distance away. He watched Bolles open the driver's door and sit down. Robison was holding a remote radio-control device in both hands. He pressed a button, but the bomb failed to detonate. As the Datsun backed out of the parking space, Robison clambered out of the truck and stabbed at the button. Bolles had just begun to pull forward when the bomb went off.

"[Robison] said he couldn't understand why it didn't blow that little car all over the place," Woodall testified. "He didn't understand why it didn't kill Don Bolles right then." Remorseful over his sloppy workmanship, Robison berated himself for not running a test on the bomb. He speculated that Bolles survived for eleven days after two amputations because the magnets Robison used to attach the dynamite to the Datsun's undercarriage did not hold, and the bomb expended much of its force downward into the macadam surface of the parking lot."

After the explosion, Robison drove to a nearby restaurant and ordered coffee. He stepped into a pay phone and called Adamson at The Ivanhoe, where he and Neal Roberts were waiting to hear from him. Robison told his partner the job was done. Adamson testified later that when he asked Robison whether the bomb had done its work, Robison replied, "Eyeball to eyeball."

Woodall kept a diary to record the details of his talks with Robison. From time to time, Robison would pass him notes. Woodall collected the notes, written in Robison's own hand. In one, Robison complained that Marley had never paid him for his part in the murder, and in another he proposed that he and Woodall write a book together in which they would combine his knowledge of the Bolles case with Woodall's familiarity with Arizona land fraud. Woodall passed everything on to the FBI, which turned it over to state prosecutors for submission as evidence.

Under questioning before the state trial jury, Woodall acknowledged he had told Robison that his sources in the mob said Kemper Marley had put out an offer to pay $100,000 to anyone who would kill Adamson. Years later, a police detective asked the imprisoned Adamson whether he knew of anyone who had tried to kill him. Adamson said he did. "An associate of [Adamson's] by the name of Freddie Fiegle had told him that [Henry] Aleman had a contract on him. Freddie was locked up with Aleman [and] said Aleman told him he was supposed to kill Adamson for people in Chicago. The Chicago people were afraid of something he might say and not something he has already said."

For their testimony, the FBI accepted Woodall and Adamson in the national witness-protection program, Adamson for confessing to the Bolles murder and testifying against his fellow conspirators, and Woodall for tricking Robison into making a confession to him in writing. Adamson served a twenty-year term and was released. Woodall eluded all but about five years of his prison sentence, and his testimony put Robison away for several decades.

WHAT DID GOLDWATER KNOW?

There is little doubt that Barry Goldwater had a direct if covert association with Neal Roberts. What is not clear is what Goldwater might have known, if anything, about Roberts's role in the Bolles murder.

Contemporaneous records cast some light on the relationship between Goldwater and Roberts and what the senator knew about Roberts's participation in the plot. First-person accounts have survived from witnesses who gave independent reports about conversations they had with Roberts or overheard between Goldwater and Roberts around the time of the bombing.

Phoenix police interviewed three women who were on intimate terms with Roberts and in contact with him in late May and early June of 1976. They were Roberts's wife, Antje Samter Roberts; his secretary, Eileen Roberts; and a girlfriend, Kay Kroot. Police also interviewed Max Dunlap.

A fifth witness was Claude Keller, a lawyer who briefly shared space with Roberts in his law office and overheard a raucous telephone conversation between Roberts and Goldwater on the day Bolles was killed and again on the day after. Keller gave his account of the exchange to his colleague, Michael Stuhff.

Taken together, the reports permit a consideration of a critical question: did Barry Goldwater have foreknowledge of the Bolles murder?

Until June 2, the phone conversations between Goldwater and Roberts were frequent and intense, but their intensity seemed related almost entirely to the senator's ongoing preoccupation with removing Navajo President Peter MacDonald from office. The immediate context for the conversations was ongoing political agitation in Window Rock over a $13 million embezzlement of tribal funds. Hundreds of anti-MacDonald activists demonstrated to demand MacDonald's resignation in protests that were organized and publicized in part with the help of Goldwater's operative in the Navajo capital, Joe Patrick. Goldwater's power struggle with MacDonald was coming to a head just as Adamson, Robison, and Roberts were planning the last details of the Bolles murder.

The accounts of the witnesses who either overheard conversations between Goldwater and Roberts or had access to privileged information cover a period starting about two weeks before the bombing on June 2, 1976, and ending the following day. They are given here in chronological order of the events described.

Witness #1
Goldwater called Roberts two weeks prior to Bolles's murder
On June 29, 1976, Max Dunlap called Phoenix police to make this statement. "Approximately two weeks prior to the Bolles incident, he was with Roberts when Roberts was discussing a situation involving the Indian affair on the reservation centering around Peter MacDonald. He said that as a result of this conversation, Neal Roberts told him [Dunlap] that Barry Goldwater had called him and was mad as hell at Peter MacDonald and wanted him off the reservation... Dunlap stated that to his knowledge, Neal Roberts is not a name dropper, and he believed Neal Roberts did in fact receive a phone call from Barry Goldwater." A shorter version of Dunlap's phone call found its way into the *Republic* three months later. Reporter Charles Kelly wrote that Dunlap told him he was at the Roberts compound two weeks before the Bolles murder when Goldwater called Roberts to say "he wanted Peter MacDonald's head."

Witness #2
Goldwater met with Roberts three or four days before Bolles's murder
Sometime over the 1976 Memorial Day weekend, three or four days before the Bolles bombing, Goldwater and Roberts met face-to-face. Dan Barker, a Phoenix homicide detective working on his own time for the Navajo Tribal Council, tracked down a woman who had been dating Roberts for several years,

Kay Kroot, then thirty-seven years old. Barker asked Kroot whether she knew of any meetings between Roberts and Goldwater. She responded that she had a phone call from Roberts during the last week of May in which he said several times that he had to meet with Goldwater that weekend. Roberts's last mention of the meeting was in a call to her on Sunday, May 30, the day before Memorial Day, when he asked for a date. Her impression from the conversation was that by the time of that Sunday call, Roberts and Goldwater had already met. The bomb exploded that Wednesday.

Witness #3
Goldwater called Roberts the day before the Bolles bombing
John P. Frank, a former chairman of the Arizona Democratic Party whose advice Goldwater sought during the Bolles crisis, wrote a memo in which he referred to a conversation between Goldwater and Roberts that was held "on approximately June 1, 1976"—that is, the day before the Bolles bombing— "at which time Senator Goldwater called Roberts and 'said he wanted Peter McDonald's head.'" The witness to this conversation, according to Frank, citing a police report, was Max Dunlap. Frank became involved when Goldwater asked him to write a confidential legal memo on how to respond to questions he might be asked about his relationship with Roberts.

Witness #4
Goldwater called Mr. Roberts three times on June 2
Antje Roberts was the source for a police report in which she referred to three heated phone calls between Goldwater and Roberts on the day Bolles's car was bombed. The report is one of the supporting documents attached to the Navajo *Preliminary Report*. Detective Marcus Aurelius (his real name) interviewed Antje Roberts on June 20 and wrote the report the same day. In Aurelius's highly condensed version, she gave this account of her conversation with her ex-husband:

Barry Goldwater—Close friend of Mr. Roberts. Mr. Roberts was his campaign manager 1964 in Calif. Called Mr. Roberts three times during evening, Wed. 6-2-76 and Thurs. 6-3-76 "excited"——"what the hell's going on, how far is thing going to go, and how much is it going to cost to shut people up." Mr. Roberts admitted being his pay-off man for several years. Reportedly set up and directed Roberts to obtain $25,000 in small bills to pay off Adamson. Since Goldwater was in Good Samaritan Hospital at the time, Roberts obtained the money from Dunlap. All under direction of Kemper Marley.

Witness #5
Goldwater: "What will it take to shut people up?"
Claude Keller, a former director of securities for the Arizona Corporation Commission and a lawyer who had just rented space in Roberts's law office, overheard part of a telephone conversation between Goldwater and Roberts soon after the bombing.

At the time Keller related the anecdote to Stuhff, he was the supervisor of the Navajo Tribal Council legal office. In 1973, *Wall Street Journal* reporter Jonathan Kwitney celebrated Keller for shutting down the Picture Island fraud, an advance-fee scheme linked to Chicago mobster Alex Gaus that operated in Scottsdale in the late 1960s. "Keller was my immediate supervisor," Stuhff recalled. "I went to his office because I was dismayed by [the Arizona state prosecutor's] cavalier treatment" of Roberts's involvement in the Tuba City bomb. Keller described how he had come to Window Rock and the Navajo government. Keller was weary of battling wealthy criminals in securities frauds on the limited budget of a state agency, Stuhff wrote. "He told me that at the time of the bombing, he had just recently begun using an extra office in Neal Roberts's complex...He knew Roberts, but not well, and the terms and location were favorable."

"In the immediate aftermath of the [Bolles] bombing," Stuhff continued, "there was a lot of publicity, of course, but little detail...Claude was aware that Roberts was close to Goldwater. He [Keller] came in to Roberts's office on one occasion after the bombing and heard part of the conversation in which Goldwater was angry and asking, 'How far is this going and what will it take to shut people up?' At that point, Claude said he realized that there was far more than an attorney-client situation…Claude told me, with some trepidation, that he just walked out of the building. He said that he left the diplomas and certificates on the wall. He said he did not yet have any client files or papers that he would have needed to retrieve."

Keller looked around for a job and found the opening for the supervisor's position in the legal department on the Navajo Nation in Window Rock. After the Roberts experience, he wanted to get out of Phoenix and thought the reservation "would be as far removed as he could practically get." Then he realized that "he had just jumped out of the frying pan into the fire."

'YOU DIDN'T THINK I'D DO ANYTHING LESS?'

In 1999, as part of a late attempt to free Max Dunlap from prison, Dunlap's lawyers videotaped a deposition with a woman who worked as an office secretary for Neal Roberts for about six months in 1976. They became intimate. Some years later, after he was unable to care for himself because of his advanced alcoholism, she took him into her home.

Eileen Roberts was, as noted elsewhere, an Englishwoman who coincidentally possessed the same surname but was not related to Neal Roberts. On videotape, she related that Neal had hired her in April 1976 but that she quit the job in October that same year because the publicity over his role in the Bolles bombing led to a decline in his law practice and an inability to pay her salary.

"After three months," she said under questioning, "he became extremely abusive" and "could not control his alcohol intake."

Did he ever mention the bombing?

"Our lives revolved around it," she told Dunlap's lawyers.

Was Roberts involved in the bombing?

She had asked him that very question, Eileen Roberts replied. It was in January 1996, according to her deposition, "a month after I took him into my home." She extended the act of mercy because by this time her former boss was too debilitated to care for himself. He was angry that she had asked him "about his role in the bombing," she said, and became "very profane," calling her "stupid" and "horrible names."

"His answer convinced me he was guilty. I asked him, 'Was it worth it?'"

"He looked at me and smiled like someone who had just won the gold [at the] Olympics and said, 'Someone had to do it. I was at the top of the totem pole. You didn't think I'd do anything less, do you?'"

'GOLDWATER UNDERSTANDS INSULATION'

After he was convicted and sentenced for his part in the Bolles murder, James Robison offered to tell state prosecutors what additional information he had about the role of "certain individuals" in the crime. They turned him down. In August 1978, Robison's lawyer, David G. Erickson, wrote to Assistant Arizona Attorney General William J. Schafer III:

> I have previously stated to you and Jon Sellers of the Phoenix Police Department regarding the murder of Don Bolles and the participation of certain individuals in it. When I first talked to you in June, you said that you did not wish to do anything about it until after the sentencing in the federal case involving the attempted bombing of the Indian Health Services building...In our telephone conversation after the Federal sentence was imposed, you stated that you were not interested in what Mr. Robison had to say nor negotiating the circumstances under which he would make such a statement...

There were at least two people who were interested in what Robison had to say about the Bolles case. One had been Woodall; the other was Michael Stuhff, acting for the Navajo government.

In June 1979, Stuhff interviewed Robison on death row at the state prison in Florence, Arizona. Stuhff asked Robison the question the Navajo Tribal Council most wanted answered: was there a plan to stage a coup against the Navajo government? Yes, Robison said.

> "Robison stated that a plot to institute 'martial law' on the Navajo Reservation did exist and had been implemented," Stuhff wrote. Robison "stated that it involved some of the same people who were

involved in the Bolles homicide. Robison indicated that Goldwater understands 'insulation' and that Neal Roberts is the insulation between the plot and Goldwater. The prosecution in both the Indian Health Service attempted bombing and the Bolles homicide cooperated with Adamson in suppressing Neal Roberts's involvement in both crimes in order to protect the plea agreement, themselves, and prominent Arizona figures who were involved. He characterized the prosecutions as a 'cover up.'"

ADAMSON'S ESCAPE

On June 3, 1976, the day after the white Datsun exploded, Neal Roberts, Max Dunlap, and Harry Noye met at Durant's restaurant. They said later they had assembled to deal with the problem created by Bolles's last words before losing consciousness. He named Adamson and said, "Find him."

At Durant's, the men said, they decided to set up a defense fund for Adamson. A second and related purpose might have been to coordinate alibis. At that moment, police and FBI agents were compiling a chronology of the movements of Adamson and his closest associates, including Roberts. They were concentrating on Adamson's escape to Lake Havasu City, a town on the Colorado River, hours after the car bomb.

One of the first things law enforcement learned was that on June 2, Roberts called a private air-charter service and booked a flight for Adamson and his wife, Mary, to Lake Havasu City for later that night. Then he called Ted Krum, desk manager of the Rodeway Inn, to reserve a room for "Mr. and Mrs. Jim Johnson," telling Krum not to expect them until after midnight or 1:00 a.m.

FBI agents wanted to know the exact time of Roberts's calls to the air-charter company and to Krum. They also wanted to find out why Roberts called Harry Noye, a Roberts client, prominent Lake Havasu City businessman, and owner of the Rodeway Inn. Roberts called Noye right after booking the room for the "Johnsons." The agents learned that Roberts called Noye to ask him to meet the Adamsons at the airport and drive them to the motel. He obliged.

Noye dropped Mary at the front entrance to register and then drove Adamson around to the back. Adamson walked through the rear entrance and joined his wife in Noye's personal suite, Room 444.

By the time Adamson awoke in the Rodeway the next morning, his name was already circulating in the news media. He was now an at-large murder suspect. When reporters later asked Roberts why he'd booked the Adamsons on the flight to Lake Havasu City, he responded that his client had been "in fear of his life." He would give no further explanation. When there was nothing to be gained by remaining in Lake Havasu City, Roberts told Adamson to return to Phoenix.

Noye would become important to the case because he vouched to authorities for Roberts's account of the timing of his June 2 phone calls to Lake Havasu City. Because Noye vouched for Roberts's alibi, a closer look at his association with Noye and the Rodeway Inn is necessary.

Noye controlled the Rodeway property through a private shell corporation named the Apollo Development Company, organized in Seattle. Upon incorporation, it issued one million shares, which served as collateral on loan applications to banks and mortgage companies, including the State Bank of Havasu, Great Western Bank of Phoenix, and Metropolitan Mortgage of New York. The three lenders put up more than $3 million for construction of the 175-room motel. After the motel faced financial problems, Roberts filed a loan application for $4 million to the Small Business Administration. He cited the energy crisis of 1973 as the cause for the Rodeway's losses. The application was discovered among Barry Goldwater's personal papers at the Arizona Historical Foundation, with no record of whether the SBA approved it, although one source said it was. Whatever the outcome, Noye seemed grateful. In 1975, he gave Roberts a two-year-old gold Cadillac.

ROBERTS FINDS A SAFE HOUSE

A week after the meeting at Durant's, Neal Roberts drove into Lake Havasu City with a pair of FBI agents on his tail. Both parties had similar missions. The agents were investigating the circumstances of Adamson's flight from Phoenix on the day the Bolles bomb exploded. Roberts was there to shore up the alibi he had devised for Adamson in which he claimed his client fled to Havasu "in fear of his life."

First to arrive was Roberts and a companion. After driving west from Phoenix during the early morning hours, Roberts pulled into the Rodeway Inn parking lot at 5:15 a.m. on June 9. His companion was Arlene Lyons, president of the Apollo Development Company. She was also one of Roberts's longtime girlfriends. Roberts was driving a car he had given to Lyons, a blue Lincoln Continental with a white hardtop. Ted Krum registered the guests into Room 444, the same suite John and Mary Adamson had checked into.

The same morning FBI Special Agents Laird L. Hiestand and Mark William Kennedy arrived in Lake Havasu to investigate Adamson's flight there. One of their first interviews was with Krum. They asked Krum at what hour on June 2 Roberts had telephoned him to reserve the room for "Jim Johnson" and his wife.

"On June 2, 1976," the agents reported, "Krum received a telephone call on his private telephone line from Roberts. The time of the telephone call is not certain in Krum's mind, but he does know that it was received in the morning of the second of June. Krum normally arrives for work at the Rodeway around seven a.m. and did so on the day in question. Krum then stated that he is sure the call from Roberts did not arrive between seven or eight a.m., nor between eight and nine a.m. and, therefore, must have come between nine and ten a.m. on June 2, 1976. Krum reiterated that although he is not entirely sure as to the exact hour of the call, he is fairly certain that it arrived between nine and ten a.m., and he is sure without a doubt that the call from Roberts arrived in the morning."

The exact hour of Roberts's call to reserve the Rodeway room was, of course, vital to establishing Roberts's role in the case. James Robison hit the trigger on the bomb at 11:34 a.m. With one assertion of fact, Krum could simultaneously and unwittingly blow up Roberts's alibi and implicate him in a murder.

The next day, the FBI men returned to the Rodeway Inn to reinterview Krum. He told them after the agents left. he received a phone call from his boss, Harry Noye. Noye wanted to know what Krum had told the FBI.

"Krum stated to Noye," Hiestand and Kennedy reported, "that the inter-viewing agents were concerned with the time at which a reservation had been made for Jim Johnson. Krum told Noye that Neal Roberts had made the reser-vation sometime between nine a.m. and ten a.m. on June 2, 1976."

Noye then told Krum that he must have been mistaken because Noye had spoken with Neal Roberts after the Phoenix Suns–Boston Celtics basketball game on June 2, 1976, about 9:00 p.m., twelve hours later.

"Krum was then asked by the interviewing agents which version of the time of the telephone call from Neal Roberts was the correct one," that is, the one he had given to them earlier or Noye's recollection. "Krum stated that after speaking with Noye, he was not sure of the time of the call from Neal Roberts." Then the manager returned to his original statement. "Krum believes his initial recollection of the call arriving from Roberts may still be correct."

Sixteen months later, the matter would be brought up at the murder trial of Max Dunlap and James Robison. Dunlap's attorney called to the stand Rex Asderberg, public-affairs manager for Mountain Bell. Asderberg brought along Roberts's subpoenaed phone records. The Mountain Bell records showed that Roberts placed the June 2 call to the Rodeway Inn at 6:55 a.m.—three hours and thirty-nine minutes before the Bolles bomb exploded.

Paul Smith, Dunlap's lawyer, told the jury during his opening statement that he would prove that Roberts "engineered" the bombing and arranged for a safe house for John Adamson in Lake Havasu after the deed was done. Smith presented the phone records, but they stirred no interest among the authorities, and the best evidence of Roberts's role as a coconspirator subsided into the silt of a million other facts forgotten or ignored in the Bolles case.

A Peculiar Immunity

In 2011, Robert Blair Kaiser and Don Devereaux reported an extraordinary dis-covery. Phoenix police knew about Roberts's incriminating 6:55 a.m. phone call from the earliest days of the investigation. "[Detective Jon] Sellers found telephone records that proved Roberts was making calls to Lake Havasu on the morning of June 2," Kaiser and Devereaux reported in their book, *Desert Injustice.*

Why did police fail to arrest and charge Roberts when they found his phone records? Kaiser and Devereaux, apparently quoting Sellers, described it as an excess of caution. "Sellers waited...for Roberts to make a dumb move. Roberts made a smart one. The day after Bolles died, he hired John Flynn, the state's most celebrated criminal lawyer, so Flynn could negotiate immunity for him." The deal was cut before the meeting between Flynn and County Attorney Moise Berger. Berger would soon leave Phoenix for exile in California after his role in protecting land-fraud king Ned Warren was exposed.

The grant of immunity is surprising in light of the fact that Roberts's 6:55 a.m. phone call to Lake Havasu was known to police within days and perhaps hours after the Bolles bomb exploded.

It remains a mystery why the Phoenix police, who possessed direct evidence that Roberts was at the very least an active coconspirator, did not arrest him on the spot, on their own authority.

More surprising was County Attorney Moise Berger's bizarre decision to offer Roberts immunity before he opened his mouth. Equally odd were the two conditions attached to the immunity: he was obliged to tell prosecutors everthing he knew about the murder, and the immunity could be revoked if he lied.

The first condition collapsed right away. Rather than tell prosecutors what he knew about the killing, Roberts proposed a "theory" about its motive. Kemper Marley, one of the state's wealthiest landowners, wanted Bolles killed because he was angry about the reporter's assertions in news stories that a conflict of interest might disqualify Marley from serving on a state board. "Kemper was out of money, but if he got the appointment to the racing commission, all that would be solved," Roberts told prosecutors. Just how the racetracks would provide such a large flow of cash to the wealthy Marley was not explained, and the Berger either did not bother to ask Roberts about the source or the amount of the money or withheld the information from Roberts's statement when it was made public. It made little difference in any case because no evidence was offered beyond anecdotes of the sort that might have been collected at The Ivanhoe. The second condition—that Roberts's immunity would be rescinded if he lied—was never tested. Roberts was never permitted to give further evidence in the case, even when he made an offer.

The Roberts immunity remained a point of embarrassment to state officials. Arizona Attorney General Bruce Babbitt, before he took control of the case, said the agreement was "disastrous" but did not explain further. William J. Schafer III, who became Babbitt's top prosecutor in the Bolles case, told Kaiser and Devereaux he did not believe the immunity was valid but that unnamed others had bound him to it. "I have always disputed the fact that Roberts had immunity in the murder. But I could never force a ruling," Schafer said. "We couldn't talk to him."

FEDS: ADAMSON IMPLICATED ROBERTS

In 1982, Michael Stuhff retrieved a document from the FBI titled "Synopsis," dated February 18, 1977, which summarized the events of January in the Bolles case, including Adamson's plea agreement with the state. One of the few legible paragraphs in its heavily redacted five hundred pages let slip some closely held information that put the state's "yard theory" of Roberts's involvement in Bolles's murder in a new light:

> In return for the grant of immunity, Adamson was allowed to plead to a second-degree murder charge in return for his testimony implicating subject Roberts and a third individual *[The Justice] Department has immunized Adamson in captioned case for his testimony implicating Roberts and Robison*, whom he implicated, along with himself, in captioned matter. Federal charges filed against Roberts and Robison 2/14/77. [Emphasis added.]

What the "captioned matter" was, precisely, it is impossible to tell. The caption was also partly blacked out by the FBI. But the meaning was clear enough because there was only one murder case in which all three men were involved. Clearly, Adamson's description of Roberts's role in the murder had to have been considerably more detailed than the "yard theory" to knock down the murder charge against him from the first to the second degree, thus saving him from the death penalty. Yet it is Adamson's description of Roberts's role in the murder, the undergirding of Adamson's plea agreement, that is missing from the public record, apart from this single allusion, itself apparently an oversight of the federal censor.

'HE JUST HUNG OUT WITH THE WRONG PEOPLE'

In the received and official view of Arizona law enforcement, Neal Roberts had nothing to do with the Bolles murder and possessed no direct knowledge of it. An authoritative example of this view was presented in a public lecture in 2006 and rebroadcast on Arizona public radio. William Schafer explained why the state had not sought to develop evidence against Roberts, and it had nothing to do with immunity.

> I never talked to Neal Roberts about immunity. That was done by, I think, someone from the County Attorney's Office. And it was never consummated. He just never got it. And there was no reason to give it to him...
>
> Neal Roberts never really had anything to do with Max Dunlap's case. And that's another question I get. Somebody's probably going to ask this, "Why wasn't Neal Roberts charged?" Well, there was nothing to charge him with. And Adamson even said, "I never told Neal Roberts. And the conversation I had with Dunlap when he offered me the job was outside of Neal Roberts's house." Maybe he did that on purpose. But there was nothing to tie Neal Roberts in except he was an associate of all these guys.

Schafer's reference was to Adamson's description of the way Dunlap approached him to arrange the Bolles murder. The critical moment, in the state's view, occurred not in Roberts's compound but outside—"in the front yard, not the backyard," as Adamson testified. It was a distinction Sellers carefully elicited from Adamson in the Tucson hearing. This critical distinction between Roberts's two yards was the beginning and the end of official curiosity and questioning about the lawyer's role in the crime.

Schafer described the scene this way. "One morning in 1976, when he was entering Roberts's office complex, Dunlap pulled [Adamson] aside and told him he had a job for him. He said a man named Kemper Marley...had been badly hurt by an article by Don Bolles and that he would like to have him killed."

For Schafer, the fact that the conversation was held outside the law offices, the "yard theory," was proof enough that Roberts knew nothing of the murder plot. His only infraction was in making injudicious friendships. "He [Roberts] seemed to use to like to rub elbows with these guys. You know, there's people like that, who really like to rub elbows with those dirty people, yes?"

In reply to a question, Schafer elaborated, saying that Adamson never implicated Roberts. "If you go on Adamson, there was no Neal Roberts there at all. Nice-looking guy, everybody said, 'Very good lawyer.' I didn't know him as a lawyer. He just hung out with the wrong people."

'I COULD GIVE YOU OTHER NAMES'

The official lack of interest in Roberts was clarified with the discovery of a memo in the files of the Arizona Attorney General, written in 1989 by lead investigator George Weiss, that referred to two important conversations between Sellers and Roberts that took place two years after Roberts was granted immunity. On the tape, Roberts offered to come forward to tell what he knew without the benefit of immunity.

After listening to two tape cassettes of the eleven-year-old conversation between Roberts and Sellers, Weiss wrote the following summary:

Follow-up, 9/20/89

On 9/14/89, approximately 11:15 hours, I [Weiss] met Jon Sellers at the State Fairgrounds Office at the Coliseum...Sellers gave me two [audio] cassette tapes which he said consisted of two conversations he said he had with Neal Roberts, labeled "6/27/78, Neal Roberts." According to Sellers, the tapes consisted of conversations in which Roberts offers to talk to the Attorney General's Office about the Bolles case and agrees to do so in a three-step process. Sellers says that in the first step, Roberts is willing to sit down and talk without a grant of immunity and not wanting anything in return. This offer was made at Helsing's restaurant. Sellers says he is willing to pass the offer on to Bill Schafer.

Telephone conversations, according to Sellers, consist of Sellers talking to Roberts after Schafer has refused to meet with Roberts. Sellers recalls that after he brought this information to Schafer, Schafer subsequently told Sellers that he, Schafer, would not meet with Roberts. When Sellers asked why not, Schafer reportedly said something to the effect that "Bob," indicating Bob Corbin, did not want to have it done.

On 9/19/89, I [Weiss] asked Bob Corbin if he recalled this incident and what transpired between Schafer and him on this issue. Corbin says that he does not recall being told anything about Roberts's desire to talk and notes that he did not take office as attorney general until January 1979, six months after the Roberts-Sellers conversation. Corbin says his only conversation with Schafer regarding the possibility of Roberts talking was a general discussion about the legitimacy of the immunity granted to Roberts in the early stages of the case. The attorney general in June 1978 was Jack LaSota, and LaSota is mentioned by Roberts in the second tape as someone to get clearance from regarding a possible need for immunity. (Attachments: two interviews between Sellers and Roberts.)

Sellers referred to the tape recordings in almost wistful tones during an interview with a reporter in 1999. "At one point, I met with Neal at the old Helsing's coffee shop and tape-recorded him saying that he could 'give you other names' in exchange for immunity," Sellers said. "I took the tape to the AG's office, and it died there. I don't know what it all means to this day."

Chapter 8

THE CASINO-SKIM DIARY—
KEMPER MARLEY

The last thing Bolles said was, "Emprise...the Mafia...John Adamson...Find him," and his fellow journalists preserved an almost mystical belief that these seven words contained all the clues necessary to find the person who blew up Don Bolles on a June morning in 1976. This belief prevailed even though it was far from clear what connections joining John Adamson to the Mafia and the Mafia to the Emprise Corp could have led to such a moment. In his own investigation, Bolles had found little more than a receding historical association between the Detroit-Cleveland mob and the greyhound dog track in Phoenix.

Apart from the promise of a cash payment for the two men who handled the bomb, the state never established a clear motive for either. The third man, Max Dunlap, was said to be a courier who acted out of a sense of loyalty to his mentor, Kemper Marley. *The Arizona Republic* accepted the idea that Marley was the man behind the murder and agreed in some respects with Neal Roberts's theory. Marley was said to be angry over Bolles's reporting because it had cost him an appointment to the state racing commission. Bolles wrote that Marley had a conflict of interest because he sold liquor to the same horse and dog tracks he would be regulating as a commissioner. But revenge on this scale over a few newspaper articles seemed disproportionate. Why would someone as rich and powerful as Marley care about an appointment to a minor state-regulatory agency?

Still, Bolles's last words really are clues to his killers' motives. They take on a different significance if we consider that Marley, in a very specific sense, *was* Emprise and the Mafia. He had a direct connection to the Phoenix Greyhound Track and the Detroit-Cleveland Combination, which managed the biggest Las Vegas casinos through Morris (Moe) Dalitz, owner of the Stardust Resort and Casino and a friend to many at the top levels of the Phoenix network.

There was a specific connection. John Adamson had worked for Marley at one time. The old rancher paid him to keep an eye on his interests at the greyhound track. The relationship between the two men is recorded in a report on an "unauthorized purge"—actually, a theft by insiders—of Phoenix police-intelligence files.

Marley's relationship with the Las Vegas casino mob had a surprising dimension, a business tie between Marley and the Stardust that revealed a deeper motive in the Bolles murder. In 1978, the FBI acquired an internal Mafia financial journal that implicated Marley in the Las Vegas "skim," or money-laundering operation. According to witnesses who spoke to Bolles shortly before his death, the reporter got a tip about a so-called Mafia ledger showing that Marley was the gatekeeper to a casino-skim operation that laundered cash from the Stardust and other casino slot machines.

In 1982, the document surfaced in Arizona, when Marley filed a civil lawsuit against Investigative Reporters and Editors in which he claimed the journalists' association had libeled him in its 1977 *Arizona Project* report. An unnamed source in the FBI handed to James Henderson, the lead defense attorney for IRE and a longtime lawyer for *The Arizona Republic*, a copy of the document before the trial started.

The FBI and police referred to the document as "the Ledger" or more often "the DeNono Papers" after Gerard DeNono, the person who discovered it. For the sake of clarity, it will be referred to here as the casino-skim diary or the slots diary. Its authenticity is not beyond doubt. But nearly all of the analysts in the FBI and in state and local law enforcement in Arizona, California, and Utah, and journalists who have examined it closely, generally agree that it's an authentic record of the illegal coin skim taken from slot machines at the Stardust Hotel and eight other Las Vegas casinos over a fifteen-month period from 1972 and 1973.

The FBI learned a great deal about the operation of the casino skim from 1960 to the mid-1980s, a period of bitter struggle between the Mafia and the US government but finally won by the federal forces. At stake were millions of dollars in tax-free profits, much of which had been diverted into real estate, drug deals, and payoffs.

News of the government's discovery of a large Las Vegas skim operation first reached the public late in 1963 on the front page of *The New York Times*, which boosted the story with a series of eight jackhammer headlines. The editors rejected the mob's dairy metaphor in favor of its own invention, "black money." When the reader's eye worked through the stack of headlines and fell on the first paragraph, the language was no less sweeping. "The huge earnings of Nevada's legal gambling industry have created a new force in American life, a force with a hidden impact so great that it is of deep concern to top law-enforcement officials throughout the nation." The phrase *black money* might have caught on, and the national press might have taken up the story, if not for its timing. It ran on November 18, four days before the assassination of President John F. Kennedy in Dallas.

An idea of how the skim worked and the amount of money involved can be found in a federal indictment of Meyer Lansky in 1970. According to prosecutors, Lansky's end of the skim from a single casino, the Flamingo, amounted to $36 million during the 1960s. It was distributed around the country by Mafia couriers flying out of Las Vegas to cities around the Midwest in satchels stuffed with $100,000 in bills. The couriers traveled to Kansas City, Milwaukee, Cleveland, and Chicago, where they turned the cash over to mob bosses who were silent partners in the Mafia casinos. They also flew to Miami to see Lansky, who set up a complicated system of laundering hot money through Swiss banks using sophisticated couriers who were trained to handle any emergency. They carried as much as a quarter-million dollars apiece for deposit in numbered accounts hidden by Swiss tax laws through corporations nested like Russian dolls, each owning another through legally untraceable connections. Some of the money went to payoffs in the highest circles of politics. One of Lansky's couriers, Benjamin Siegelbaum, made sure a share went to Washington insider Bobby Baker, an intimate of Senate Majority Leader Lyndon Johnson.

TRANSLATING THE SKIM DIARY

The casino diary was kept in a kind of shorthand of abbreviations that could be read and understood only by someone with a close knowledge of casino financial operations. It was a weekly record written in a fine, looping hand, suggesting that it was dictated and used to prompt the memory of someone already familiar with the transactions. Crucially, the diary indentifies the participants in the laundering scheme by name or in shorthand. Kemper Marley is identified by his last name in three entries that appear to record the fact that he had given his formal approval to coin laundering at the Emprise greyhound track in Phoenix.

Marley's name first appears early in the diary's second entry, which records the coin skim from the Stardust on Jan. 15, 1972.

> 1-15-72
> Local 226—Al Bram—OK Hot Springs Corp. Shen OK—K. Marley—(Funk) Emprise Phoenix pu Tony S. to Chi pd (met with (Chi) on Dogs Arz (Emp) pts Chi pd Shen) Stardust—Slots to Dogs pd.
> [In the right margin, these numbers appear:]
> 1,—
> 115,—

Most of the entries are annotated in a translation and analysis written by FBI agent and historian of the Mafia, William F. Roemer Jr. He wrote the following about the Jan. 15 entry:

> That Al Bramlet, business agent of Culinary Local Union 226, loaned one million dollars to Murrieta Hot Springs resort near San Diego, which was authorized by Morris Shenker.
> That Kemper Marley (Phoenix millionaire) and the Funk Brothers (from dog tracks) had something to do with the Emprise Corporation from Phoenix furnishing one million dollars to Tony Accardo Chicago Mob Boss thru his bagman Tony Spilotro.
> Also that a meeting took place with Chicago Mob people and thru Morris Shenker skim money, $115,000, from the Stardust was

furnished to Arizona Dog interest [sic] for unknown reasons. Possibly bribes or to further the establishment of dog racing in Nevada.

In all, the diary records thirty instances of transporting coins, three of them to the Phoenix Greyhound Park, then held in a majority interest by Emprise and in a minority interest by the Funk family of Phoenix. The diary shows that the casinos alerted Kemper Marley in advance of any shipment of coins to the Phoenix track and that he was given a 5 percent commission. The resulting clean money, in currency, was sent on to Tony Accardo, boss of the Chicago mob, and to other national mob leaders according to the number of "points" they held as owners of the various casinos. This procedure is alluded to in the entry for January 27, 1972:

> Emprise pts to Chi T.A, Slots to Dogs to Chi Marley OK. Moe OK pts—dogs—Stardust coins—OK

If these entries were accurate descrption of the transactions, Marley's motivation in the Bolles case ran deeper than a series of articles on his conflict of interest in selling liquor to racetracks, and he really did have income at stake in acquiring some administrative control over the dog tracks. According to the entry for January 15, 1972, the Stardust ran $115,000 in silver through the Phoenix track's coin counters from the preceding week. At the mob's standard 5 percent laundering fee, Marley's payoff for approving that transaction would have been $5,750.

Skeptics of the idea that Las Vegas slot machines could be skimmed by laundering coins have objected that their sheer weight and the difficulty of transporting them under the noses of Nevada Gaming Control made the practice unrealistic. However, a former FBI agent dispelled this idea by describing how the Stardust slot manager in this period, Jay Vandermark, turned casino coins into banknotes through an internal casino system he called "unauthorized auxiliary banks."

Vandermark revolutionized the coin skim by using sensitive electronic scales to weigh the coins that remained in the slot machines as house winnings after payouts. He weighed the winning coins twice. The first count determined their actual weight and value for internal recordkeeping. Vandermark then removed the coins intended for the skim—the untaxed portion, usually about one-third—and flipped a switch to record the second, lower weight. That count would be reported to the Internal Revenue Service for tax purposes.

After setting aside the skimmed coins and falsifying the records, Vandermark returned the remaining two-thirds of the coins to the casino for recirculation. He moved the skimmed coins to the unauthorized auxiliary banks, whose existence was unknown to government inspectors. The coins sat in the banks awaiting a weekly pickup for transporting and laundering. One of the destinations for the Stardust coins was the Phoenix greyhound racetrack.

Through telephone taps on Moe Dalitz in the 1960s, the FBI learned that nearly every casino gambling operation in Las Vegas skimmed each of its operations at about 33 percent. The slots diary shows that in 1972, the skim from coin operations in nine casinos yielded about $800,000 a week. Because $10,000 in quarters weighs almost exactly ten pounds, a truck or a small cargo trailer to haul that much money would require load capacity of no more than 800 pounds, well below the limit for most pickup trucks.

How the FBI Found the Diary

The origin story of the skim diary belongs to a mob associate and convicted felon, Gerard DeNono, who said he stole it from the floor safe of Edward "Marty" Buccieri, a made member of the Chicago Outfit. Buccieri himself appears frequently in the diary as someone important enough to be entrusted with reporting skim transactions over the phone to Meyer Lansky in Miami.

Buccieri died one evening in 1975 after finishing his shift as a pit boss at Caesar's Palace. He climbed into the front seat of his car in the Caesar's parking lot. Someone was waiting in the backseat with the traditional .22-caliber silenced handgun. Buccieri died before he could turn the key.

Sometime early in 1978, in the course of arresting DeNono on a traffic stop, a Utah highway patrolman learned that DeNono was wanted on a Las Vegas warrant. The patrolman also discovered that DeNono had in his possession "a ledger of mob activities." The agent, Wayne Wickizer, passed the ledger on to the FBI, where it was examined and ignored. A frustrated Wickizer, after he had moved on to become a special agent with the Utah Attorney General's Office, asked the bureau to return the ledger. It arrived in the mail one day in September 1978, one vinyl-bound green ledger with five pages of notes written by an agent named Bender.

Wickizer had contacts in California law enforcement and turned to Daniel H. Bultman of the California Department of Justice Organized Crime and Criminal Intelligence Branch for help in analyzing the diary, including any traces of physical evidence. Wickizer drove to San Diego with the diary and met with Bultman on Oct. 16, 1978. Bultman's analysis followed in February 1979. "Although the authorship of the ledger remains unknown and laboratory tests have so far failed to link the document itself to known OC [organized crime] figures," Bultman wrote, "the correlation between the ledger and previously confirmed intelligence data indicates that it is genuine." Although Bultman later developed doubts, his initial findings reflected those of most other analysts.

By 1979, the FBI was sending copies of the diary to journalists and making DeNono available to the press. Columnist Jack Anderson wrote about it in some detail in August 1978. Reporter Jerry Seper described it in *The Arizona Republic* in August 1980, and in 1984, the BBC interviewed DeNono for an affiliate with outlets in American television.

Seper learned of the diary from a confidential source in law enforcement. He told his editors that his source was puzzled by the inclusion of Kemper Marley's name and believed it discounted the idea that the ledger was a forgery. Seper wrote in an in-office memo:

How did he [the ledger writer] know about Kemper Marley? [Quoting the source:] "For that one name, I tend to believe the ledger probably was not the invention of this guy [DeNono]. It seems that the inclusion of Marley's name in the ledger is very unusual." The source said California authorities did not place any particular importance on the Marley name until they happened to run across it in connection with the Don Bolles murder. They do not have much information on Marley. The source said authorities from Arizona, and the clear indication was the Phoenix PD, have expressed an interest in the ledger. "They're aware of it," the source said. "Actually, they now have a copy of it."

Phoenix police had been in possession of a copy of the diary since at least the spring of 1978, seventeen months before Seper's source described it to him. On March 28 of that year, a Phoenix homicide detective working on the Bolles case wrote a blind memo to an unnamed recipient, with no date and no signature. Even references to two other analysts of the diary in other law-enforcement agencies were recorded as rows of *X*s. The Phoenix analyst, Detective Andy Watzek, was deeply interested in the three mentions of Marley's name. "It should be noted," he wrote, "that in early 1972 [the first mention of Marley], very little was known of Kemper Marley or any of his clandestine dealings, and there was no public information concerning Marley having any dealings with Las Vegas business enterprises or the Emprise Corporation.

"The information contained in these entries that refer to Kemper Marley and the Emprise Corporation points or percentages going to the dog-racing interest was never uncovered by investigating agencies or news sources. Thus, it would be known only by someone on the inside," Watzek concluded.

WHAT DID MARLEY KNOW?

Was Kemper Marley aware of the existence of the diary or suspect someone was leaking it or its contents to Bolles? Oddly, this question never appears in the analyses of the diary dated after the murder. There is indirect evidence in Adamson's description in his January 1977 statement in Tucson about Dunlap's increasingly insistent demands that Adamson speed up his plans for the assassination. In May 1976, in Adamson's account, after Dunlap discovers that little actual planning has been done, he confronts Adamson at The Ivanhoe and complains that he has paid Adamson thousands of dollars in advance for expenses and wants action.

ADAMSON: Max came up to me one day in The Ivanhoe, and he said, "Look, you're responsible for me spending a lot of money." And he said, "I'm tired of it." He says, "This has got to be done soon"—he was talking about Bolles. He says, "Bolles is going to do something here pretty damn quick, and we have to get this done."

I can recall meeting Max at The Ivanhoe and him saying, "When is it going to happen? I want to be out of town."

And again, soon afterward, Dunlap said, "Look, it's got to happen…Bolles is working on something, and it's going to occur in about two weeks. He's got to be killed."

'Hell of a Lot of Skimming from Vegas'

As we have seen, Bolles's years of investigation of the Phoenix greyhound track and its possible connections to organized crime ended mostly in frustration. He was taken off the investigative beat and reassigned to the statehouse after the racetrack owners filed a successful libel suit against the newspaper. For the newspaper, it was perhaps the biggest legal setback since the publisher's loss of a libel suit to former Arizona Attorney General Wade Church. Bolles made the best of his reassignment to the state legislature, but in late May, he seemed suddenly reenergized. In the weeks before June 2, Bolles told a few friends and coworkers that he had learned something important that was connected to Las Vegas money laundering. To track it down, he was planning a trip to San Diego.

A Bolles friend, Kathy Kolbe, wife of a prominent columnist for *The Phoenix Gazette*, described her conversation with Bolles to *Wall Street Journal* reporter John R. Emshwiller. "He outlined a complex story involving the Mafia, Emprise, racetracks, and some sort of skimming operation, she says, though she no longer remembers the specifics of all he said. He told her of an imminent trip to San Diego to get information for the story…Ms. Kolbe says that right after the murder, she tried in various ways to tell the police of what she knew. 'But the police never interviewed me,' she says."

A Bolles coworker, *Republic* medical reporter Julian DeVries, told investigators he ran into Bolles in a supermarket at First Street and Indian School Road on June 1, the day before the car bomb. "Bolles was buying some things, and he seemed very elated and excited, and I asked him what was new," DeVries told an investigator. He quoted Bolles directly: "Oh, boy, I wish I could tell you but—Marley. There's a hell of a lot of skimming from Las Vegas going on and—I'm gonna shut up. I told you too much already." It was going to be, Bolles told DeVries, "a terrific story."

In his Tucson statement in 1977, Adamson testified that Dunlap told him it was Marley who wanted the murder. Years later, before he was released from prison, Adamson said he had concluded that Marley wanted Bolles dead to prevent him from finding the skim diary. In 1990, Joe Koretski, an investigator for the Arizona Attorney General's Office, filed a report about a meeting Adamson had with DeNono while both men were in custody in an unnamed federal protective facility in San Diego:

> Adamson stated he now thinks the reason Bolles was going to San Diego was the Las Vegas diary. He said that he [Adamson] did not know anything about the diary or the people mentioned in it in 1976, but that in 1979, while he was in the federal prison there [in San Diego], he met Gerry DeNono. Denono told him about the diary, where and how he got it, and told him what was in it. Adamson stated that he never saw the diary, DeNono just told him about it. He further stated that he advised Assistant US Attorney Ray Jennings and [Detective] Lonzo McCracken about what DeNono had said and suggested they look at it.

THE PURGE OF PHOENIX POLICE FILE #851

Why was Detective Andy Watzek so cautious? Why was the Phoenix police detective determined that no identifiers, including names of other analysts in out-of-state law-enforcement agencies, be identified in his memo on the skim diary? Was it a professional risk to take an official interest in Kemper Marley? The answer came in the form of a scandal remembered in the Phoenix Police

Department as the purge of File #851, when someone stole sensitive intelligence files related to the Bolles case. The thefts occurred in September 1976, three months after the bombing.

Police administrators said they first learned of the thefts on May 11, 1979, the day after a sergeant in the organized-crime bureau, Jack Weaver, suddenly quit the department. It was Weaver who ordered the "unscheduled purge," as administrators called it. Three days after Weaver cleaned out his desk and left the station for the last time, police brass ordered an internal investigation.

The case was a tangle from the start. Weaver claimed he had ordered the purge at the direction of Lt. Glen Sparks. Sparks denied it. As soon as Weaver left the building, Detective Harry Hawkins stepped forward. Hawkins informed his boss, Detective Mike Butler, that it was he who purged File #851 on direct orders from Weaver.

Weaver was an unusual officer, a cop whose behavior suggested that he was too powerful to fire. When he resigned, he and two partners, one of whom was also a member of the organized-crime bureau, decided to go into business for themselves. In September 1978, they formed a corporate partnership and leased a bar at 32nd Street and Washington Avenue called Guys and Dolls. It was an odd choice for cops on the organized-crime beat. For one thing, it was a favorite nightspot for Joseph "Buddy" Tocco. From time to time, Tocco was joined by guests from New York who were under investigation for buying up bars in Arizona through straw purchasers. In 1987, an FBI source told Joe Koretski that Weaver was fronting for Tocco in buying the bar and that Tocco "paid him a quarter million dollars in cash."

When they re-opened the bar after remodeling, Weaver and his partners renamed the place Villa de Margarita. To celebrate, they invited old friends from the department to a grand opening. About a dozen officers, including members of the organized-crime unit, showed up. They found themselves staring over their drinks at what the *Republic* called "local hoodlums," which is to say, some of the same people they spent their days watching.

Weaver's departure from the police force marked the beginning of the purge scandal, not the end. After Hawkins admitted on May 15 that Weaver told him to hide File #851, the internal investigation began in earnest. For a month, nothing happened. In mid-June, it was announced that four officers, including the principal detective in the Bolles case, Jon Sellers, would lead an investigation into the file purge. On June 14, the second day of the probe, Detective Andy Watzek informed Butler, one of the investigators, that as Weaver was cleaning out his desk on May 14, he handed Watzek several index cards containing information on John and Mary Adamson and Kemper Marley. Weaver told him to "hang on to these until after Bolles," Watzek said, meaning until the Bolles homicide was closed.

On June 26, the investigative team interviewed Jack Weaver. Two weeks later, on July 13, the team ordered a "complete review of the entire file system of the organized-crime bureau" to find every file that mentioned John Adamson. The idea was to determine whether any of those files remained unindexed.

On July 16, Butler wrote an eighteen-page memo to Police Captain Jerry Kimmel and sent a copy to the chief prosecutor for the state in the Bolles case, William Schafer. Butler said some material in File #851 had been "inadvertently deleted by himself." He described the four files as 1) a twenty-six-page business history of the Jacobs family of Buffalo and its relation to Emprise; 2) an intelligence report dated June 24, 1975, on the Arizona Racing Commission; 3) an intelligence report dated June 20, 1972, also on the racing commission, and 4) an intelligence report dated June 3, 1971, that identified a contract held by the City of Phoenix with SportsService (formerly Emprise). Two additional and unidentified files were still missing.

Soon after, Butler wrote a memo to Schafer as the sole recipient. "Attached and made part of this memo," Butler wrote, "are all [relevant] items known to exist within the file system of the Organized Crime Bureau. The total attachment numbers forty-five pages in length and contains any and all references to the names John Adamson, Mary Adamson, or Kemper Marley."

That was still not the end of the story of Jack Weaver and the purge of File #851. On July 20, Sgt. Al McKenzie informed Butler that "some weeks after the [Bolles] bombing," Weaver ordered McKenzie to remove the master index card for John Adamson, which listed all of the documents in the police-intelligence files that related to Adamson and where they could be found in the filing system. Weaver had told him to remove the master index to protect the Adamson information from subpoena. McKenzie said he complied out of "professional courtesy." On July 23, Butler wrote an addendum to his earlier memo to Schafer. He informed the prosecutor of McKenzie's admission. In July 1982, Max Dunlap filed a lawsuit charging twenty-two Phoenix police officers with fraudulent concealment and conspiracy, with File #851 at the center of the suit.

Dunlap's Lawsuit Against the Cops

Some accounts of Dunlap's lawsuit have mischaracterized its intent, which was not to disassociate himself from all guilt in the Bolles murder but to claim that his role had been deliberately exaggerated because members of law enforcement destroyed evidence that would have implicated others. It was evidence that would have at least alleviated his punishment, he argued. Phoenix police had found evidence "tending to establish that persons other than Dunlap were criminally responsible for Bolles's murder," Dunlap argued, evidence that would have "unshrouded those who were in league with Adamson in the murder of Bolles."

Dunlap's lawsuit blew up in the tenth week of the contentious trial of the eleven former and current Phoenix cops named as participants in the file purge. One of them, Weaver, testified that the defense had shown him evidence privately that, contrary to the attorney's statements in court, said the purportedly missing original files still existed. Weaver was accusing his own lawyer of perjury. It was the legal equivalent of attaching a bomb to the undercarriage of the case, which was promptly declared a mistrial. The other ten defendants claimed that Weaver had been "planted" on their side of the case and was working for someone else, unnamed. A defense lawyer warned the court Weaver's action might give a future jury, if there were one, the mistaken impression that "the cover-up has continued through this trial." Despite the legal chaos, all of Dunlap's appeals were denied.

There was an epilogue to the File #851 scandal. In 1987, as part of the same article in which *The Wall Street Journal*'s Emshwiller reported on Bolles's last reporting project, he described a memo, now apparently lost, about the origins of File #851. The memo contained some vital new details. "[A] file on Emprise was given to Harry Hawkins, a detective in the department's Organized Crime Bureau," Emshwiller reported. "As Mr. Hawkins later recalled in a memorandum, two superiors told him to pull out any information tying Mr. Adamson to the Funks and Emprise—an unusual request because the parties have denied having any ties. He said he removed several items and was then told to renumber the pages of the file to hide the purging." The "two superiors" were not named.

There was more. "Shortly after the murder," Emshwiller wrote, "the bureau's file cards on several individuals were taken and hidden. Without the files, information in the voluminous files about individuals was essentially unfindable. Among the cards pulled were ones on Mr. Adamson, Emprise, one of the Funks, Mr. Marley, and Senator Barry Goldwater. When authorities found the cards years later, they discovered that some of the information referred to was no longer in the files."

Through it all, Weaver maintained that he had merely been trying to protect police sources. That he was protecting them from prosecutors seemed to make no difference. In any case, no one in authority bothered to check his story. Weaver was neither charged with a crime nor required to take a lie-detector test. The opportunity was lost to establish the identity of whoever it was, likely outside the department, for whom he was working. He was, it appeared, untouchable. Sellers said he and other police investigators tried to get Weaver to sit down with them and explain himself, but he refused. Meanwhile, Hawkins was demoted. He offered to submit to a polygraph but was turned down. Sellers said he asked for just such a test for Sparks as well, but that, too, was denied.

WHAT WAS IN FILE #851?

A reading of the police department internal-investigation report sets out only a few new facts in referring to the purged documents. Some of the more revealing concerned John Adamson.

Adamson had been an informer for the police-intelligence squad for at least two years before the bombing. This was the probable source of Adamson's boast to Dennis Kelley in the parking lot of the Nu-Towne Saloon that he and the police were on such good terms that he was virtually immune to arrest. It's possible that the mentions of Adamson were part of the purge in part because it could have been embarrassing to the department if records surfaced showing that Bolles's assassin was a police informant even while he was plotting murders.

There was also this. In the days when he was running a string of dogs at the Phoenix Greyhound Park under the name Viking Kennels, Adamson put in an appearance at the dog track nearly every day. That put him in frequent contact with the track's manager and co-owner, Bradley Funk. When Adamson was at the track, he had an additional job. He was paid to spy on, or take care of, members of the Funk family when they became incapacitated from drink. Adamson's employer for this task was Kemper Marley. Adamson was to make sure that when any of the Funks were too drunk to drive, he would get them home safely.

There were many unanswered questions. Why would Marley want someone to look out for the Funks? How did Marley and Adamson meet? Why was Goldwater's card among those purged?

But perhaps that was the point of the purge. If it had become generally known that Goldwater was being protected from something—and that Bolles's assassin had once worked for Marley—both men would have been pulled directly into the unwelcome spotlight of the Bolles investigation and its press coverage. Someone within reach of the files at the Phoenix PD had to take action. That it was Jack Weaver raised even more questions, the kind of questions that had to be, and were, avoided.

WHO IN THE PHOENIX PD WAS HELPING ROBERTS?

In their reports, the frustration of Jon Sellers and other investigating officers over police administrators' refusal to allow a thoroughgoing probe into Weaver's motives was evident. There weren't many explanations possible other than the obvious one. At some level, organized crime had penetrated the department's organized-crime bureau.

Weaver was not the only insider who could manipulate internal police-record systems. So could Neal Roberts. In late 1977, it was discovered by accident during the investigation of an otherwise routine crime in a west-side neighborhood that someone in the department had been feeding Roberts police-intelligence files on the Don Bolles case virtually from the start.

On October 19, neighbors called Phoenix police to intervene in a burglary at the Westwood School at the corner of 22nd Avenue and West Pierson. When a detective named Walsh and several uniformed officers responded, they saw teenagers, a girl and several boys, walking away from the school carrying musical instruments. The kids spotted the cops and ran to a concrete-block apartment house on nearby West 21st Avenue. Police chased the malfeasants into an apartment, located the instruments, and sat the teens down in the living room. During the questioning, an officer L. Baker cased the apartment. In the closet of the girl's bedroom, he discovered a foot-high stack of Phoenix police reports relating to the Bolles murder.

When she was confronted with the papers, the girl told Baker they belonged to "Uncle Neal."

Detective Walsh riffled through the papers and found that none of them had departmental stamps showing they had been reviewed and authorized for release to other agencies or to the public. Alarmed, Walsh called the patrol supervisor on duty at the time, Lieutenant Lou Absher, and told him what Baker had found. Absher said he would be right over.

As he waited, Walsh made a phone call and found that the apartment the kids had fled to was rented to Arlene Lyons. He recalled that Lyons had worked with Neal Roberts in some capacity. Absher arrived, looked at the documents, and ordered the officers to put them in the trunk of his patrol car. After Absher left, an indignant Neal Roberts appeared at the door of the apartment "and objected to the removal of the documents by the police." Walsh told him he was too late. When Walsh later inquired about the fate of the foot-high stack of internal intelligence, he was told that someone in authority had returned the documents to Roberts.

No Phoenix police report of this incident has survived in the usual archives. The only known account is an FBI report found among the Bolles case files in the Arizona Attorney General's Office. On February 23, 1989, an FBI agent named Zahn reported to the bureau that the Detective Walsh in question had just informed him about the discovery in 1977 of Roberts's collection of police files. It was a matter of concern, Zahn wrote, that Roberts had "obtained files unauthorized or unlawfully removed from the police department information bureau."

No part of the Bolles investigation, it seemed, lay beyond the reach of the Phoenix network.

THE END OF THE FORMER WORLD

The twenty-three-year battle between the mob and the FBI for control of the Las Vegas skim ended in Phoenix in September 1986. At a small hotel on fashionable Camelback Road, a large, rough-looking man could be seen pushing a man in a wheelchair across the lobby and out the front door of the Arizona Manor. The slumped-over figure appeared to be seriously ill. A closer look would have revealed that he was dead.

When the man pushing the wheelchair reached the curb, he yanked the corpse out of the chair and pushed it into the backseat of a waiting car. Within the hour, it would be lying in a ditch in the desert, distant from the lights of the city.

By killing George "Jay" Vandermark, the mob was getting rid of a key grand-jury witness against the casino skim in Las Vegas.

Until a few months before his murder, Vandermark was the manager of the slot-machine operation at the Stardust. His problems began when he started skimming too much of the skim. While he was supervising the phantom coin operation and collecting an estimated $7 million from the coin skim for his bosses, he managed to set aside nearly $3 million for himself. When he escaped with the money, supposedly to Mexico, he soon had three posses on his trail. The FBI and investigators for Nevada's Gaming Control Commission wanted to find him and force him to tell what he knew about the Stardust slots. The mobsters wanted their $3 million back. The State of Nevada sent an officer to find Vandermark's son to tell them where in Mexico the father was hiding. The son wouldn't talk. The mob must have been following the Nevada officer, for soon afterward, the son was found dead, his head stoved in.

No one knows what happened to Vandermark between the time he left Las Vegas and registered under a false identity at the Arizona Manor,. Whether the mob kidnapped him and stowed him at the Manor or he arrived there voluntarily, Phoenix was a bad choice. If Vandermark was hoping that the Manor's manager, Emil "Mal" Vaci, a friend from Las Vegas, would save his life by acting as a go-between with the Chicago Outfit, he miscalculated. Vaci was also a confidant of Paulie "the Indian" Schiro, who lived in Scottsdale for years and was the Outfit's enforcer in Arizona. If Vaci discovered that Vandermark had come to Phoenix and failed to tell Schiro, it would be like putting a gun to his own head.

Vaci had come under FBI surveillance after the bureau spotted him at the Stardust deep in conversation with a casino vice president they were interested in. When they put a tail on him, Vaci led them to Phoenix and the Arizona Manor, where they put a bug in his phone. Agents apparently learned from the phone tap that Vandermark had arrived in Phoenix. But before they could pick him up, they found that Vandermark had checked out, leaving no forwarding address. So they arrested Vaci instead.

Soon, a replacement witness was called to testify to the Las Vegas grand jury about the skim. It was Vaci. Federal prosecutors forced him to testify to a grand jury several times, and he was pressed repeatedly to divulge Vandermark's whereabouts. He couldn't very well tell jurors that his friends from Chicago had already killed Vandermark, so he refused to talk. Frustrated, prosecutors gave him immunity, meaning he could not be prosecuted for any information he shared but that he could be jailed for contempt for as long as he refused to talk. At that point, Vaci was exposed to the threat of a contempt citation and might have been tempted to save himself by joining the government's witness-protection program. He agreed to talk if he was subpoenaed.

By this time, Vaci was in his seventies, He had a reputation as someone who could keep his mouth shut, but he was still financially insecure enough that he moonlighted as the maitre d' at Ernesto's, a pretentious mob-connected restaurant a block south of the Manor.

Late one night in June 1986, Vaci walked to his car in Ernesto's parking lot. As he took a set of keys out of his pocket, the side door on a van parked next to his car rolled open, and several hands reached out to grab him. One of the hands belonged to Nick Calabrese. Another held a handgun.

A couple of men watched the scene from a lookout car nearby. One of them, monitoring a police scanner, was Paulie Schiro.

A few days later, desert hikers in an area east of Phoenix found Vaci's body lying in a drainage ditch, wrapped in a plastic tarp. He had been given the usual good-bye: a handful of .22-caliber slugs in the back of the skull. The newspapers treated the news with interest but had little to work with. Law enforcement, chagrined at the death of an important federal witness, was not generous with details.

Soon after the Vaci murder, Schiro left Arizona and returned to Illinois, where he was given two more assignments. As the Outfit's enforcer in Las Vegas, Tony Spilotro had the responsibility to keep the skim "honest," and the discovery that Vandermark had left Las Vegas with $3 million of the coin skim in his possession was evidence of Spilotro's incompetence. Schiro and his associates killed Spilotro and his brother, Michael, and buried them in an Indiana cornfield.

GOLDWATER SAYS FAREWELL TO AN OLD FRIEND

Marley's death on June 25, 1990, in La Jolla, California, attracted little notice outside Arizona. He had been wise to avoid his home in his waning days. On June 26, Phoenix broke all heat records. The thermometer at the airport that date hit 122 degrees Fahrenheit, an event noted with grim delight on the front page of newspapers all over snow country. A few days later, at the funeral, Marley's friend Barry Goldwater, supported by a pair of canes after hip surgery, struggled into the packed sanctuary of the Church of the Beatitudes in northwest Phoenix.

From his casket, Marley allowed himself a last wink at his old friend Barry. The Reverend Winthrop Stone, to honor Marley's request, and accompanied by the church organist, sang the deceased's favorite song, Frank Sinatra's mob hymn, "My Way."

Conclusion: Men of
Private Influence

Phoenix "has a curious disposition not to prosecute people like bankers, law-yers, title-company executives, ranchers, and real-estate promoters," *New York Times* reporter Robert Lindsey wrote in February 1977. That was months before the law settled the Don Bolles case with the convictions of two low-level assassins and a go-between for Kemper Marley. Most Arizonans agreed with Lindsey when he wrote that the Bolles case remained "unsolved," and they reluctantly resigned themselves to the idea that it never would be. Curiosity about who wanted a reporter dead was replaced by a different question: who had the power to bury a crime of such notoriety?

The answer, as we have seen, is that the Bolles murder occurred in the middle of a struggle for the control of energy resources on the Colorado Plateau. For decades, large national corporations that leased the largely Indian-owned oil, coal, and uranium deposits controlled energy policy in northern Arizona. In the 1970s, as energy resources came under dispute everywhere, with the Arab-oil embargo the sharpest example, the president of the Navajo Nation organized a coalition of tribes of the Mountain West into an associa-tion of energy producers to enter the energy markets on their own terms and free themselves from exploitive relations with large corporations. The federally appointed bureaucrats and politicians who promoted corporate interests viewed the Indian-energy association as a cartel, "an Indian OPEC," and a threat to their plan for rapid economic expansion in the desert Southwest.

To an extent that can hardly be exaggerated, the development project depended on the reputation, goodwill, and influence of Barry Goldwater, who had mentored the same Navajo leader who was defying him. He was the president of the Navajo nation, Peter MacDonald, whose drive for Indian self-determination had transformed him from a friend into one of Goldwater's bitterest political enemies.

In Goldwater's view, MacDonald's ambitions were so threatening to the buildup of the urban Southwest and to his own position as a leader that they required drastic countermeasures. In what could be described as an application of the policy that is now called regime change, Goldwater devised a plan to force MacDonald from office. He introduced federal legislation hostile to Indian-energy interests. He prevailed on a close political ally, Attorney General Richard Kleindienst, to launch a criminal investigation against MacDonald. And he or his staff developed a covert operation that depended on criminals to execute.

In January 1976, Goldwater staff hired a Phoenix criminal lawyer, Neal Roberts, and through him the arsonist and gangster John Harvey Adamson, to devise the covert operation. Adamson proposed to plant a propaganda bomb—six sticks of dynamite with a defective fuse, designed not to explode but to ignite panic in those who found it—in the chambers of the Navajo Tribal Council, where its discovery during a memorial service would, in theory, send a wave of fear through the tribal capital. The intention was to blame the bomb on MacDonald to discredit him. In the end, Adamson's role in the larger Navajo scheme proved to be minor after he panicked and discarded the bomb in a public trash basket located miles from the capital. Its discovery left barely a ripple in the news. But if Adamson's bomb was a dud, his willingness to talk about it was not.

The FBI learned of Adamson's role in the Navajo plot when the State of Arizona indicted him for murder and turned him over to federal custody for questioning. When he was told of the Navajo episode in the Bolles murder, US Attorney for Arizona William G. Smitherman flew to Washington, DC, with a subpoena in his pocket. He was ready to hand it to Goldwater if the senator resisted his request that he return home to testify. The federal prosecutor wanted the senator to tell a grand jury what he knew about Adamson's statement: was it true that Roberts hired him on Goldwater's behalf to "raise havoc" among the Navajo people?

Goldwater waived the subpoena and returned to Arizona to testify. But when he took the chair before the grand jury, he was never asked about Adamson or the Navajo plot. Smitherman had had a change of heart. The one chance to get Goldwater on the record, even as part of a sealed grand-jury record, was lost.

Still, documents in the archives of Investigative Reporters and Editors in Missouri and elsewhere tell part of the story about what Goldwater knew. The most useful are transcriptions of Phoenix police interviews with witnesses who said they overheard telephone conversations between Goldwater and Roberts on June 2, 1976, the day of the attack on Bolles.

The tone of Goldwater's angry exchanges with Roberts as reported by witnesses strongly suggests that the senator had no foreknowledge of the Bolles bomb plot. Goldwater's questions to Roberts seem to show that the senator was surprised and angry upon learning of the carbombing of Bolles. It seems likely that Roberts, who was working for another client in the Bolles job, probably had not informed Goldwater beforehand.

Nonetheless, in the same phone conversations with Roberts, according to a witness, Goldwater ordered the lawyer to "shut people up" about the murder and promised to pay for Adamson's silence. According to the police records, Goldwater "reportedly set up and directed Roberts to obtain $25,000 in small bills to pay off Adamson." In other words, despite his apparent lack of foreknowledge of the Bolles incident, Goldwater was willing to pay hush money to Adamson. The reason is not hard to guess: he had to prevent the public from discovering that either he or his team had assigned Roberts to participate in a covert operation that was part of his ongoing effort to overthrow Peter MacDonald. The related secret that had to be protected at all costs was that Roberts had hired the assassin of Don Bolles as part of the Goldwater operation against MacDonald.

How could information of this importance to a high-profile criminal case be suppressed?

We have seen how the context for the social evolution of political power in Phoenix after World War II was similar to that of many large cities in the United States. Friendships between individual gangsters and politicians were often overlooked as "colorful" exceptions to the rule of civic virtue. But in Phoenix, these friendships were unusually deep and persistent.

The Willie Bioff case showed how a celebrity gangster could find refuge in Arizona. Bioff was permitted a winking notoriety in private while successfully hiding his identity in public until his murder exposed his background. Among many other details reported for the first time in the daily press, it was learned that he had been a "staunch Republican." But there were limits to merely political protection. The mob demonstrated that their assassins could reach into Phoenix when they wanted to make a statement in blood.

The same point was made more forcefully three years later, when the Chicago mobsters ordered the death of Gus Greenbaum, one of their own. He started out as a backroom bookie, but within a little more than a decade, he expanded his business to include brothels and union racketeering. In the meantime he became, like Bioff, something of a social insider. During World War II, based largely on his strength with the unions, he emerged as a boss in the urban wing of the Democratic Party, with the proceeds from his various enterprises underwriting his preferred candidates for legislative, gubernatorial, and congressional offices. So expert was Greenbaum in negotiating his way through the Phoenix political economy that after the war, local bankers required his personal signature on loans for the construction of casinos in Las Vegas.

Greenbaum's role in Phoenix history was considerably larger than Bioff's, but in the end, not even Greenbaum could be protected from the Chicago Outfit. After World War II, he abandoned the Democratic Party and with Bioff joined the Goldwater-led, anti-gangster municipal-reform movement and became a generous contributor to the cause. His assassination in 1958 came just a few years before Goldwater prepared his run for the presidency. The Greenbaum murder posed a possible threat to the presidential campaign after widespread national publicity created the impression that organized crime in Phoenix had become an

independent and perhaps uncontrollable force. Those fears would soon be confirmed by Don Bolles's reporting.

Bolles's investigative series about Ned Warren's criminal real-estate empire
and its political influence was something of an easy target because Warren had
made the mistake of seeking cover for his schemes among Democratic lawmakers at a time when Goldwater was consolidating his influence over many
if not most government operations. By the time Warren found his political
footing in the early 1970s by cultivating some of the most influential people
in Goldwater's inner circle (though not the senator himself), the doors of the
federal bankruptcy courts and state regulatory agencies had been thrown open
to him, with many officials turned into silent partners. Boxes of written complaints from fraud victims were shuttled into the state incinerator. Witnesses in
civil actions received unfriendly visitors at their front doors from members of
Warren's gang and on occasion from a member of the Outfit's Chicago Heights
crew. Thus armed, Warren operated with impunity for more than a decade.

The Warren land fraud became so notorious that federal authorities felt
compelled to step in. With the help of the Phoenix police and FBI, the Los
Angeles Organized Crime Strike Force put Warren behind bars. But the protection of Warren by well-placed members of the Phoenix network had its cost.
The system that allowed Warren to flourish undisturbed permitted a figure as
compromised as Neal Roberts to enjoy an impunity even greater than the king
of real-estate fraud.

The demobilization of justice in the Bolles case owed its success largely
to the near-universal regard for Goldwater. Members of most social, political, official, and government circles in Arizona, including many members of
the Democratic Party, regarded Goldwater with affection and admiration. But
there was also apprehension. After Bolles's death, IRE reporting demonstrated
with great clarity that Phoenix insiders had close connections to organized
crime. When Bolles's murder remained unsolved, it was understood to be a
silent confirmation of that fact.

Archival documents establish that the Bolles murder in the last instance
was a criminal conspiracy between Adamson and Roberts. For reasons outlined
in this book, it was almost certainly Kemper Marley who hired Roberts for the

job. Roberts hired Adamson to devise and execute it. Roberts hired Adamson's getaway plane hours before Adamson clamped the bomb to the underside of Bolles's car. Then Roberts arranged for Adamson's remote hideout owned by a client and business partner. In short, Roberts was the mastermind of the murder.

Roberts and Adamson also participated in the Goldwater effort to overthrow the Navajo president. At least some state and federal officials who were close to the Bolles case knew this and decided to protect Goldwater's reputation at the expense of pursing the investigation to its conclusion. This was the solution to the otherwise puzzling decision to grant Roberts immunity from prosecution when the police already had direct evidence of his organizational management of the murder. The Roberts immunity produced no evidence because none was desired. The intent of the immunity was to protect the boundaries of the investigation.

US Attorney Smitherman, after flying to Washington to discover the relationship between Goldwater and Roberts in the Navajo case, was in a similar position. After he returned to Phoenix, he decided he no longer wanted the answer.

All of this happened with the cooperation of otherwise conscientious citizens, public servants, and men of private influence. It was a collective act of fealty from witting insiders for whom loyalty was sometimes indistinguishable from obedience. It was the fruit of a system created by Arizona's strongest men, for whom impunity was the natural reward of wealth and power.

Endnotes

Introduction

Under the Gaze. Robert Lindsey, "Organized Crime Spreads to Fast-Growing Arizona," *The New York Times*, June 14, 1976. **Detectives had lost their optimism.** Lindsey, "Grand Jury May Check Press Reports on Crime in Arizona," *The New York Times,* May 9, 1977. **Lindsey made a declaration.** Lindsey, "Unsolved Slaying of a Reporter Is Focus as Phoenix Trial Opens," *The New York Times,* Jan. 21, 1980. **Cooperation and silence.** Lindsey, "The Anatomy of a Reporter's Murder," *The New York Times, Feb. 20, 1977.* **Illicit practices leave few trails.** Renate Bridenthal, "The Hidden History of Crime, Corruption, and States: An Introduction," *Journal of Social History* Vol. 5, No. 3 (2012): 575–581. **The patron-client model of organized crime.** Block and Chambliss, *Organizing Crime.* **Organized crime as a political phenomenon.** Chambliss, *On the Take,* 9–11, 55.

Chapter 1

Barry Goldwater's Beechcraft. Reid and Demaris, 44. **"I" meant "Chicago."** Malcolm Johnson, 14–33. **The conclusion of the trial.** Abels, 33. **Cold cuts and conversation.** Phoenix Police Department Report, circa 1958. **Police found two legs.** "Blast Blows Hand, Legs from Victim," *The Phoenix Gazette*, Nov. 4. 1955; "Victim Had Put House Up For Sale," *The Phoenix Gazette*, Nov. 5, 1955. **A colored window washer.** Westbrook Pegler, *The San Francisco Examiner*, "Sidelights on the Bioff Case," April 11, 1956. **John Birch Society in Phoenix.** Buckley, 77–80. **Parasites of political unionism.** Pegler, *The San Francisco Examiner*, "Bioff Helped to Educate a Senator," March 29, 1956. **Kefauver Committee publicized the case.** Messick, 159. **Bioff lived modestly.** "Bioff's Widow Named to Administer Estate," *The Arizona Republic*, n.d., circa 1956. **A prominent Californian.** "Bioff Collection Auction Stirs

Little Interest," *The Arizona Republic*, March 31, 1957. **The person who made off with the money.** Gene McLain. "Lump Sum Deposits Mystery," *The Arizona Republic*, Nov. 19, 1955. **Half of the country club knew him.** Letter from Alfred G. Rasor to Goldwater, March 1977; Goldwater's reply, April 1, 1977. Folder: "Goldwater notes, 1977," Box 6, Goldwater Collection, Arizona Historical Foundation (now at the Arizona Historical Society). **Loot the syndicate was anxious to get back.** Herb Lyon column, *The Chicago Tribune*, Nov. 23, 1955. **Arizona Downs.** Alex Drehsler, Re: Willie Bioff. Maricopa County Sheriff's Office Homicide File, Nov. 2, 1976. IRE Collection #5473. **Help Bioff get a Presidential pardon.** "Barry Morris Goldwater: Information in Bureau Files," 1962. FBI Case #62-98961-324. See also Carol Sowers, "FBI had files on Goldwater," *The Arizona Republic*, May 10, 2000.

CHAPTER 2

"It was a wide-open town." Sheridan (1995 ed.), ix. **The three things we like best.** Evanne Kofman, Harry Rosenzweig Interview, 1984. Shema Arizona: Arizona Jewish Historical Society Oral History Database. **"I'm not a gambler."** Goldberg, 79. **"This wider world of action."** Alan A. Block, "Organized Crime: History and Historiography," in *Space, Time and Organized Crime* (New Brunswick, NJ: Transaction Publishers, 1994, 2nd ed.), 55–56. **Offices high in the Luhrs Tower.** George Weisz, Memo to Files, Dec. 6, 1976, "Talk with Adam Diaz in lobby of Luhrs Office Building." IRE #5473, Box 2. Folder: "Adam Diaz." **Clanking silverware and plates.** Adam Diaz interview and Mickey Cohen's description in his testimony to the Kefauver committee. **Capitalize prostitution and drugs.** Turkus and Feder, *Murder, Inc.: The Story of the Syndicate* (New York: Da Capo Press, 1992), 284. A California Crime Study Commission agreed: "The [horse-racing wire] service is a framework on which a whole series of criminal rackets can be organized and operated." **Grand jury indicted Gus, Sam, and William.** "Sanders Testifies At Start of Greenbaum Fraud Trial," *Phoenix Gazette*, April 7, 1937, and "Fraud Charge Retrial Opens," *The Arizona Republic*, April 7, 1937. **Greenbaum spent long hours.**

Diaz also recalled that Kemper Marley was a "good friend" of Greenbaum's and a frequent visitor to the Luhrs ninth floor. In an otherwise evasive deposition taken years later, Marley acknowledged that he knew Greenbaum well "from the 1930s until his death" and was also acquainted with his wife and daughter. **An investigation in 1950.** Dean Jennings, p. 141. **She was found unconscious.** AP, "Slain Gangster's Girlfriend Found," *Lodi* (Calif.) *News-Sentinel*, Dec. 13, 1947. **Greenbaum's growing circle.** "George Raft Cast on Side of Law," *The Los Angeles Times,* April 22, 1946. While vacationing [in Phoenix], Raft borrowed a car from a friend, Jack Chiate, and drove it to his hotel. A few hours later, the car disappeared. It had been stolen by an eighteen year old for a joyride. **Ben Siegel and I sat in an office in Phoenix.** Appearance by Michael ("Mickey") Cohen before the Kefauver Committee. US *Senate, 81*[st] *Congress, Second Session, Senate Special Committee to Investigate Organized Crime in Interstate Commerce,* Part 10, 1950, 194. **Negotiating over the rewards.** "Harless Candidacy Stalled as 'Financial Angels' Tangle," *Arizona News*, May 14, 1948. Harless's papers at Arizona State University show that Neri Osborn was an active correspondent and made frequent requests to Harless to arrange hotel accommodations for him in Washington. **Greenbaum packed up his handbook.** FBI Phoenix Field Division, "Crime Survey," Nov. 6, 1945. **Siegel had cased Las Vegas.** Michael Woodiwiss, *Crime, Crusades and Corruption: Prohibitions in the United States* (London: Pinter Publishers, 1988), 88. **Undisclosed percentage of the ownership.** Robert Lacey, *Little Man: Meyer Lansky and the Gangster Life* (New York: Little, Brown and Company, 1991), 152. **Ragan pulled up at the stoplight.** Allan May, "History of the Race Wire Service," CrimeMagazine.com, n.d. **They slipped him the salt.** Susan Berman, *Lady Las Vegas: The Inside Story Behind America's Neon Oasis* (New York: A&E Network and TV Books, 1996), 56–57. **A new underworld banking system.** Alan A. Block, *Masters of Paradise: Organized Crime and the Internal Revenue Service in the Bahamas* (New Brunswick, NJ: Transaction Publishers, 1991). **Rosenzweig wasn't asked.** Burton Bernstein, "AuH2O," *The New Yorker*, April 25, 1988, 55. **Greenbaum arranged the loan.** Dave Offer, "Del Webb, L. C. Jacobson Overview," Jan. 23, 1977. IRE #5473. **A condition for the loan.** Thomas E. Sheridan, *History of Arizona* (Tucson: University of Arizona Press, 1995),

337. **Organized crime was formally accepted.** Untitled Alex Drehsler
memo, Oct. 17, 1976, IRE #5473. See also Lacey, 152–53, and Denton and
Morris. **Webb Co. broke ground.** "Webb Co. Speeds New *Republic & Gazette*
Plant: Southwest's Finest News Building Planned." *Webb Spinner*, Vol. 1, No. 6,
1947. Webb Spinner was the in-house newsletter for the Webb Co. **The great
chasm.** "Gala Party Features Opening of Flamingo," *Webb Spinner*, Vol. 1, No.
4, 5. **Teach Gus a lesson.** Reid and Demaris, 41. **A few nights after the
meeting.** Russo, 215. **Leone was killed a week after the Riviera opened.**
Leone Greenbaum death certificate, Maricopa County medical examiner, April
28, 1955. **One of Siegel's "henchmen."** "Dead Woman Feared Henchman,
Police Told," *The Arizona Republic*, May 3, 1955. **Enforcer Marshall Caifano.**
"The Greenbaum Murder," AmericanMafia.com, October 2001. **Completely
dissipated.** Reid and Demaris, 46.

CHAPTER 3

Warren sold fraudulent sales contracts. Richard Frosts' unpublished
nonfiction book manuscript. The Western Historical Manuscripts Collection
provided a copy to the Arizona Historical Foundation. See also *Crime!*, a special
section of *The Arizona Republic*, June 25, 1978, R2. **There were seven foot
of them.** Frost, sworn statement to David Metz McArthur, assistant US attorney, Santa Fe, NM, and investigator Edward J. Stafford Jr., Sept. 30, 1975,
Albuquerque, NM, 160–161. **Frederick Jackson Turner searched the
future.** Turner, 258–259. Nearly a century after the publication of Turner's
influential essay, a modern historian of the West, Donald Worster, looked
back on the twentieth century and agreed. "Where larger and larger dams and
more and more elaborate canals were built, political power came to rest in the
hands of an elite...[who] wielded absolute control over the common people."
Worster, *Rivers of Empire*, 12. **"Internal colonialism on a colossal scale."**
Sheridan (2012 ed.), 314–15. **It was fundamentally a political project.**
Andrew Needham, "Sunbelt Imperialism: Growth Politics and Navajo Energy
Development," unpublished manuscript. Thanks to Allen Hunter. See also
John Logan and Harvey Molotch, *Urban Fortunes: The Political Economy of Place*

(Berkeley: U. of California Press, 1987), 32, 53. Cited in Needham. **Phoenix grew from a population.** Gerald D. Nash, *Creating the West*, (Albuquerque: University of New Mexico Press, 1991), 172. **Postwar federal subsidies.** Todd Andrew Needham, "Power Lines: Urban Space, Energy Development and the Making of the Modern Southwest," PhD dissertation, University of Michigan, 2006. See also Alan Brinkley, *The End of Reform: New Deal Liberalism in Recession and War* (New York: Knopf), 1995. **Arizona was a one-party state.** Daniel J. Elazar, series introduction to David R. Berman, *Arizona Politics & Government* (Lincoln: University of Nebraska Press, 1998), xxiv-xxv. **"A wholesale transformation in Indian leasing policy."** Andrew Needham, "Sunbelt Imperialism: Boosters, Navajos and Energy Development in the Metropolitan Southwest," in Nickerson and Dochuk, 260. **One federal expert on organized crime.** William C. Kavanaugh, a special agent for the Bureau of Alcohol, Tobacco and Firearms in Phoenix, speech to Phoenix law enforcement, Aug. 20, 1973. Thanks to James Henderson. **One hundred of the state's community leaders.** James E. Patrick, Valley National Bank president from 1962 to 1967, quoted in IRE memo to file; IRE #5473. The Arizona Academy is a civic organization that sponsors annual gatherings of influential citizens who discuss and publish their views on statewide issues. **Fit the definition of a "shadow government."** Block and Chambliss, *Organizing Crime*, 96. **The future King Ned.** *The New York Daily News*, June 3, 1948. **She *loves* hay.** Wampler, 31. **The New Millionaires.** Harold H. Martin, "The New Millionaires of Phoenix," *The Saturday Evening Post*, Sept. 30, 1961. **Ackerman flew DC-3s.** Much of the Ackerman biographical material is taken from an IRE document by John Rawlinson, John Winters, and Myrta Pulliam, "Lee Ackerman, Interview: Oct. 28, 1976," IRE #5473. Supplemented by the Ackerman entry in Paul W. Pollack, *Men of Achievement* (Phoenix: Paul W. Pollack, n.d.). **The case against Ned Warren's operation.** Richard Remender, "Motion to Vacate Plea Agreement and Reset for Trial," *Arizona v. James Cornwall*, CR-80166, Aug. 27, 1975. See also IRE documents "Chronology of Ned Warren and the local system" by Jerry Uhrhammer and Ray Schrick, Jan. 31, 1977, and "Supplementary info on Ned Warren-Justice chronology" by the same authors, Feb. 2, 1977. IRE #5473. Berger's response apparently has not survived. **A small cash payment.** "James Richard Tancill," *Crime!*, a special section of *The Arizona Republic*, June 25, 1967. **J. Fred Talley died.** In his "Activity List," a chronological record of crimes he participated in or knew about (and shared with Phoenix police), John Adamson included Talley's death. See Chapter Five. **Lazar had been Warren's accountant.** Zachary Lazar, *Evening's Empire: The Story of My Father's Murder* (New York: Little, Brown and Company, 2009). **A young lawyer named William Rehnquist.** *Crime!*, a special section of *The Arizona Republic*, June 25, 1978, R-2. See also John Winters, "Memo from Winters," Dec. 17, 1976, IRE #5473. **The transaction required discretion.** Rosenzweig said ECS stock belonged to family members, and the buyer was never identified. **Berger and McCracken pulled up their chairs.** Memo by IRE reporters Jerry Uhrhammer and Ray Schrick, "Supplementary info," Feb. 2, 1977, IRE #5473. Based on their reading of the court transcript and police reports, including McCracken's record of his dialogue with Berger. **By tipping off Harry.** IRE found a transfer notice recording six thousand shares of ECS stock worth twelve dollars and fifty cents per share (about $75,000) were sent to Bache & Co. of New York. **US senator Paul Fannin.** Fannin was a three-time Republican governor, later US senator and part of Goldwater's circle. He was arrested for drunken driving on Nov. 17, 1972. The Phoenix network swung behind Fannin, and the charge was dismissed. When the scandal failed to die down after seven months, Berger called a grand jury to investigate the matter and found a witness who had seen Fannin drinking at the Favorite Lounge on Thomas Road on the night in question. The matter ended when Fannin called a news conference on Aug. 15, 1973, confessed his guilt, and paid a hundred-dollar fine.

CHAPTER 4

Some pretty prominent politicians. Wendland, 31. **"Harry set me up, and I fell for it."** Roy Elson interview, Dec. 21, 2006, in Sonoita, Arizona. **News of the Marley brothels.** *The Arizona Republic*, Nov. 30, 1980. **I would have to take the case to all the judges.** *Bankruptcy Fraud Oversight: Hearings*

Before the Subcommittee on Improvements in Judicial Machinery of the Committee on the Judiciary, US Senate, 96th Congress. Serial No. 96–52, p. 91. **Less organized than the criminals. Ibid,** p. 95. **The bureau contacted the senator and warned him.** "Goldwater biographical material attached to FBI internal memo from W. V. Cleveland to Mr. Evans. [Redacted] Special Inquiry," Oct. 19, 1964. IRE #5473. **Soldiers of the 364th infantry regiment.** Luckingham, 143–145. **How it was possible for black soldiers to obtain firearms.** *Arizona News*, Dec. 4, 1942. **The red-light district.** Zarbin, 171. **Vice detectives were making the rounds.** Hunsaker, 105. **Free rein to clean up the city.** Zarbin, 172. **Reform slate governed the city.** Zarbin, 173. **The paper had been sold.** Zarbin, 175, 178. **Those boys...are friends of mine.** "Underworld Graft, Gaming Charged in Phoenix Probe," *Arizona News*, Sept. 13, 1946. **A small bagnio called The Cozy.** *Arizona News*, Sept. 14, 1946. **There was five, six, seven thousand to divide among five or six guys.** Bridges, 107n. **Western News Exchange.** "Alleged Betting Headquarters in Phoenix Raided," *Prescott Evening Courier*, Feb. 6, 1948. Western News had existed in one form or another at least since before Maricopa County Attorney John W. Corbin tried to shut it down in 1938. The resulting lawsuit, *Engle v. State*, led to a review of the laws on gambling parlors by the Arizona Supreme Court. The court upheld the legality of Corbin's attempt to close Western News, but by the time the decision was handed down, Corbin had moved on, only to be replaced as county attorney by Greenbaum ally and future US congressman Richard Harless. **Fifteen brothels operating openly.** Hunsaker, 105. **"We had corruption in government," Goldwater replied.** *Arizona Memories*, 1999. Produced by KAET-TV. **Fifteen brothels operating openly.** Bob Greene, "Memo to Files," Dec. 9, 1976. Folder: "Herb Lieb." IRE #5743. **Teak Baldwin and his gang ran the Steak House.** IRE reviewed the ownership history of the Steak House and found that it had been acquired by Goldmar, Inc., a corporate entity that combined the last names of the Goldwater and Martori families. Goldmar, Inc. was a holding company for twelve subsidiaries and fifteen or more affiliates, all previously independent entities owned by one or the other family. The parent company issued loans to its subsidiaries through a segregated investment fund. The focus was on citrus production, farming, real-estate development, taverns and restaurants. Bob Goldwater Sr., the senator's younger brother, was the chief stockholder. The Goldwater family invested in other properties with the Martoris, including Hobo Joe's, owned by a transplanted Detroit associate of Tucson mobster Peter Licavoli. None of the tavern operations could compare to the Steak House for the scale of its interconnections with the Phoenix underworld and its business and political elite. Character witnesses on behalf of applicants for the liquor licenses included Chet Johns, president of the Maricopa County sheriff's posse, and Joe Hunt, a Scottsdale restaurateur who sat on the boards of several dog tracks and was state treasurer and state tax commissioner. Another character witness was the former owner of Navarre's Restaurant, where Ned Warren was part-owner. IRE memo, "Goldmar," n.d. Folder: "Chet Johns." IRE #5473. **A bookkeeper for the Yuma bus company.** Alex Drehsler, "Re: C.B. 'Teak' Baldwin," Oct. 20, 1976. IRE #5473. **Thrown out of the Gilded Cage.** *Picow v. Baldwin*, 77 Ariz. 395 (1954). **A monthly betting handle of $300,000.** IRE, *The Arizona Project*, Day 10. **The victims had voluntarily accepted the drinks.** "Baldwin Tells of Gambling Over [sic] Phoenix, *Prescott Evening Courier*, June 9, 1954. **Baldwin cheated him out of $4,500.** "Teak Baldwin Loses Dope Case Judgment," *Prescott Evening Courier*, April 18, 1952. **Statutes against gambling were rarely enforced.** "New Lien Tossed at Teak Baldwin," *Prescott Evening Courier*, May 16, 1952. **Marley called Baldwin as a character witness.** "Marley Testimony Continues," *Prescott Evening Courier*, Oct. 26, 1980. **The reporter described Newman.** "U.S. Delays Bookie Trial," *The Arizona Republic*, Jan. 16, 1958. **Senator Goldwater had intervened.** Wendland, 83. **No political obstacles remained.** Stephen Shadegg, *What Happened to Goldwater?* (New York: Holt, Rinehart, 1965), 20–21. **I go with nothing but love.** "Jimmy Aaron, Ex-Partner of Greenbaum, Kills Self," *The Phoenix Gazette*, Oct. 19, 1959. **The notorious Bernard Cornfeld.** Charles Raw, *et al.*, *Do You Sincerely Want to Be Rich?: The Full Story of Bernard Cornfeld and IOS* (New York: Viking Press, 1971.) See also Arthur Herzog, *Vesco* (New York: Doubleday, 1987). **Vesco robbed him of $250 million.** Herzog, 31–32. **Publicity over the letters was brief but intense.** Al Sitter, "Goldwater Is Unsure Who Sought Letter," *The Arizona Republic*, Oct. 19, 1976. **He wrote to a close** friend. Goldwater letter to Jack Ross. Aug. 10, 1976. **An unusual memo.** Goldwater papers, Folder: "Organized Crime," Arizona Historical Society. In the memo, Frank explained that he was filling in for Goldwater's personal attorney, who was not available at the time. **Carson testified about Warren.** Al Sitter, "Witness Held Top Crime Post," *The Arizona Republic*, Oct. 4, 1977. **Woodall's fraud was uncovered.** Sitter, "State's Infamy for Corruption Draws Fraud, Con Man Claims," *The Arizona Republic*, Nov. 10, 1977. **The matter was dropped for good.** The only accounts of the committee hearing on Del Rio that have been preserved are in the daily press. When a researcher asked the Clerk of the House for a copy of the hearing minutes in 2007, he was told they had been lost or misplaced. **The names of a few people he had bribed.** Sitter, "State's Infamy for Corruption Draws Fraud, Con Man Claims," *The Arizona Republic*, Nov. 10, 1977. **A plot to kill Stan Tanner.** Frank Turco, "Lawyer Claims Ex-Judge Admitted Murder-Role Plot," *Republic*, Feb. 17, 1978. **Robison lawyer David G. Derickson.** *State of Arizona v. Max Anderson Dunlap and James Albert Robison*, CR-96127, Proceedings in Chambers of the Hon. Howard F. Thompson, Oct. 4, 1977, 4. Derickson cited a fee of $100,000 for the letters, which apparently was not paid after the scandal erupted. **"He wrote a letter to Coulter."** Folder: "James Cornwall." IRE #5473.

CHAPTER 5
Plane crashes, heart attacks, and suicides. John Carpenter, "9 Connected to Land Fraud Cases Died," *The Phoenix Gazette*, n.d. IRE #5473. In 1976 and 1977, five more partners died, including Tony Serra. **Mr. Adamson met Jimmy Robison.** Undated police report by Jon Sellers on an interview with Carl Verive. **He wanted to know how much I would charge for three murders."** Jon Sellers, "Interview with John Harvey Adamson," Phoenix Police Department Report #75018779, May 3, 1995. Adamson said later that police had pressed him on whether the third contract was for Don Bolles, but he knew it was from someone else whose name he could not recall. It might have been Richard Frost, who told investigators that Warren had put a price of $5,000 on his head. There was also the unresolved mystery of the death in

1974 of Arizona Real Estate Commissioner J. Fred Talley, a chief recipient of Warren's hush money. In the official accounts, the death was attributed to heart failure. But on July 30, 1976, *The Phoenix Gazette* reported that Talley deputy James Kieffer believed his boss had been killed in his hospital bed. The fifth entry on Adamson's "Activity List," dated Nov. 3, 1974, was the name "Fred Talley," and next to it, the word *murder.* Thanks to Zachary Lazar for sharing the unredacted police report. **Dennis Kelley was comfortable in the Phoenix demimonde.** FBI files acquired under a Freedom of Information Act request on Ned Warren covering the period October 1974 to May 1979. Case files 179–69 and 179–1037. See also E. Dean Prichard, *Certain Concessions*, an unpublished book manuscript at the Arizona Historical Foundation, which is based on extensive interviews Prichard conducted with Kelley in the 1970s. Prichard died in 2007. Both accounts are supplemented with police reports and contemporaneous news reports. **A provision noted when it was too late.** Prichard, 93–97. **John Adamson's "Activity List."** Adamson gave the list to investigators from the state and Phoenix police in May 1995 as part of their investigation into the murder of Edward Lazar after his killers were identified. **Junior handled the financial transactions.** Prichard, 156. **Drunk and disorderly in Phoenix.** Cook County State Attorney's police report, LEIU #2416, Feb., 16, 1972. IRE #5473. **The execution of stool pigeon Louis Bombacino.** *United States v. John Philip Cerone Sr., et al.*, 52 F. 2d 274; 1971 US App. Lexis 8066, Sept. 15, 1971. **Only two or three crews remaining.** Gerry Smith, "Weakened by Convictions, Chicago Mob Still Running Schemes, Experts Say, *The Chicago Tribune*, June 20, 2011. **A "terrific explosion."** "Store Blaze Loss is $25,000: Explosion in Costello Bros. Wholesale Confectionary Causes Total Loss," *The Chicago Heights Star*, Jan. 25, 1923. **Millions of gallons of 160- to 190-proof alcohol.** Luzi, 22–23. **Zelko disappeared after putting the** *Spectator* **to bed.** John Conroy, "Where in the World is Molly Zelko?" *The Chicago Reader*, March 11, 1993. **LaPorte was the boss.** Luzi, Chapter Five, and Demaris, 368–369. **The Chicago Outfit was out of control.** Adrienne Drell, "Hit Man Tells of Tocco Orders to Kill 4," *The Chicago Sun-Times*, Nov. 21, 1989. See also Tom Rybarczyk, "Chicago Heights Mob Boss Dies Serving 200-Year Term," *The Chicago Tribune*, Sept. 25, 2005. Roemer, *The Enforcer*,

275–276. Corbitt and Giancana, 255. **Joe Tocco was identified.** US Senate Committee on the Judiciary, *Oversight on Civil RICO Suits: Hearings Before the Committee on the Judiciary*, 1986, 355. **Warren turned belligerent.** Prichard, 103–111. Dialogue in quotes are Prichard's; those not in quotes are paraphrases. **Let's start with five thousand dollars.** There are discrepancies between Kelley's accounts of the incidents at Durant's and Nu-Towne as told separately to the FBI and Prichard. Kelley told the federal investigators that the trouble at Durant's started when Adamson demanded $300 for striping the parking lot at Little Hughie's, not the $5,000 he cited to Prichard. And rather than going to Nu-Towne to warn his roommate, Kelley said Adamson "instructed" Kelley to meet him there because he knew Kelley had an ownership interest in the bar. That is, Adamson likely knew that Kelley could order the bartender to hand over cash from the till. **"Your cop friends can't help you."** Kelley's statement to the FBI about Adamson's threat at the Nu-Towne was broader. "Your friends at the city and the FBI can't help you. We can snatch you off the street if we want to." FBI case files 179—69 and 179–1037, 12. IRE #5473.

CHAPTER 6

Waved it at The Ivanhoe patrons. "Statement of John Harvey Adamson," Jan. 4, 1977, *State of Arizona v. John Harvey Adamson*, CR-93385. Thanks to James Henderson. **Warren said he would pay $25,000.** Clarke, 124—125, 155. See also Greg O'Brien, "Neal Roberts Put Off Scheme to Kill Felon, Former Hit Man Says," *The Arizona Republic*, June 25, 1978. **Roberts was awakened before dawn by gunshots.** Arizona death certificates for Nathaniel Taylor Roberts and Vernetta Sweet Roberts, Nov. 19, 1948. Neal was the informant for the county medical examiner. **Reported the highjinks.** "Pranksters Play Gov. Long for Phoenix Laugh," *The Flagstaff Sun*, July 20, 1959. **"A sort of mini Brady Bunch."** "Fire Upsets Plans of Phoenix Families," *The Gallup Independent*, May 22, 1974. **A book on simple bomb manufacturing.** "Adamson Discussed Homemade Bombs," *The Gallup Independent*, n.d.; probably summer 1976. **He struggled through life, a flop at nearly everything.** Lindsey, "The Anatomy of a Reporter's Murder," *The New York Times*,

Feb. 20, 1977. **"A mind like a snake."** Tallberg. See also Charles Kelly, "Bolles Jury Told Dunlap Feared Becoming 'Patsy,'" *The Arizona Republic*, Oct. 7, 1977. **Boyden was also working for Peabody.** Wilkinson, *Blood Struggle*, 122, 309. **Morton was irate.** MacDonald,183, 187. **Morton was named energy czar.** Joel Havemann, "Energy Report: Ford Rearranges Organization to Give Morton Policy Control," *National Journal Reports*, Nov. 2, 1974, 1655– 56. **When Goldwater appeared before a House committee.** *Partition of Navajo and Hopi 1882 Reservation.* CIS 74-H441–8. House Committee on Interior and Insular Affairs, May 14–15, 1973. **The bar where the gandy dancers drank.** Interview with Vlassis, January 2007. **The AFL-CIO delightedly took the credit.** MacDonald, 194–195. **Smitherman will reopen the grand-jury investigation.** "Harold Mott letter dated January 1975," *Preliminary Report to the Navajo Tribal Council*, February 1980. **Joe Patrick made a show.** Interview with Kenneth Fields, Nov. 14, 2007. **He referred to the senator as "Kit" Goldwater.** W. H. Bowart, *Without Reservation*, unpublished manuscript. Thanks to Michael V. Stuhff. **Six hundred Navajo activists.** Grace Lichtenstein, "U.S. Investigating Navajos Over Handling of Millions," *The New York Times*, May 16, 1976. See also "Members of Navajo Tribe Hold Protest on Allege Fund Misuse," *The New York Times,* May 19, 1976. **It was hardly enough to justify martial law.** Official interest in the Navajo bomb and its intended havoc was confined to members of the Navajo Tribal Council. They pursued it on the specific question of whether Goldwater's plan to topple the Navajo president had included anything as radical as a declaration of martial law, as Adamson claimed. Michael Stuhff interviewed Eugene F. Suarez, Chief of the Division of Law Enforcement Services for the Bureau of Indian Affairs in Washington, DC. Suarez acknowledged that there existed a BIA "contingency plan for unrest on Indian reservations," but said that it could not characterized as preparation for martial law. Instead, Suarez said, "an agreement had been reached among the Department of Interior, Department of Defense, and BIA that the DOD would supply jeeps, half-tracks, and," he added facetiously, "a B-52, if necessary." There was reason to believe that Goldwater was serious about idea of deploying some kind of armed presence in a confrontation. He was quoted in one Western newspaper as saying about his Navajo problem, "Well, if they want to make trouble out here, I have the Arizona National Guard all ready, and we'll give them all the trouble they want." See Gregg Wager, "Land Grab." *L. A. Weekly*, July 11-17, 1986, 16. **Neal Roberts and the attempted firebombing.** *United States v. Neal T. Roberts and James Albert Robison*, No. 77–0073M, Phoenix, Feb. 16, 1977. **A more concise account.** Adamson gave the statement to his lawyers, William Feldhecker and William Friedl, on Dec. 30, 1976, the day before he signed a plea agreement. Navajo counsel Michael V. Stuhff discovered it as part of his investigation into connections between events on the reservation and the Bolles murder and included it in his *Preliminary Report* to the Navajo Tribal Council. It has been slightly edited for clarity. **He threw the dynamite in a trash bin.** In his confession to the Bolles murder, Adamson said his source for the dynamite was a powder house in Peoria, a Phoenix suburb, owned by Stan Tanner. Adamson's claim that Tanner was the source for his explosives has been challenged from time to time, However, two agents for the federal Bureau of Arms, Tobacco and Firearms testified at a federal preliminary hearing that they had traced the dynamite in Roberts's and Adamson's attempted firebombing of the Indian Health Service building on Feb. 17, 1976, to the shed on Tanner's ranch. **Ties between Goldwater and Patrick.** Jerry Kammer, "Stories about Spies, a Meddling US Senator, and Plots to Throw the Navajo Reservation into Turmoil," *Navajo Times*, Vol. 19, No. 4 (1978). **"We were all suspicious of Patrick."** Interview with Ken Fields, Nov. 13, 2007. Dennis Ickes had worked on the Navajo reservation as a staff attorney for NASBA before joining the Justice Department. US Attorney General Kleindienst, a member of Goldwater's inner circle, hired Ickes to monitor events during the federal military occupation at Wounded Knee. There he met Fields, another fledgling DOJ staff attorney, on the same mission. When Ickes was transferred to the US Attorney's Office in Arizona to organize the FBI investigation of MacDonald, he asked Fields to join him, and eventually Fields handled the prosecution. It was during this period that Patrick began showing up "out of nowhere" to pick up what he could on the progress of the MacDonald case. One of the men who joined Patrick at the meeting at Roberts's law office was Harold Mott, the former chief counsel to the Tribal Council under Nakai. In a copy of a letter included in the *Preliminary Report*, Mott wrote in January

1975 that he knew how many FBI agents were assigned to Justice Department investigation into MacDonald's affairs and how many Navajo witnesses the FBI had interviewed. **FBI interviews with Adamson had produced a troubling story.** Interview with one of Smitherman's assistant prosecutors, Jan. 9, 2008. **A kilo of cocaine in an identical Gucci bag.** Jon Sellers, interview with Robert Daniel Sprouse, April 9–10, 1982, at the Adult Correctional Institution, Chesterfield, Missouri. Sprouse died in prison not long after the interview. Thanks to Mike Dunlap.

CHAPTER 7

Emprise's ties to organized crime were tenuous. Roemer, *Man Against the Mob*, 277. **An account of the arrest ran on the front page.** Denny Walsh, "Coast Bugging is Linked to Aide in House Inquiry," *New York Times*, June 11, 1973. See also: Paul L. Montgomery, "Ex-Congressman, a Bitter Critic of Emprise, Now Comes to its Defense," *The New York Times*, Jan. 23, 1977. **Its exact terms remain sealed.** The source for the terms of the settlement is a Phoenix attorney who spoke to the author only in exchange for a signed promise of anonymity. **A giveaway if anyone rigged the car with explosives.** Roger Rapoport, "The Reporter Who Was Silenced by the Mob," *New Times* (Phoenix), July 26, 1976. **The next stop would be death row.** Statement of John Harvey Adamson, 28–60. **Neal threw Max out of his office.** Adamson statement, 39. **Councilman or something.** Don Aldridge (1937–1999) was a Republican legislator from Lake Havasu City who served ten months as speaker of the Arizona House of Representatives in 1998 before resigning for health problems. **I asked Don his size.** For a time in the 1970s, Adamson and Carl Verive fenced clothes stolen from semitrailers in a storefront in Mesa. **King Alphonse.** Nickname of Al Lizanetz, a former advertising director for Kemper Marley's wholesale operation, United Liquor. After suffering an injury on the job, he sued for workman's compensation, was denied, and fired. He briefly published a newsletter critical of Marley and talked to reporters at the state capitol and passed his last days at the capitol plaza as addled figure, his arms outstretched, his face obscured under the flapping wings of pigeons. **The price**

was $50,000. The price Adamson asked for was identical to what Ned Warren agreed to pay two Chicago hit men for killing Edward Lazar two others. **A "dese an' dose" guy.** Interview with former Assistant U.S. Attorney Joe Keilp, August 2007. **Agents recorded the event laconically.** FBI teletype from Phoenix to Washington, Indianapolis, and Detroit titled HOFFEX 00: DETROIT, Dec. 16, 1976. Thanks to Michael V. Stuhff for these and related documents not included in his *Preliminary Report*. **HOFFEX memo.** Among those interrogated about Hoffa was Anthony Joseph Zerilli Jr., who had been active in Arizona. The forty-eight-year-old uncooperative prisoner was the son of Detroit boss Joseph Zerilli Sr., then doing time in the federal lockup in Sandstone, Minnesota, for his part in the illegal takeover of the Frontier Hotel and Casino in Las Vegas. **"Aleman had a contract on him."** Maurice Possley and Rick Kogan, *Everybody Pays* (New York: G.P. Putnam's Sons, 2001). See also Robert Cooley and Hillel Levin, *When Corruption Was King* (New York: Carroll & Graf, 2004). Harry Aleman loomed large in the history of Chicago organized crime in the 1970s for murdering thirteen people. He was a member of the Melrose Park group of the Outfit's west-side crew and a nephew of its *caporegime*. In 1997, Aleman was sentenced to three hundred years in prison for killing a Teamster official. There was an Arizona connection to Aleman. On the day he was convicted, Robert Cruz, Aleman's cousin, disappeared. Cruz was out of jail on appeal for the brutal murder of a Phoenix printer whose shop Cruz wanted to use to launder casino skim money. In the spring of 2007, Cruz's remains were found in a DuPage County, Illinois, mob burial ground, his trigger finger chopped off to show that he would never kill again. Cruz allegedly had given Aleman some bad advice on choosing a lawyer. **"Two weeks prior to the Bolles incident."** Detectives Jon Sellers and Dan Dryden filed their incident report the same day, June 29. Dunlap appeared to be warning them away from an impending newspaper article linking him to the delivery of payoff money to Adamson. **A shorter version of Dunlap's phone call.** Charles Kelly, "Bolles Jury Told Dunlap Feared Becoming 'Patsy,'" *The Arizona Republic*, Oct. 7, 1977. **"Three or four days before the Bolles bombing."** Dan Barker #391 (badge number), "Interview of Kay Kroot," n.d., attachment to the *Preliminary Report to the Navajo Tribal Council*. **"The day before the Bolles**

DAVE WAGNER

bombing." John P. Frank, "Confidential Material for Senator Goldwater," n.d. Goldwater personal papers, Arizona Historical Association. The Phoenix police report to which Frank refers has not been located. It might have been part of a September 1976 unauthorized purge of Phoenix police intelligence documents. **Had just rented space in Roberts's law office.** Keller's temporary use of an office in Roberts's compound is confirmed by a Phoenix police report from June 24, 1977. It refers to an unrelated meeting in May 1976 at which Roberts asked Keller to sit in. **The Picture Island fraud.** Jonathan Kwitney, *The Fountain Pen Conspiracy* (New York: Knopf, 1973). **Keller was my immediate supervisor.** E-mail to the author, Feb. 15, 2007. **On videotape she related.** The deposition is dated Aug. 5, 1999. Thanks to Mike Dunlap. **After the sentencing in the Federal case.** The letter is dated Aug. 11, 1978. **"'To protect the plea agreement, themselves and prominent Arizona figures.'"** *Preliminary Report to the Navajo Tribal Council,* 1-2. **Booked a flight for Adamson.** There are two contemporaneous accounts of Adamson's arrival in Lake Havasu on June 3. One is a memo written by IRE editor Bob Greene based on a confidential interview. The other is an FBI account of agents' on-the-record interviews conducted in Havasu on June 9 and 10. **In fear of his life.** Wendland, p. 12. **Noye controlled the Rodeway property.** *Description* and *History of the Business of the Apollo Development Company, Inc.,* an attachment to a loan application for $4 million to the Small Business Administration, July 21, 1975. Roberts is listed on the application as Apollo's lawyer. **Special Agents Laird L. Hiestand and Mark William Kennedy.** Hiestand and Kennedy dictated FBI report PX 174–559 based on interviews conducted June 9 and 10, 1976, in Lake Havasu City. The three surviving pages were attached to the *Preliminary Report to the Navajo Tribal Council.* The first two pages record their interview with Krum on June 9 and dictated on June 10. The third page records a follow-up interview with Krum on June 10, dictated on June 11. **The Mountain Bell records showed.** "Records Indicate Dunlap Placed Call to Lake Havasu," *Arizona Daily Sun,* Oct. 14, 1977. (Note: The headline writer erred in writing *Dunlap* rather than *Roberts,* which was correctly used in the body of the report.) **Roberts's incriminating 6:55 a.m. phone call.** Kaiser and Devereaux, Kindle Direct Publishing e-book loc. 156. **John Flynn, the**

state's most celebrated criminal lawyer. Tom Galbraith, "John Flynn," *Arizona Lawyer*, September 2005. **Kemper was out of money.** "Millionaire Named in Murder Theory," *The Prescott Courier*, July 9, 1976. The Associated Press story was based on a court filing that included the statement Roberts gave to police on July 6 after he was immunized. *The Courier*, contrary to journalistic practice—and perhaps in a wink to its readers—gave Roberts, the subject of the story, a byline over the wire report. **The agreement was disastrous.** Sheridan, 339 (1995 ed.). **[Adamson] testimony implicating subject Roberts.** Stuhff received the Synopis from the FBI on August 19, 1982. The legible portion of the caption reads, "Neal Taylor Roberts, John Harvey Adamson, James Albert Robison," with additional names blacked out. The names of the drafters and recipients, and nearly all of the following 526 pages, were also redacted. **In a public lecture in 2006.** "The Don Bolles Murder Case," transcript of address by Schafer to the Arizona Historical Foundation, broadcast on KJZZ-FM, July 26, 2006. **Official lack of interest in Roberts was clarified.** The memo was written in the context of the scheduled retrial of Max Dunlap in January 1990, at which Howard Woodall was to testify. The author found the memo in 2008 among the Bolles files at the Office of the Arizona Attorney General. The tape cassettes referred to in the memo were not attached. **I don't know what it all means to this day.** Eileen Bailey, "Bolles-Case Clues May Have Died With Roberts," *The Arizona Republic*, Feb. 13, 1999.

CHAPTER 8

These seven words. Zarbin, 323. **James Henderson, the lead defense attorney.** Henderson did not use the diary during Marley's civil trial because no one at the bureau was willing to testify about it. **Jackhammer headlines.** Wallace Turner, "Las Vegas: Gambling Take Creates New Force in U.S.," "Millions in Untaxed 'Black Money' Give Obscure Figures Power That Extends From Underworld to Government," "A Broad Impact," "Roots of the Problem," "Las Vegas: Huge Gambling Take Creates Force That Pervades Life in U.S.," "Millions Cached, Safe from Taxes," *The New York Times*, Nov.

18, 1963. **IOUs in the form of post-dated checks.** Fried, 276. See also "Casino Credit Records Seized in Las Vegas Casino," *The Los Angeles Times,* Jan. 22, 1971. **Payoffs in the highest circles.** Sandy Smith, "Mobsters in the Marketplace,"*Life*, Sept. 8, 1967. There were many more schemes described in the so-called "Goodfellas Tapes." In transcription form, these filled thirteen volumes of conversations from mob wiretaps harvested by the FBI in the late 1960s. See also US Federal Bureau of Investigation transcripts on exhibit in *USA v. De Calvacante, Vasotal and Annunziata,* US District Court, District of New Jersey. Index number: Criminal 111–68 (New York: Lemma Publishing Corp., 1970). **William F. Roemer Jr.,** *The Enforcer* (New York: Ivy Books, 1994), 125. **One vinyl- bound green ledger.** Thanks to Wayne Wickizer for sharing this log. **It is genuine.** Bultman later changed his mind, saying the diary's reference that the Nixon administration accepted a bribe to release Teamster boss Jimmy Hoffa "was just too over the top for me." That is, the Nixon reference was evidence that the diary was a forgery because it was conspicuously out of place and likely designed to attract publicity for De Nono to show that he had cooperated with authorities. (E-mail to the author, July 17, 2012.) Others have challenged the diary's authenticity on the ground that the crimes referred to in its pages had been reported earlier in the national press and thus could have been used as sources in a forgery. Examination of the relevant journalism shows the claim to be untrue. All of the events adverted to in the diary occurred well before law enforcement discovered the diary. Other events were never publically reported. On the issue of the bribes to the Nixon administration to pardon Hoffa, the earliest newspaper reporting appeared on April 27, 1973, in the *Manchester* (New Hampshire) *Evening Leader*, with *The Los Angeles Times* following the next day. The skim-diary entry referring to these events is dated well before either, on Jan. 3, 1973. **We have to get this done.** Statement of John Harvey Adamson, *State of Arizona vs. John Harvey Adamson.* (No. CR-93385) Jan. 4, 1977. Vol. I, 54-55. **Described her conversation.** Kolbe is quoted in John R. Emshwiller, "Bungled Case? Bolles Murder Probe Still Haunts Arizona with Many Questions – Inquiry into Reporter's Death Is Marred by Accusations of Cover-ups, Lost Files." *The Wall Street Journal* (Eastern edition), New York, Feb. 23, 1987. Emshwiller's story is presumably the source for this statement in the history of the Mafia in Las Vegas by Sally Denton and Roger Morris, *The Money and the Power.* 36. (NewYork: Knopf, 2001). "At the time of his death, [Bolles] was in the middle of an exposé linking skimmed money from Las Vegas casinos to the racing monopoly in Arizona." **I'm gonna shut up.** Arizona Attorney General's Office Memo to files, 1989. **A federal protective facility in San Diego.** Two law-enforcement sources have confirmed independently that DeNono was held in a federal facility in the San Diego area in 1976, when Bolles was murdered. **He met Gerry DeNono.** Joe Koretski, "Investigative Report," April 20, 1990. Loose folder (untitled). Record series AGI 86–0045 (Don Bolles), Box 5061. Jennings was Adamson's handler for the Justice Department. DeNono was reportedly in failing health in 2012 and did not respond to requests for an interview to inquire whether he had contacted Bolles in 1976. **Why was Andy Watzek so cautious?** Watzek did not respond to a request for an interview. **Seper learned of the diary.** Memo "From: Jerry Seper, Subj: The Ledger," Aug. 19, 1979. Arizona Historical Association Organized Crime Collection. **Guests from New York.** John Winters and Randy Collier, "3 Phoenix Officers Leased Mob-Linked Bar," *The Arizona Republic*, Dec. 7, 1980. **Tocco paid him a quarter-million dollars.** Joe Koretski, interview with unidentified FBI source, Sept 18, 1987. Folder A. Bolles Files, Arizona Attorney General's Office. **Richer than Cibola.** Marley's story is rooted in his family's history in the cattle business in Idaho and Wyoming in the late nineteenth century. His father, John Marley, converted his cattle fortune to cash and then to real estate and stock after he brought his wife and sons to Arizona in 1909 for his wife's health. **The total attachment numbers forty-five pages.** The attachment could not be located in the twenty or so boxes of Bolles case file reviewed by the author at the Attorney General's Office. **"Unshrouded those who were in league with Adamson."** *Dunlap v. City of Phoenix* **The cover-up has continued through this trial.** Sellers v. Superior Court, 284. See also Emshwiller. The Hawkins memo apparently has not survived. **Skimming too much of the skim.** Jeff Coen, *Family Secrets: The Case that Crippled the Chicago Mob* (Chicago: Chicago Review Press, 2009), 232–40.

BIBLIOGRAPHY

Congressional and Government Records

Bankruptcy Fraud Oversight: Hearings before the Subcommittee on Improvements in Judicial Machinery of the Committee on the Judiciary, US Senate, 96th Congress. Serial No. 96–52.

FBI files acquired under a Freedom of Information Act request on Ned Warren covering the period October 1974 to May 1979. (Case files 179–69 and 179–1037.)

First Report, Organized Crime Control Commission, State of California, May 1978. (Re: Louis and Carl Verive.)

Kavanaugh, William C. *Organized Crime in Arizona* (unpublished, Aug. 20, 1973). Kavanaugh was a special agent with the Bureau of Alcohol, Tobacco and Firearms.

Navajo Tribal Council, *Preliminary Report to the Navajo Tribal Council* (unpublished), February 1980.

Organized Crime in Sports (Racing): Hearings before the Select Committee on Crime, US House of Representatives, 92nd Congress, Second Session. (Bolles testimony at 317.)

US Senate Committee on the Judiciary. 1986. "Oversight on Civil RICO Suits: Hearings before the Committee on the Judiciary."

US Senate Special Committee to Investigate Organized Crime in Interstate Commerce. Part 10, 1950. US Senate, 81st Congress, Second Session. ("Kefauver Committee.")

Court Records

John Marley, wills of 1927 and 1932 Maricopa County Clerk of Courts, PB 9016 (1932).

Picow v. Baldwin. 77 Ariz. 395 (1954).

Sellers v. Superior Court, Maricopa County, 742 P.2d 292, 154 Ariz. 281. (Ct. App. 1987.)

State of Arizona v. John Harvey Adamson, CR-93385.

State of Arizona v. Max Anderson Dunlap and James Albert Robison, CR-96127.

United States v. De Calvacante, Vasotal and Annunziata, US District Court, District of New Jersey, Criminal 111–68 (New York: Lemma Publishing Corp., 1970).

United States v. James Cornwall, CR-80166.

United States v. John Philip Cerone Sr., et al. 452 F.2d 274; 1971 US App. Lexis 8066, Sept. 15, 1971. Includes carbombing of Louis Bombacino in Tempe, Arizona.

United States v. Neal T. Roberts and James Robert Robison, 77–0073M, Phoenix, 1977.

Collections

John Doherty Organized Crime Collection, Arizona State Library (formerly archived at the Arizona Historical Foundation).

Records of Investigative Reporters and Editors, Inc., Western Historical Manuscripts Collection, University of Missouri-Columbia Accession #5473; *Marley v. IRE*, Series AGI 86–0045 (Don Bolles), Arizona Attorney General.

Shema Arizona: Arizona Jewish Historical Society Oral History Database.

Media

Crime, Inc. All in the Family: Mobsters Tell Mob Secrets (BBC/HBO VHS tape, 1984). Thames Television. On-camera interview with Gerard DeNono.

Books

Abels, Jules, *The Truman Scandals* (Chicago: Regnery Publishing, 1956).

Aucoin, James L., *The Evolution of American Investigative Journalism* (Columbia: University of Missouri Press, 2005).

Benedek, Emily, *The Wind Won't Know Me: A History of the Navajo-Hopi Land Dispute* (New York: Knopf, 1992).

Berman, David R., *Arizona Politics and Government: The Quest for Autonomy, Democracy and Development* (Lincoln: University of Nebraska Press, 1998).

————, *Politics, Labor and the War on Big Business: The Path of Reform in Arizona, 1890–1920* (Boulder: University Press of Colorado, 2012).

Berman, Susan, *Lady Las Vegas: The Inside Story Behind America's Neon Oasis* (New York: A&E Network and TV Books, 1996).

Block, Alan A., *Masters of Paradise: Organized Crime and the Internal Revenue Service in the Bahamas* (New Brunswick, NJ: Transaction Publishers, 1991).

————, *The Business of Crime: A Documentary Study of Organized Crime in the American Economy* (Boulder: Westview Press, 1991).

Bridges, Amy. *Morning Glories: Municipal Reform in the Southwest* (Princeton, N.J.: Princeton Univ. Press, 1997).

Brill, Steven, *The Teamsters* (New York: Simon & Schuster, 1978).

Buckley Jr., William F., *Flying High: Remembering Barry Goldwater* (New York: Basic Books, 2010).

Calabrese Jr., Frank, *Operation Family Secrets* (New York: Broadway Paperbacks, 2011).

Caromony, Neil (ed.), *Whiskey, Six-Guns & Red-Light Ladies: George Hand's Saloon Diary, 1875–1878* (Silver City, NM: High-Lonesome Books, 1994).

Chambliss, William J. *On the Take: From Petty Crooks to Presidents* (University of Indiana Press, 1978. (2nd ed., 1988).

Clarke, James W., *The Last Rampage* (Tucson: University of Arizona Press, 1988).

Coen, Jeff, *Family Secrets: The Case That Crippled the Chicago Mob* (Chicago: Chicago Review Press, 2009).

Corbitt, Michael, and Sam Giancana, *Double Deal* (New York: Avon Publications, 2003).

Davis, John H., *Mafia Kingfish* (New York: Signet, 1989).

Demaris, Ovid, *Captive City* (New York: Pocket Books, 1970). See also Reid, Ed, *Green Felt Jungle*.

Denton, Sally, and Roger Morris, *The Money and the Power* (New York: Knopf, 2001).

Everett, Leila P., "The Rise of Jewish National Politics in Galicia, 1905–1907," in Andrei S. Markovits and Frank E. Sysyn (eds.), *Nation-Building and the Politics of Nationalism: Essays on Austrian Galicia* (Cambridge: Harvard Ukrainian Research Institute, 1982).

Fried, Albert, *The Rise and Fall of the Jewish Gangster in America* (New York: Columbia University Press, 1993).

Goldberg, Robert Alan, *Barry Goldwater* (New Haven: Yale University Press, 1995).

Gordon, Linda. *The Great Arizona Orphan Abduction* (Cambridge, MA: Harvard U. Press, 1997).

Headley, Lake, with William Hoffman, *Loud and Clear* (New York: Henry Holt, 1990).

Herzog, Arthur, *Vesco* (New York, Doubleday, 1987).

Hunsaker, Gordon A., *Gunfights and Gunfighters: Reflections from a Phoenix Police Officer* (iUniverse, 2010).

Iverson, Peter, *Barry Goldwater: Native Arizonan* (Norman: University of Oklahoma Press, 1997).

Jennings, Dean, *We Only Kill Each Other* (New York: Pocket Books, 1967).

Johnson, Malcolm, *Crime on the Labor Front: The Inside Story of Murder, Violence, and Organized Gangsterism in Labor Unions* (New York: McGraw-Hill, 1950).

Kaiser, Robert Blair, *Desert Injustice* (Kindle Direct Publishing, e-book, 2011).

Kammer, Jerry, *The Second Long Walk: The Navajo-Hopi Land Dispute* (Albuquerque: University of New Mexico Press, 1980).

Kleindienst, Richard, *Justice: The Memoirs of an Attorney General* (Ottawa, Ill.: Jameson Books, 1985).

Kwitny, Jonathan, *The Fountain Pen Conspiracy* (New York: Knopf, 1973).

Lacey, Robert, *Little Man: Meyer Lansky and the Gangster Life* (Boston: Little, Brown and Company, 1991).

Lazar, Zachary, *Evening's Empire: The Story of My Father's Murder* (New York: Little, Brown, and Company, 2009).

Leo, Mabel, *The Saga of Jack Durant* (Phoenix: MIBS Publishing, 2011).

Luckingham, Bradford, *Phoenix: The History of a Southwestern Metropolis* (Tucson: University of Arizona Press, 1989).

Luzi, Matthew J., *The Boys in Chicago Heights* (Charleston, SC: History Press, 2012).

Martori, Joe, *Street Fights: A Novel Based on a True Story* (Santa Barbara: Paragon, 1987).

MacDonald, Peter, *The Last Warrior* (Library of the American Indian, 1993).

Magnesen, Gary, *Straw Men: How the FBI Crushed the Mob in Las Vegas* (Minneapolis: Mill City Press, 2010).

Messick, Hank, *The Silent Syndicate* (New York: Macmillan, 1966).

_____, *Lansky* (New York: G.P. Putnam's Sons, 1971).

Moldea, Dan, *The Hoffa Wars* (New York: Paddington Press, 1978).

Needham, Andrew, *Power Lines: Phoenix and the Making of the Modern Southwest* (Princeton and Oxford: Princeton University Press, 2014).

Nickerson, Michelle and Danen Dochuk, *Sunbelt Rising: The Politics of Space, Place and Region* (Philadelphia: University of Pennsylvania Press, 2013).

Moore, William Howard, *The Kefauver Committee and the Politics of Crime 1950–1952* (Columbia: University of Missouri Press, 1974).

Peterson, Virgil W., *Barbarians in Our Midst: A History of Chicago Crime and Politics* (Boston: Little, Brown and Company, 1952).

Pileggi, Nicholas, *Casino: Love and Honor in Las Vegas* (New York: Simon & Schuster, 1995).

Pulliam, Russell, *Publisher: Gene Pulliam, Last of the Newspaper Titans* (Ottawa, Ill.: Jameson Books, 1984).

Reid, Ed and Ovid Demaris, *The Green Felt Jungle* (New York: Pocket Books, 1963).

Reppetto, Thomas, *Bringing Down the Mob: The War Against the American Mafia* (New York: Macrae/Holt, 2006).

Roemer Jr., William F., *The Enforcer: Spilotro: The Chicago Mob's Man over Las Vegas* (New York: Ivy Books, 1994).

_____, *Roemer: Man Against the Mob* (New York: Ivy Books, 1989).

Russo, Gus, *Supermob: How Sidney Korshak and His Criminal Associates Became America's Hidden Power Brokers* (New York: Bloomsbury USA, 2006).

Schafer III, William J., *Schafer's Cases: The Hard-to-Find Ones* (Springfield, Ill.: Charles C. Thomas, 1972).

Shadegg, Stephan, *What Happened to Goldwater?* (New York: Holt, Rinehart, 1965).

_____, *The Remnant* (New Rochelle, NY: Arlington House, 1968).

Sheridan, Thomas E., *History of Arizona* (Tucson: University of Arizona Press, 1995).

_____, *History of Arizona* (Tucson: University of Arizona Press, 2nd ed., 2012).

Shermer, Elizabeth Tandy, *Sunbelt Capitalism: Phoenix and the Transformation of American Politics* (Philadelphia: University of Pennsylvania Press, 2013).

Tallberg, Martin, *Don Bolles: An Investigation into His Murder* (New York: Popular Library, 1977).

Turner, Frederick Jackson, "Contributions of the West to American Democracy" in *The Frontier in America History* (New York: Henry Holt and Co., 1921).

Wampler, Vance, *The Prince of Garden Hills* (Prescott, Ariz.: Wolfe Publishing, 1988).

Ware, Harry David, *Alcohol, Temperance and Prohibition in Arizona,* PhD thesis, Arizona State University, 1995.

Wendland, Michael F., *The Arizona Project* (Mesa, Ariz.: Blue Sky Press, rev. ed., 1988).

Wiley, Peter and Robert Gottlieb, *Empires in the Sun: The Rise of the New American West* (New York: G.P. Putnam's Sons, 1982).

Wilkinson, Charles, *Blood Struggle: The Rise of the Modern Indian Nations* (New York: Norton, 2005).

_____, *Fire on the Plateau: Conflict and Endurance in the American Southwest* (Island Press, 2004).

Woodiwiss, Michael, *Crime, Crusades and Corruption: Prohibitions in the United States* (London: Pinter Publishers, 1988).

Worster, Donald, *Rivers of Empire: Water, Aridity and the Growth of the American West* (New York: Pantheon, 1985).

_____, *Under Western Skies: Nature and History in the American West* (New York: Oxford University Press, 1992).

Zarbin, Earl, *All the Time a Newspaper: The First 100 Years of The Arizona Republic* (Phoenix: The Arizona Republic, 1990).

ACKNOWLEDGMENTS

First thanks go to James Henderson, longtime attorney for *The Arizona Republic*, for his early help and encouragement, and to Michael V. Stuhff of Las Vegas for sharing documents unobtainable elsewhere. Thanks also go to the late Roy Elson of Sonoita, Arizona; to Allen Hunter for scholarly sources; and to Zachary Lazar for sharing personal insights about his father's case, along with unredacted police reports.

I am indebted to sources in law enforcement and government who participated in this project on the condition of anonymity. Gratitude is due also to Investigative Reporters and Editors, Inc. for access to Arizona Project records at the Western Historical Manuscript Collection at the University of Missouri, as well as for the trial records of Kemper Marley's 1980 libel lawsuit against IRE; to the staffs of the Arizona State Library and the former Arizona Historical Foundation; and to the staffs of the Maricopa County Superior Court and the Office of the Arizona Attorney General. Thanks go as well to the staffs of the Luhrs Reading Room and the Federal Depository, both at Arizona State University, for their help in accessing congressional records and specialized collections. Finally, I am grateful to the FBI for fulfilling sizeable records requests under the Freedom of Information Act.

Personal thanks go to my longtime writing partner, Paul Buhle, and to Ron McCrea and Philip Ball for their aid in matters large and small, and to my editor, Valerie Kalfrin. For valuable help in graphic matters, I thank Robert Aulicino (aulicinodesign.com) and Tad Wagner (tadwagnerstudio.com). And for her many hours of research, consultation, close reading, and patience, I especially thank Grace Wagner.

INDEX

Made in the USA
Middletown, DE
17 May 2016